6th Seminar on Industrial Control Systems: Analysis, Modeling and Computing

ITM Web of Conferences Volume 6 (2016)

Moscow, Russia
25 - 26 February 2016

Editors:

Evgeny V. Nikulchev
Evgeny I. Veremey

ISBN: 978-1-5108-2267-2

Printed from e-media with permission by:

Curran Associates, Inc.
57 Morehouse Lane
Red Hook, NY 12571

Some format issues inherent in the e-media version may also appear in this print version.

Printed by Curran Associates, Inc. (2016)

For additional information, please contact EDP Sciences – Web of Conferences at the address below.

EDP Sciences – Web of Conferences
17, Avenue du Hoggar
Parc d'Activité de Courtabœuf
BP 112
F-91944 Les Ulis Cedex A
France

Phone: +33 (0) 1 69 18 75 75
Fax: +33 (0) 1 69 28 84 91

contact-edps@webofconferences.org

Additional copies of this publication are available from:

Curran Associates, Inc.
57 Morehouse Lane
Red Hook, NY 12571 USA
Phone: 845-758-0400
Fax: 845-758-2633
Email: curran@proceedings.com
Web: www.proceedings.com

TABLE OF CONTENTS

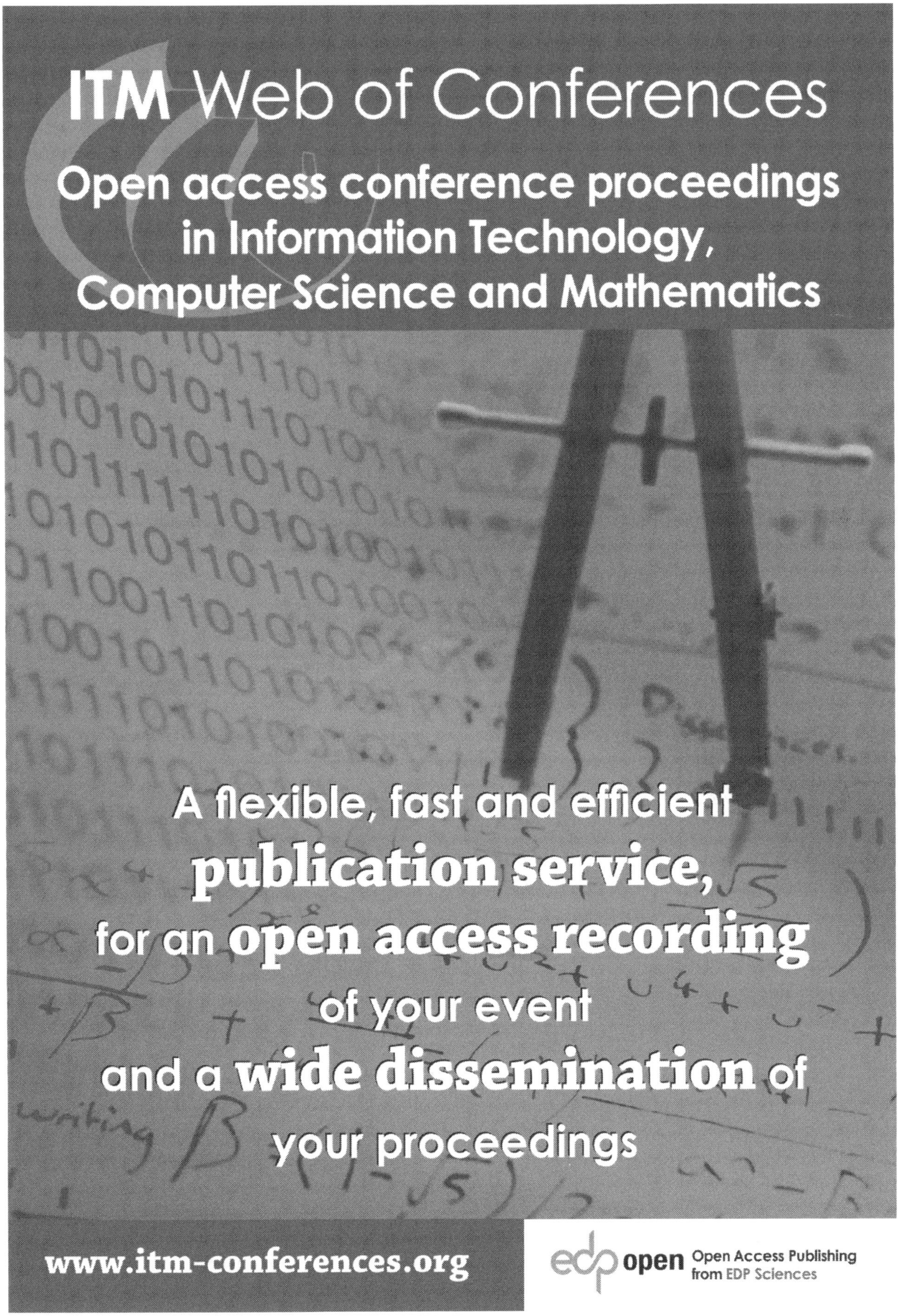
ITM Web of Conferences
Open access conference proceedings in Information Technology, Computer Science and Mathematics
A flexible, fast and efficient publication service, for an open access recording of your event and a wide dissemination of your proceedings
www.itm-conferences.org
edp open Open Access Publishing from EDP Sciences

Aims & scope

ITM Web of Conferences is an open-access journal devoted to the publishing of conference proceedings dealing with all areas related to information technology, computer science and mathematics.

ITM Web of Conferences aims to make conference proceedings visible, citable and widely usable by the scientific community. It offers outstanding services for the publication and dissemination of contents in order to ensure long-term archiving and maximum exposure of scientific events.

Coverage includes the whole spectrum of pure and applied mathematics, as well as all domains related to computer science such as programming, operating systems, databases, software engineering, web technologies, human-computer interaction, etc.

Why publish with ITM Web of Conferences?

- **Open access:** conference papers available worldwide.
- **Fast publication:** less than 3 months.
- **Total flexibility:** no page restrictions, free unlimited use of colour in the online version, any kind of scientific document welcomed (traditional articles, posters, abstracts and slideshows).
- **High visibility:** all documents indexed in main databases and easily found online.
- **Fair author rights:** CC-BY Creative Commons license.
- **Range of additional publishing options:** printed proceedings, CD-ROMs, copy-editing, etc.

Contact: Isaline Augusto
itm@webofconferences.org

ISSN (electronic edition): pending

www.itm-conferences.org

edp open Open Access Publishing from EDP Sciences

Moscow Technological Institute

6th Seminar on

Industrial Control Systems:

analysis, modeling and computation

Moscow, Russia
Moscow Technological Institute
25–26 February 2016

Address: Moscow, Leninsky prospect, 38A.

Main topics of the conference:

- Control systems
- System Analysis
- Sensors
- Computational problems
- Data communication

Program Committee

- E.Nikulchev, professor, Moscow (General Chairs)
- V. Belov, professor, Ryzan
- G. Bubnov, professor, Moscow
- E. Veremey, professor, Saint-Petersburg
- L. Demidova, professor, Ryzan
- A. Diveev, professor, Moscow
- A. Goryashko, professor, Moscow
- E. Kovshov, professor, Moscow
- E. Loginova, professor, Moscow
- B. Lushnikov, PhD, Kursk
- E. Pluzhnik, DBA, Moscow
- A. Prutzkov, PhD, Pyzan
- A. Pylkin, professor, Ryzan
- G. Rogachev, Dr., Saratov
- K. Gigalov, PhD, Moscow

The language of the documents — English
Contact address: e_nikulchev@mti.edu.ru

edp sciences

ITM Web of Conferences

Statement of Peer review

In submitting conference proceedings to ITM Web of Conferences, I certify to the Publisher that I adhere to the **Policy on Publishing Integrity** of the journal in order to safeguard good scientific practice in publishing.

1. All articles have been subjected to peer review administered by the proceedings editors.
2. Reviews have been conducted by expert referees, who have been requested to provide unbiased and constructive comments aimed, whenever possible, at improving the work.
3. Proceedings editors have taken all reasonable steps to ensure the quality of the materials they publish and their decision to accept or reject a paper for publication has been based only on the merits of the work and the relevance to the journal.

Title, date and place of the conference

6th Seminar on Industrial Control Systems: analisys, modeling and computation / Moscow, Russia, 25-26 Feb. 20

Proceedings editor(s):

Prof. Evgeny V. Nikulchev
Prof. Evgeny I. Vekemey

Date and editor's signature

26.02.2016

17, avenue du Hoggar - PA de Courtabœuf – BP 112 - 91944 Les Ulis Cedex A (France)
Tél. : 33 (0)1 69 18 75 75 - Fax : 33(0)1 69 07 45 17 – www.edpsciences.org

ITM Web of Conferences **6**, 01001 (2016)
DOI: 10.1051/itmconf/20160601001

Algorithm for motion control of an exoskeleton during verticalization

Sergey Jatsun[1, a], Sergei Savin[1], Boris Lushnikov[1] and Andrey Yatsun[1]

[1]*Southwest State University, Department of mechanics, mechatronics and robotics, 305040 Kursk, Russia*

Abstract. This paper considers lower limb exoskeleton that performs sit-to-stand motion. The work is focused on the control system design. An application of a null space projection methods for solving inverse kinematics problem is discussed. An adaptive multi-input multi-output regulator for the system is presented with the motivation for that choice. Results of the simulation for different versions of the regulator are shown.

1 Introduction

The design of exoskeletons is a relevant complex scientific and engineering task. The importance of exoskeleton design can be explained by the wide spectrum of their application in medicine, the military and industry, rehabilitation and improving the life of elderly and disabled people. The complexity of designing effective exoskeletons lies in high demands on the quality of the control system's operation.

At the moment there is a large amount of scientific literature devoted to exoskeleton control, reception and processing of commands from the operator of the exoskeleton (see, for example, [1-2]). Publication [3] discusses issues related to the design of the control system of the exoskeleton as a whole and notes that the low robustness of the resulting control system requires the use of a high-precision control system dynamic model of the mechanism. Many publications focus on application of assistive and medical exoskeletons (see [4-7]).

There is a series of work describing exoskeleton control during verticalization (see [8-12]). Article [8] proposed an analytical method of solving the inverse kinematics problem and the control system's structure based on a modified version of a proportional-integral regulator. The stated approach is developed in [9] where it is supplemented by an adaptive module that allows us to change the time allotted to verticalization depending on the load on the exoskeleton. The regulator's region of parameters allowing for verticalization of the exoskeleton without tipping was determined in [10] by numerical experiments. A two-stage control strategy for the process of ascent from a chair is developed in [11].

One of the disadvantages of the proposed approaches to exoskeleton control is that the input parameters of the control system are the coordinates of the center of mass and the body's angle of inclination and control system does not cater for a soft transition to another set of control actions. To solve this problem we propose in this work a control strategy that uses the null space projection method (see [13]) of solving the inverse kinematics problem.

2 Description of the lower-limb exoskeleton

We consider a remote controlled lower-limb exoskeleton which is a multi-link system mounted on the operator by means of belts. Each leg of the exoskeleton is a three-link mechanism with successive hinged joints. The exoskeleton's links are driven by electric drives installed in the joints. Fig.1 shows a photograph of an experimental prototype of the exoskeleton.

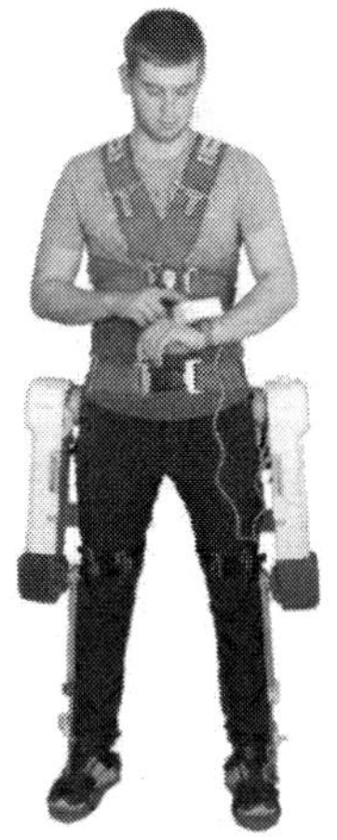

Figure 1. Photograph of a lower-limb exoskeleton.

The dimensions of the links and the location of the hinges are designed in such a way that the links move

[a]Corresponding author: teormeh@inbox.ru

together with the person's body parts to which they are connected.

3 Mathematical model of the mechanism

In this work we look at the exoskeleton's motion during the process of verticalization. We assume that the links and the legs perform planar motion. This allows us to model the exoskeleton as a four-link mechanism with successive hinged joints. The analytical diagram for the mechanism is shown in Fig. 2.

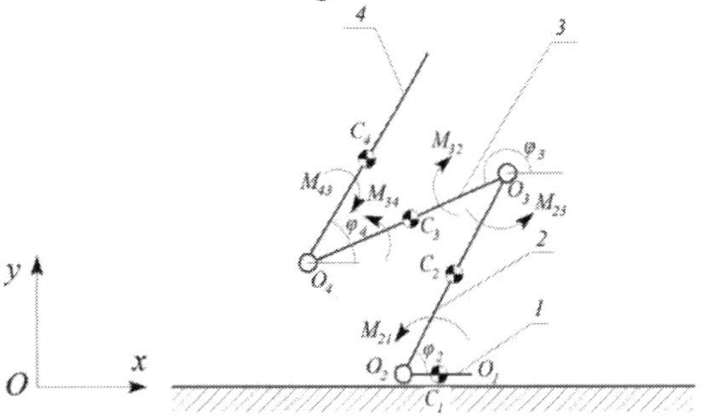

Figure 2. Analytical diagram of the exoskeleton; 1-4 – first – fourth links.

On Fig. 2 we have C_i – the centers of mass of the links and points O_i – locations of the hinged joints. Angles φ_i determine the orientation of the links relative to the horizontal plane, $M_{i,i-1}$ – torques applied to the links by the mechanism. The links have masses m_i, lengths l_i and moments of inertia relative their centers of mass equal to I_i. We make the assumption that the first link is fixed during motion.

We introduce a vector of joint coordinates: $\vec{q}=\begin{bmatrix}\varphi_2 & \varphi_3 & \varphi_4\end{bmatrix}^{\mathrm{T}}$. Kinematic and dynamic equations of the given mechanism can be written using the introduced denotations. Here we confine ourselves to the vector form of the equations of motion (the scalar form can be found in [11]):

$$\mathbf{A}(\vec{q})\ddot{\vec{q}}=\vec{b}(\vec{q},\dot{\vec{q}})+\mathbf{B}\vec{M} \quad (1)$$

where $\mathbf{A}(\vec{q})$ – joint space inertial matrix, $\dot{\vec{q}}$ – vector of joint velocities, $\ddot{\vec{q}}$ – vector of joint accelerations, $\vec{b}(\vec{q},\dot{\vec{q}})$ – vector of joint gravitational forces and inertial forces. $\vec{M}=\begin{bmatrix}M_{21} & M_{32} & M_{43}\end{bmatrix}^{\mathrm{T}}$ – vector of the torques of the electric drives, $\mathbf{B}$ – quadratic matrix.

Matrix $\mathbf{A}(\vec{q})$ is found by the formula: $\mathbf{A}(\vec{q})=\partial^2 T/\partial\dot{\vec{q}}\partial\dot{\vec{q}}$; matrices $\mathbf{A}$ and $\mathbf{B}$ are as follows:

$$\mathbf{A}=\begin{bmatrix}a_{11} & a_{12} & a_{13}\\ a_{12} & a_{22} & a_{23}\\ a_{13} & a_{23} & a_{33}\end{bmatrix},\ \mathbf{B}=\begin{bmatrix}1 & -1 & 0\\ 0 & 1 & -1\\ 0 & 0 & 1\end{bmatrix},$$

where $a_{11}=l_2^2\left(m_2/4+m_3+m_4\right)+I_2$

$a_{12}=l_2 l_3\cos\left(\phi_2-\phi_3\right)\left(m_3/2+m_4\right)$,

$a_{13}=0.5\cos\left(\phi_2-\phi_4\right)l_2 l_4 m_4$, $a_{22}=l_2^2\left(m_3/4+m_4\right)+I_3$,

$a_{23}=0.5\cos\left(\phi_3-\phi_4\right)l_3 l_4 m_4$, $a_{33}=l_4^2 m_4/4+I_4$.

4 Control system

Here the control problem is verticalization of the exoskeleton i.e. executing vertical displacement of its centre of mass (CM). We consider the case when the desired displacement of the CM in the vertical direction is described by the polynomials:

$$x_C^*(t)=\sum_{p=0}^{n}\left(t^p\cdot c_{1,p}\right), \quad (2)$$

$$y_C^*(t)=\sum_{p=0}^{n}\left(t^p\cdot c_{2,p}\right). \quad (3)$$

The method of acquiring such polynomials which provide motion with zero velocity at the initial and final times, while observing constraints on horizontal displacement of the CM. Here we will consider the case when the CM moves vertically up.

We can find the desired values of generalized coordinates by solving the inverse kinematics problem given the desired trajectory of the center of mass. We need to define another function of generalized coordinates (in papers [13-16] such function is called "tasks" and we will use this term from here on) to obtain a unique solution of the inverse kinematics problem since we have 3 generalized coordinates and only two equations for x_C^* and y_C^*. An example is the task of controlling the horizontal position of the head of a person wearing an exoskeleton:

$$x_{O5}^*(t)=\sum_{i=2}^{4}l_i\cos(\varphi_i)=h=const. \quad (4)$$

We need task differential kinematics equations to use the null space projection method:

$$\dot{\vec{r}}_N^*=\begin{bmatrix}\dot{x}_N^*\\ \dot{y}_N^*\end{bmatrix}=\mathbf{J}_1\begin{bmatrix}\dot{\varphi}_2\\ \dot{\varphi}_3\\ \dot{\varphi}_4\end{bmatrix},\quad \dot{x}_{O5}^*=\mathbf{J}_2\begin{bmatrix}\dot{\varphi}_2\\ \dot{\varphi}_3\\ \dot{\varphi}_4\end{bmatrix}, \quad (5)$$

where $\mathbf{J}_1$, $\mathbf{J}_2$ are task Jacobians given by:

$$\mathbf{J}_1=\begin{bmatrix}-K_2\sin(\varphi_2) & -K_3\sin(\varphi_3) & -K_4\sin(\varphi_4)\\ K_2\cos(\varphi_2) & K_3\cos(\varphi_3) & K_4\cos(\varphi_4)\end{bmatrix}, \quad (6)$$

$$\mathbf{J}_2=\left[-l_2\sin(\varphi_2) \quad -l_3\sin(\varphi_3) \quad -l_4\sin(\varphi_4)\right]. \quad (7)$$

The following equations describe the operation of the null space projection method as applied to this problem:

$$\dot{\vec{q}}^*=\dot{\vec{s}}+(\mathbf{J}_2\mathbf{P})^+\left(\dot{x}_{O5}^*-\mathbf{J}_2\dot{\vec{s}}\right), \quad (8)$$

$$\dot{\vec{s}}=\mathbf{J}_1^+\dot{\vec{r}}_N^*,\quad \mathbf{P}=\mathbf{I}-\mathbf{J}_1^+\mathbf{J}_1,$$

where $\dot{\vec{s}}$ are the generalized velocities needed to perform the first task alone, $\mathbf{P}$ is an orthogonal projector, $\mathbf{I}$ is an identity matrix; the sign $^+$ denotes the Moore-Penrose pseudo inverse of a matrix. The value for $\vec{q}^*$ is obtained by integrating the previously obtained $\dot{\vec{q}}^*$.

This method also allows setting priorities to the tasks, the associated methodology can be found in paper [13].

This work considers error based control. The control error is evaluated as the difference between the desired and current values of joint coordinates:

$$\vec{e} = \vec{q}^{\,*} - \vec{q}\,. \qquad (9)$$

We pose the problem of synthesizing a regulator providing exponential tendency of error to zero. This can be achieved if the error satisfies the following vector differential equation:

$$\frac{d^2}{dt^2}\vec{e} + \mathbf{K}_d \frac{d}{dt}\vec{e} + \mathbf{K}_p \vec{e} = 0\,, \qquad (10)$$

where $\mathbf{K}_d, \mathbf{K}_p$ are diagonal matrices with positive elements.

Using (9) and expressing $\ddot{\vec{q}}$ from (1) and substituting it here we get:

$$\ddot{\vec{q}}^{\,*} + \mathbf{K}_d \frac{d}{dt}\vec{e} + \mathbf{K}_p \vec{e} = \mathbf{A}^{-1}\vec{b} + \mathbf{A}^{-1}\mathbf{B}\vec{M}\,. \qquad (11)$$

We express $\vec{M}$ from the obtained formula:

$$\vec{M} = \mathbf{B}^{-1}\mathbf{A}\left(\ddot{\vec{q}}^{\,*} + \mathbf{K}_d \frac{d}{dt}\vec{e} + \mathbf{K}_p \vec{e}\right) - \mathbf{B}^{-1}\vec{b}\,. \qquad (12)$$

The resulting regulator causes error to tend to zero. The following simplified formula can be used to simplify the realization of the regulator:

$$\vec{M} = \mathbf{B}^{-1}\mathbf{A}\left(\mathbf{K}_d \frac{d}{dt}\vec{e} + \mathbf{K}_p \vec{e}\right). \qquad (13)$$

Taking into account the written expressions the exoskeleton's control system acquires a structure shown in Fig. 3.

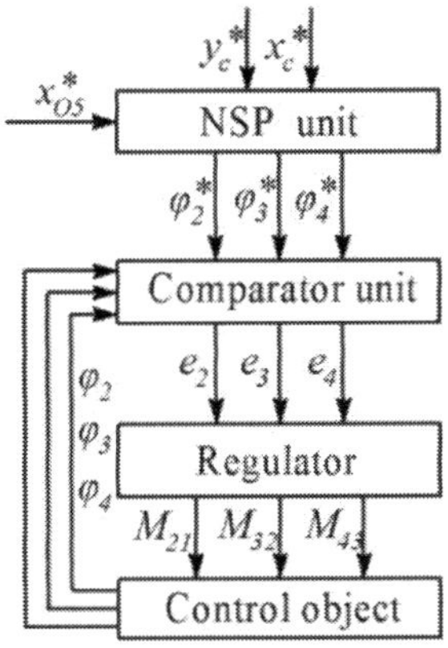

Figure 3. Structural diagram of the control system.

Fig. 3 shows five blocks of the control system. Block NSP Unit solves the inverse kinematics problem using equations (8); The Comparator block computes the control error's current values; the Regulator block generates control actions according to equation (13). The action of the block, Controlled Object is described by equation (1).

5 Results of numerical modeling conclusion

We use the following values of the mechanism's parameters during modeling: $m_2 = 9.6$ kg, $m_3 = 16.8$ kg, $m_4 = 53.6$ kg, $l_2 = 0.51$ m, $l_3 = 0.51$ m, $l_4 = 0.68$ m. The stated values were obtained using the parameter selection method, which allows consideration of weight and size parameters of both the exoskeleton and the operator. This method is described in [17].

We consider the case when the mechanism performs the following tasks:

$$x^*_{O5}(t) = x^*_{O5}(0)\,, \quad x^*_C(t) = x^*_C(0)\,, \qquad (14)$$

$$y^*_C(t) = 0.363 + 0.0161\cdot t^2 - 0.0011\cdot t^3\,. \qquad (15)$$

Formulas (14) imply that the horizontal position of the center of mass and O_5 must not change during motion. Fig. 4 shows time graphs for this case.

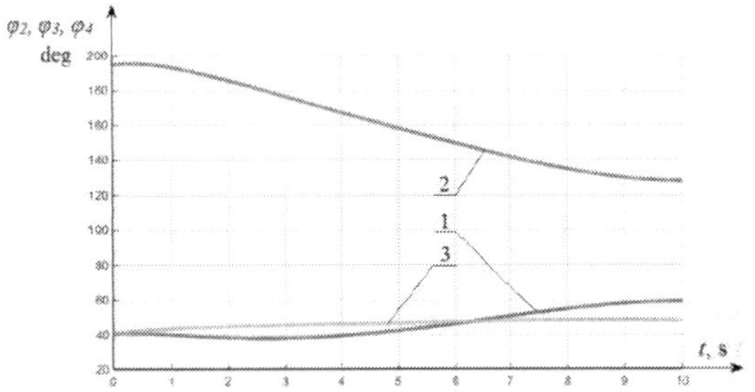

Figure 4. Time graphs of generalized coordinates: 1 – φ_2 ; 2 – φ_3 ; 3 – φ_4 .

Graphs of the desired and obtained values of coordinates visually coincide. In order to demonstrate the operation of the method we use fig. 5 to show the sequence of the positions taken by the mechanism. It can be observed that the centre of mass and point O_5 move vertically upwards without shifting in the horizontal direction, which satisfies the tasks given by formula (14).

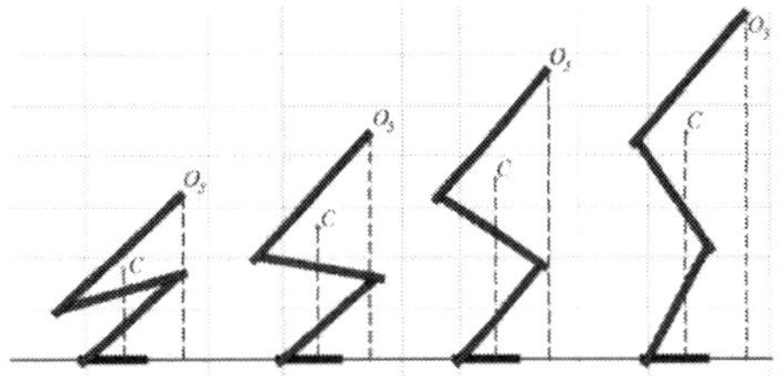

Figure 5. Sequence of positions taken by the mechanism during verticalization.

Fig. 6 presents time graphs of torques generated by the drives of the mechanism during verticalization.

After analyzing the graphs shown above it can be noted that with the exception of rapid changes in the values of moments at the beginning of motion the obtained graphs have the form of smooth continuously varying functions. We note that in practice the problem of abrupt changes in torque values at the beginning of the motion mechanism is mitigated by the fact that exoskeleton rests on chair at the beginning of motion, so that in the event that the control system is unable to execute a sufficiently rapid increase of the torques it will only result in the time lag of visible verticalization. The introduction of elastic elements in the exoskeleton's structure allows us to make the change of torques at the beginning of motion much smoother.

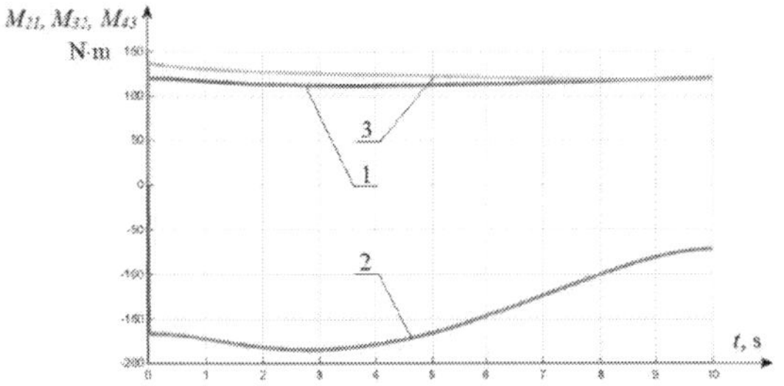

Figure 6. Time graphs of torques graphs of torques generated by the drives during verticalization: 1 – $M_{21}(t)$; 2 – $M_{32}(t)$; 3 – $M_{43}(t)$.

Let us assess the difference between controls given by expressions (12) and (13). To do that an expression for $\ddot{\vec{q}}^*$ is needed. We derive it in the following way:

$$\ddot{\vec{q}}^* = \left(\frac{\partial \vec{r}_t}{\partial \vec{q}}\right)^{-1}\left(\ddot{\vec{r}}_t - \frac{\partial \dot{\vec{r}}_t}{\partial \vec{q}}\dot{\vec{q}}\right), \quad (16)$$

where $\vec{r}_t = [x_C \quad y_C \quad x_{O5}]^{\mathrm{T}}$.

The time dependencies for generalised coordinates obtained using control given by (12) will be denoted as $\vec{q}^{<1>}$, and for the case when controls are given by (13) those dependencies will be denoted as $\vec{q}^{<2>}$. Difference between the them will be denotes as $\vec{\varepsilon}$:

$$\vec{\varepsilon} = \vec{q}^{<2>} - \vec{q}^{<1>}. \quad (17)$$

The graphs of ε_1, ε_2 and ε_3 are plotted in Fig. 7.

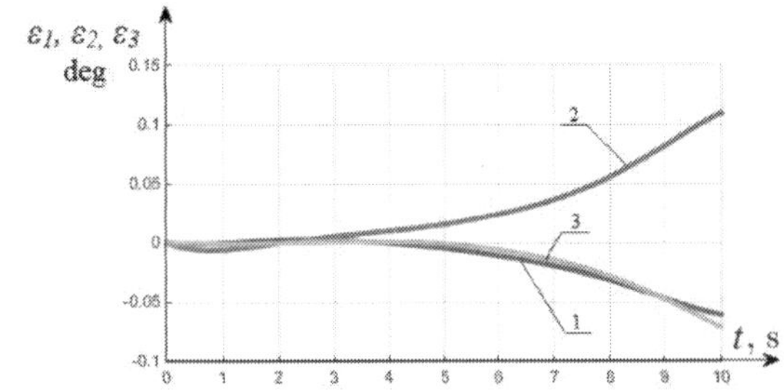

Figure 7. Time graphs of differences betwean generalised coordinates obtained using controls given by expressions (12) and (13): 1 – $\varepsilon_1(t)$, 2 – $\varepsilon_2(t)$, 3 – $\varepsilon_3(t)$.

From the graphs in the Fig. 7, we can see that the difference between the angles is less than 0.15 degree in absolute value. The difference between control errors for two controls is bounded by 0.1 degree in absolute value. That suggests that for some practical applications the difference between performances of two controls is not significant, while the scheme given by the expression (13) is simpler to implement and requires less knowledge of the control object.

6 Conclusion

An algorithm of the automatic control system's operation using the null space projection method for solving the inverse kinematics problem with multiple tasks was demonstrated in this work. The synthesis of a multichannel regulator that performs error based control was described. The efficiency of the proposed system was demonstrated by numerical experiments and an analysis of the obtained graphs was done. The developed approach to exoskeleton control during verticalization was used during in the design of the automatic control system for the prototype – ExoLite, undergoing tests at the laboratory of mechatronics and robotics at Southwest State University.

Acknowledgments

Work is supported by RSF, Project № 14-39-00008

References

1. J. Rosen, M. Brand, M.B. Fuchs and M. Arcan. IEEE Transactions on Systems, Man and Cybernetics, Part A: Systems and Humans, **31**, 210 (2001)
2. K. Kiguchi, T. Tanaka and T. Fukuda. IEEE Transactions on Fuzzy Systems, **12**, 481 (2004)
3. H. Kazerooni, J.L. Racine, L. Huang and R. Steger. Proceedings of the 2005 IEEE international conference on Robotics and automation ICRA 2005, pp. 4353-4360 (2005).
4. Y. Mao, X. Jin, G.G. Dutta, J.P. Scholz and S.K. Agrawal. IEEE Transactions on Neural Systems and Rehabilitation Engineering, **23**, 84 (2015)
5. K.Z. Takahashi, M.D. Lewek and G.S. Sawicki. Journal of neuroengineering and rehabilitation, **12**, 23 (2015)
6. E.A. Rogers. Assistive Exoskeleton for Injury Prevention During Downhill Walking. Bachelor's thesis (Harvard College, 2015)
7. X. Jin, X. Cui and S.K. Agrawal. *2015 IEEE International Conference on Robotics and Automation (ICRA)*, pp. 5578-5583 (2015)
8. S. Jatsun, S. Savin, A. Yatsun, and A. Malchikov. *Advances in Robot Design and Intelligent Control. Springer International Publishing*. pp. 165-172 (2016)
9. S. Jatsun, S. Savin, A. Yatsun and R. Turlapov. *2015 10th International Symposium on Mechatronics and its Applications (ISMA)*, pp. 1-6 (2015).
10. S.F. Jatsun, S.I. Savin, A.S. Yatsun and R.N. Turlapov. *26th DAAAM International Symposium on Intelligent Manufacturing and Automation*. (2015).
11. S. Jatsun, S. Savin, A. Yatsun, I. *Performing Standing up Motion from a Chair Proceedings of 4th International Conference on Robot Intelligence Technology and Applications (RiTA)* (2015)
12. S.F. Jatsun, L.Yu. Vorochaeva, A.S. Yatsun and S.I. Savin. *Proceedings of the International Conference on CLAWAR*, pp. 175-182 (2015)

13. F. Flacco, A. De Luca and O. Khatib. IEEE Transactions on Robotics, **31**, 637 (2015)
14. F. Flacco, A. De Luca, and O. Khatib. *2012 IEEE/RSJ International Conference on Intelligent Robots and Systems (IROS)*, pp. 3970-3977 (2012)
15. J. Nakanishi, R. Cory, M. Mistry, J. Peters and S. Schaal. *2005 IEEE/RSJ International Conf. Intelligent Robots and Systems, (IROS 2005)* (2005)
16. L. Sentis and O. Khatib. *IEEE International Conference on Humanoid Robots* (2004)
17. S. Jatsun, S. Savin, A. Yatsun. *Proceedings of 21st CISM-IFToMM Symposium on Robot Design 2016* (in publishing)

ITM Web of Conferences 6, 01002 (2016)
DOI: 10.1051/itmconf/20160601002
Owned by the authors, published by EDP Sciences, 2016

Multicriterial optimization of preventive maintenance of informational/technical stochastic system

Anna Kovalenko[1,a] and Gennady Rogachev[1]

[1]Samara State Technical University, 443100, Samara, Russia

Abstract. The problem of optimization of reliability and economical indexes is solved for informational/technical system with periodical diagnostics and restoration. The system considered is the one with users accesses and errors occurring. The probability that the error occurs increases in time. Therefore, the longer is the restoration period the more there is a risk of system operation with error. But too frequent restoration can be too expensive. To take into account all these factors two-criteria optimization is made with the restriction of reliability characteristic being of the given level.

1 Introduction

It is impossible to imagine the modern enterprise operating without informational/technical systems of various complexity and reliability. The diagnostics of such systems has gained particular significance [1]. Many authors apply queue models to model informational/ technical systems and get their adequate economical and reliability characteristics. Herewith, one should take into account their breakdowns, like in [2].

The problem of system optimization is often solved at the stage of system projection. One of the efficient solutions is planning diagnostics of the system. As the continuous diagnostics of informational/technical systems is expensive, they often apply the strategy of periodical diagnostics.

The system considered is the one with users accesses and errors occurring. The probability that the error occurs increases in time. Therefore, the longer is the restoration period the more there is a risk of system operation with error. But too frequent restoration can be too expensive. To take into account all these factors two-criteria optimization is made with the restriction of reliability characteristic being of the given level.

The system is considered to be stochastic. More specifically, we construct the model of one-server queue with immediate service and periodic diagnostics. To get system stationary characteristics the theory of regenerative processes is applied. To simplify the models they often take random variables to have exponential distributions (for example, [3]). We do not make these restrictions.

2 Problem setting

Let us consider informational/technical system with periodical diagnostics and restoration. Herewith, the system is down while restoration. The system operates in the following way.

Time period between users accesses is the random variable β with the distribution function $G(t) = P\{\beta \le t\}$ and density $g(t)$. Diagnostics period is τ. The function $p(\tau)$, depending on the diagnostics period, is the probability that there is no error and the system continues to operate. The function $q(\tau) = 1 - p(\tau)$ denotes the probability the error is found and the system restoration is begun. Restoration time is proportional to τ. The proportionality coefficient is k. The random variables β is supposed to be independent, to have absolutely continuous distribution function and finite expectation $M\beta$.

3 Mathematical model building

To describe the system operation one can apply semi-Markov process with a discrete-continuous phase state space [4]. It was done in [5, 6], for instance. But as the process describing the system is regenerative, system stationary characteristics can also be obtained another way. System operation time diagram is represented in Figure 1.

With the help of Fig. 1 one can obtain final probabilities of system restoration and normal operation respectively. As we get stationary characteristics it is enough to consider one regeneration period. In addition,

[a] Corresponding author: annushka199@bk.ru

we can do it by writing out geometrical probabilities of the system states.

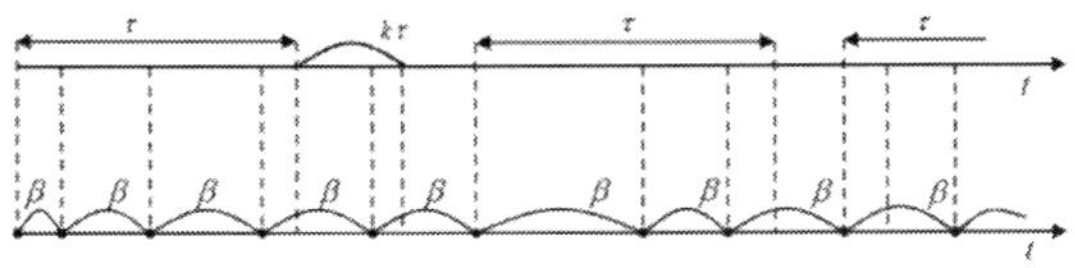

Figure 1. System operation time diagram.

If $p_0(\tau)$ is the final probability the system is under restoration, $p_1(\tau)$ is the final probability the system operates, then

$$p_0(\tau) = \frac{k\,q(\tau)\tau}{M\beta\, p(\tau)\left[1+H_g(\tau)\right]+q(\tau)M\beta\left[1+H_g(\tau+k\tau)\right]}, \tag{1}$$

$$p_1(\tau) = 1-\frac{k\,q(\tau)\tau}{M\beta\, p(\tau)\left[1+H_g(\tau)\right]+q(\tau)M\beta\left[1+H_g(\tau+k\tau)\right]}$$

In the same way, system economical indexes, such as the average specific income $S(\tau)$ per calendar time unit and average specific cost $C(\tau)$ per time unit of normal operation are:

$$S(\tau) = \frac{S_1(\tau)\,p(\tau)\left[1+H_g(\tau)\right]-c_0 k\,q(\tau)\tau - C_2}{M\beta\, p(\tau)\left[1+H_g(\tau)\right]+q(\tau)M\beta\left[1+H_g(\tau+k\tau)\right]}, \tag{2}$$

$$C(\tau) = \frac{c_0 k\,q(\tau)\tau + C_2}{M\beta\, p(\tau)\left[1+H_g(\tau)\right]+q(\tau)M\beta\left[1+H_g(\tau+k\tau)\right]-k\,q(\tau)\tau}$$

Here, $S_1(\tau)$ is the income per successive user access to the system decreasing with time as the probability of errors absence decreases: $S_1(\tau)=S_1\,p(\tau)$, S_1 is the income per successive user access to the system without errors; c_0 is the cost per time unit of system restoration; C_2 is the cost of one diagnostics, $H_g(\tau)$ is the renewal function of the renewal process generated by the random variable β.

For the system where $g(t)=\lambda e^{-\lambda t}$, $p(\tau)=\mu/(\mu+\tau)$, $\tau \ge 0$, formulas (1) and (2) take the form:

$$p_0(\tau) = \frac{k\lambda\tau^2}{\lambda(1+k)\tau^2+(1+\lambda\mu)\tau+\mu},$$

$$p_1(\tau) = \frac{\lambda\tau^2+(1+\lambda\mu)\tau+\mu}{\lambda(1+k)\tau^2+(1+\lambda\mu)\tau+\mu}$$

$$S(\tau) = \lambda\frac{(S_1\lambda\mu-C_2)\tau - c_0 k\tau^2+\mu(S_1-C_2)}{\lambda(1+k)\tau^2+(1+\lambda\mu)\tau+\mu},$$

$$C(\tau) = \lambda\frac{c_0 k\tau^2+C_2\tau+C_2\mu}{\lambda\tau^2+(1+\lambda\mu)\tau+\mu}.$$

4 Optimal period of system restoration

The following criteria of system optimal operation are taken:

1) positive criterion — average specific income per calendar time unit $S(\tau)$;

2) negative criterion — average specific cost per time unit of normal operation $C(\tau)$;

There is also a restriction given by the inequality for the probability of normal system operation $p(\tau)$.

$$\begin{cases} S(\tau) \to \max\limits_{\tau\in(0,\infty)}, \\ C(\tau) \to \min\limits_{\tau\in(0,\infty)}, \\ p(\tau) > \tilde{P}. \end{cases}$$

One of the methods of multi-criteria problem reduction to one-criteria is to take linear convolution of criteria as objective function [7]. In our case, economical indexes are of the same nature, that is why the objective goal is $V(\tau)$:

$$V(\tau) = a_s S(\tau) - (1-a_s)C(\tau).$$

Here, a_s is a weight coefficient defining the indexes of relative significance of $S(\tau)$. The function $p(\tau)$ is monotonously decreasing over the positive values of its argument. That is why in the case considered the optimization problem is the problem of obtaining the value τ^V_{opt} of absolute maximum of the function $V(\tau)$ at $\tau\in(0,\tau_p]$, $p(\tau_p)=\tilde{P}$.

Consider an example of optimization of diagnostics period. Inter-arrival time is exponential, the average time between users accesses is 2,5 hours; $p(\tau)=1/(1+0.05\tau)$, $\tau\ge 0$ $k=0{,}2$; $\tilde{P}=0{,}8$; $S_1=1000$ money units (m.u.), $c_0=400$ m.u./hour, $C_2=350$ m.u.

The solution of the problem by means of Maple application gives the following results. The linear convolution of criteria, if the weight coefficient is $a_s=1/2$, reaches its highest value, satisfying the inequality restrictions at the point $\tau^V_{opt}=3{,}21$ hours: $S(\tau^V_{opt})=219{,}92$ m.u./hour, $C(\tau^V_{opt})=67{,}52$ m.u./hour, $p_1(\tau^V_{opt})=0{,}985$, $p_1(\tau^V_{opt})=0{,}862$. Graphs of reliability criterion (the probability of system normal operation) against diagnostics period is given in Fig. 2. Graphs of economical criteria against diagnostics period are given in Fig. 3, 4. Graph of linear convolution of economical criteria against diagnostics period is given in Fig. 5.

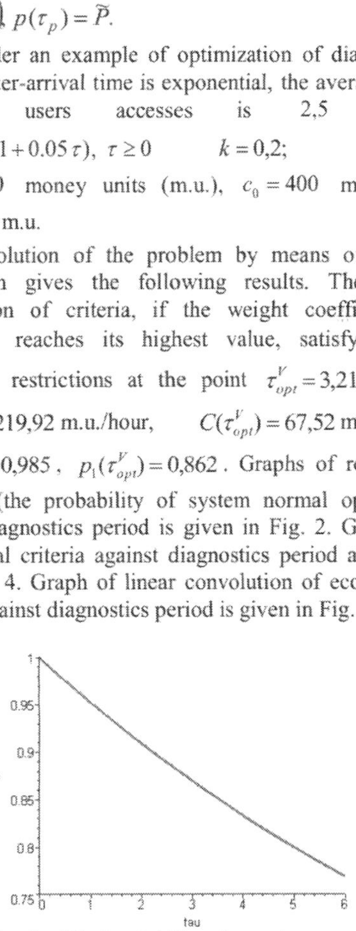

Figure 2. Graph of final probability of normal system operation against diagnostics period.

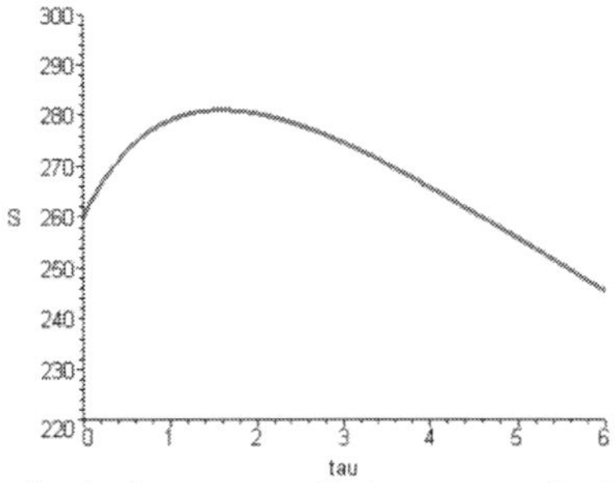

Figure 3. Graph of average specific income per calendar unit against diagnostics period.

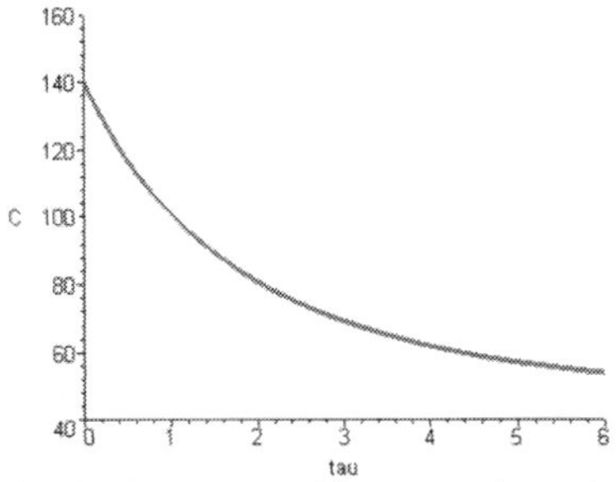

Figure 4. Graph of average specific cost per time unit of normal operation against diagnostics period.

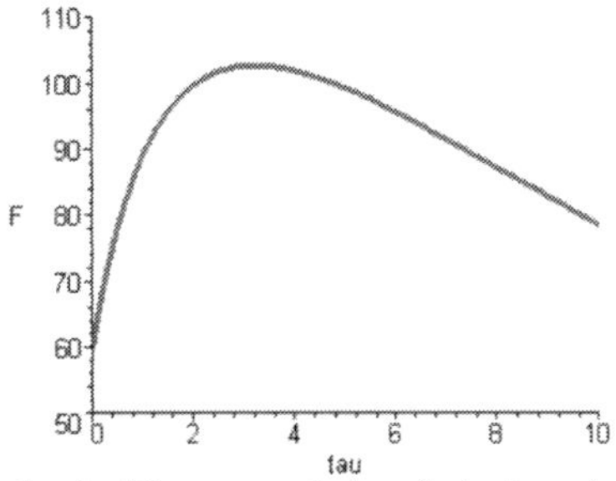

Figure 5. Graph of linear convolution of criteria against diagnostics period.

Acknowledgment

This work was financially supported by Ministry of Education and Science of Russian Federation (basic part of government contract, project No. 1271).

References

1. Ya. A. Maksimov. *8 International conference on mathematical modelling and computer science YM2007* (2007) [Rus]
2. U. Yechiali. Queueing Systems, **56**, 195 (2007)
3. N. Perel, U. Yechiali. EJOR, **201**, 247 (2010)
4. V.S. Korolyuk, A.F. Turbin. *Markov Renewal Processes in System Reliability Problems* (Nauka, 1982) [Rus]
5. A.I. Peschansky, A.I. Kovalenko. Cybernetics and Systems Analysis, **51**, 632 (2015)
6. Yu. Obzherin, El. Boyko. *Semi-Markov models. Control of restorable systems with latent failures* (Elsevier, 2015)
7. M. Emmerich, A. Deutz. *Multicriteria Optimization and Decision Making* (Springer, 2006)

ITM Web of Conferences **6**, 01003 (2016)
DOI: 10.1051/itmconf/20160601003

Constructive solution of the robotic chassis AnyWalker

Igor Riadchykov[1], Semen Sechenev[1], Sergey Sinitsa[1] and Evgeny Nikulchev[2, a]

[1]*Kuban State University, 350040 Krasnodar, Russia*
[2]*Moscow Technological Institute, 119334 Moscow, Russia*

Abstract. Presented constructive solution of the robotic system effectively solves the problem of movement in human-adapted not pre-prepared environment. AnyWalker stabilization system consists of three flywheels, implemented in the form of motor-wheels or driven with the help of transfer mechanisms each from its motor, in orthogonal planes, and the centers of mass flywheels are the same. It is proposed to formalize the functionality of the movement in the human-adapted environment in the form of a standard architecture for robotic chassis with the possibility of hardware and software extension.

1 Introduction

There are many applications of robotic systems in which robots must be able to effectively locomote in the human-adapted, not specifically prepared for the machines environment, for example, service robotics, work in rugged terrain, multistorey buildings, weightlessness. Right now there are no robotic systems, including those with anthropomorphic design, satisfying this criteria.

The external forces compensation and stabilization plays a key role during the movement of the robotic systems. At the same time there are no mathematical models of anthropomorphic robots, which have analytically solvable locomotion equations systems, provided that movement and stabilization are carried out using the same actuators [1].

It is proposed to formalize the functionality of the movement in the human-adapted environment in the form of a standard architecture for robotic chassis with the possibility of hardware and software extension.

2 Kinematic schemes

Robotic system was developed, that can move in the human-adapted environments, with the stabilization and motion being controlled by different cyber-physical systems.

The scheme of arrangement non-anthropomorphic bipedal chassis is proposed, where each leg has three links and a foot, and the center of mass of the whole structure is located on the second level from the surface of the support joint, which provides simplicity of balancing this platform, and also increases the area available to make a step or manipulate the objects, in comparison with anthropomorphic linkage (Fig. 1).

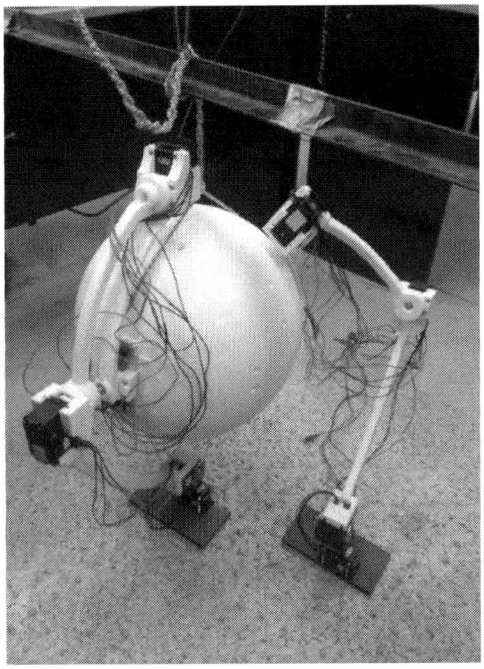

Figure 1. General view of the prototype

Kinematic scheme is shown on the Fig. 2, where 1 – body of the robot, 2 – control unit, 4 – power supply, 5 – corrective center of mass displacement unit, 6 – surface, 7 – axis of the first and second hinges rotation, 8 – axis of gravity passing through the center of mass, 9 – obstacle, 11 – first part of the upper robot leg, 12 – second part of the upper robot leg, 13 – lower robot leg, 14 – foot, 21 – first hinge, 22 – second hinge, 23 – third hinge, 24 – fourth hinge.

[a] Corresponding author : nikulchev@mail.ru

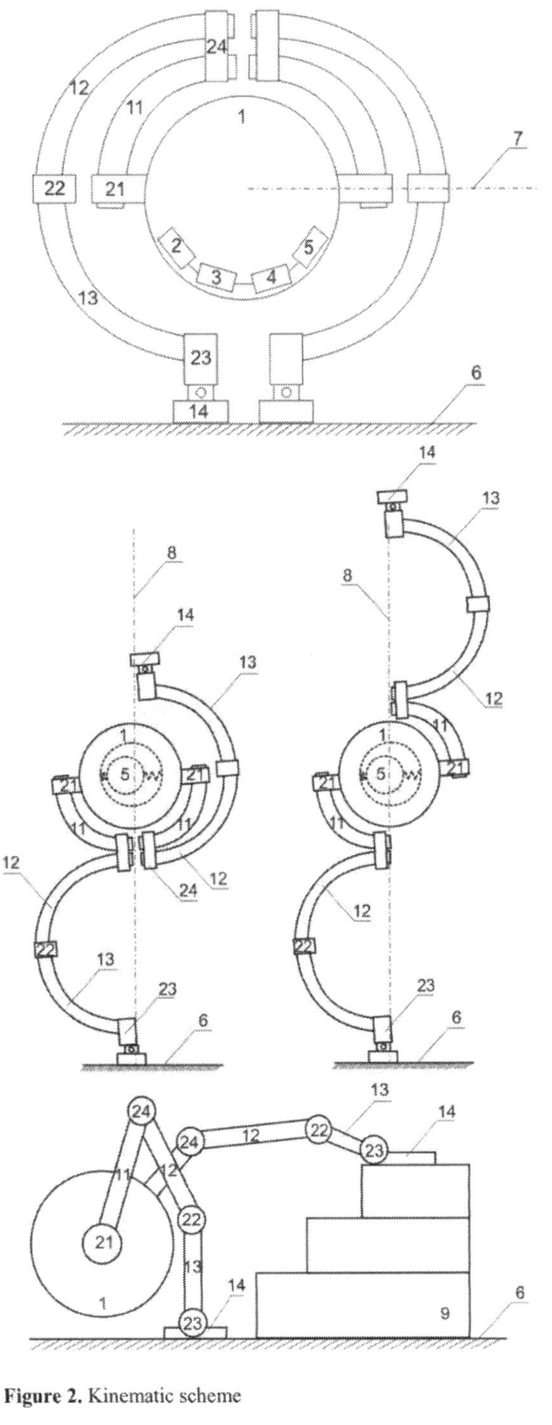

Figure 2. Kinematic scheme

The phase space of allowed manipulator states ω is specified with a Boolean function $P(\theta)$ which returns 1 if the vector displacements of the joints θ is valid. The movement θ of the kinematic scheme is a curve $\xi \subset \omega$ with initial point θ_1 and endpoint θ_2. Here θ_i $(i=\overline{1,12})$ — vector specifying the position of manipulators of the robot relative to the housing. In Fig. 2 under the numbers shown 21, 22, 24 joints are shown with one rotational degree of freedom, number 23 — joint with three rotational degrees of freedom. The endpoint of each step θ_2 is computed by solving the inverse kinematic problem for a given control algorithm coordinates in three-dimensional space relative to the robot body. Curve ξ must satisfy the following conditions:

$$\forall\theta \subset \xi P(\theta)=1;$$

$$S(\theta_1,\gamma_1)=1, S(\theta_2,\gamma_2)=1.$$

Function $S(\theta,\gamma)$ here determines whether the static state is subject to the vector of the readings of the auxiliary sensors γ.

The speed of movement of joints v_i $(i=\overline{1,12})$ are determined by the control algorithm depending on the received commands and sensor readings at each given time.

AnyWalker stabilization system consists of three flywheels, implemented in the form of motor-wheels or driven with the help of transfer mechanisms each from its motor, in orthogonal planes, and the centers of mass flywheels are the same. One flywheel is perpendicular to the ground and the direction of motion, the second perpendicular to the ground and parallel to the direction of motion, the third parallel to the ground. This stabilization system allows to compensate external influences, without altering the kinematics of walking, and moments of inertia that occur when you move the manipulators. This stabilization system is an evolution of the design presented in [2-4].

3 Hardware and software architecture of the control system

Hardware and software architecture of the control system AnyWalker consists of the following levels:

1. Reactive layer is based on a microcontroller STM32F100RB. This level is responsible for:
   - Direct control of the actuators and flywheel joints, and getting the status information;
   - Filtering of raw data from accelerometers, gyroscopes, magnetometers, pressure, distance and other sensors.
2. The Executive level is based on the controller TRIK. This level is responsible for:
   - Localization of the robot in space by using vision systems and sensors;
   - The planning of movements based on the type of surface and dimensions of obstacles;
   - Processing of the sensor readings are in the "joints", "feet" and the housing;
   - Stabilization system flywheels and stabilization of manipulators;
   - Ancillary functions, such as specialized sensors and reactive behavior.
3. Algorithmic level represents the application software installed on a personal computer or smartphone, completely or partially in the cloud. This level is responsible for:

- The user interface. Directly integrated into the chassis: bluetooth, wifi, USB. Controlled via Internet;
- Machine learning: conducting complex calculations on powerful external computing platform that communicates the sensor readings and control commands from the chassis;
- Making decisions on application behavior that is not part of the basic functionality of the chassis;
- Multi-agent interaction, robotic platforms, built on the chassis.

It is proposed to use the control algorithmic support as an information service that will allow you to give third-party API researchers to solve applied problems. The levels of the software architecture provides an API to the next level according to their functionality:

1. Reactive level: the RPC API;
2. Executive level: C++ API, API QtSrcipt;
3. Algorithmic level: the SOAP API.

AnyWalker chassis is a standardised platform for robot applications. Standards extensions:

- Hardware level: the addition of various sensors, modernization of manipulators, resize, etc. Provides the ability for third-party developers to produce and sell their own hardware that is compatible with AnyWalker architecture;
- Control level for the robotic system: programming new movements, specialization under specific conditions of external environment, etc. Provides the ability for third-party developers to create and implement their own algorithms of movements through the app store;
- Intelligent systems level: programming groups of robots or chassis in specific conditions, competitive programming, artificial intellect systems on the basis of the chassis, debugging in the simulation environment. Provides the ability for developers to create and implement their own application scenarios robots, such as competitions and performances.

4 Conclusion

Proposed robotic system is able to move in the human-adapted environment, with non-anthropomorphic kinematic scheme. In this case, movement and stabilization are attributed to different cyber-physical system, which allowed the development of a mathematical model of the controlled motion with the analytically solvable system of equations.

Proposed scheme of standardization of software and hardware architecture of the chassis provides a third party service to create hardware and software extensions and build robotic systems based on this chassis, solving different applied tasks according to their specifications and conditions of the operation.

Presented constructive solution and the hardware-software description of the robotic system effectively solves the problem of movement in human-adapted not pre-prepared environment. Provided the description of the chassis architecture for robotic systems with the aim of providing to third-party developers mechanisms to increase the functionality and specialization robots, built on hardware and software solutions for this platform.

References

1. N.A. Chaturvedi, A.M. Bloch, N.H. McClamroch. *Proceedings of American Control Conference*, 3612-3617, 2006.
2. M. Muehlebach, G. Mohanarajah, R. D'Andrea, *2013 IEEE 52nd Annual Conference on Decision and Control (CDC)*, 1283-1288, 2013
3. M. Gajamohan, M. Muehlebach, T. Widmer, R. D'Andrea. *2013 European Control Conference (ECC)*, 268-274, 2013;
4. M. Gajamohan, M. Merz, I. Thommen, and R. D'Andrea, *2012 IEEE/RSJ International Conference on Intelligent Robots and Systems (IROS)*, 3722-3727, 2012.

ITM Web of Conferences **6**, 01004 (2016)
DOI: 10.1051/itmconf/20160601004

Multipurpose stabilization of the advanced marine surface crafts

Ruslan A. Sevostyanov[1,a] and Evgeny I. Veremey[1]

[1]*Saint Petersburg University, Computer Applications and Systems Department, 198504, Saint Petersburg, Russia*

Abstract. Advanced marine surface crafts, such as SWATHs, catamarans or hovercrafts become more and more popular for a great range of various tasks. They usually operate at much higher speed than conventional ships. Moreover, in the open sea there are a lot of requirements and restrictions concerning the quality of such crafts' dynamics, especially in case of the wind or waves. This paper considers application of the control law with a special multipurpose structure for autopilot design for amphibious air cushion vehicles. Such control law allows to decompose the autopilot task into simpler optimization subtasks. Efficiency of this approach is shown in the task of stabilizing yaw angle of the air cushion vehicle in the different weather conditions.

1 Introduction

One of the main goals of creating modern advanced marine crafts is the minimization of the hydrodynamic drag by reduction of the craft's hull area in contact with water. This allows to increase craft's speed and operation range, and to reduce fuel consumption. But there are also some disadvantages, such as increased influence of the wind and waves. Moreover, moving at higher speeds and complicated methods of hull lifting imply stricter requirements and restrictions for craft's dynamics.

In this paper we focus on the particular type of advanced crafts such as air cushion vehicles (ACVs). These crafts are lifted above the supporting surface by the aerostatic pressure created by supplying air into the area below the hull fenced by flexible skirt called air cushion. Due to the air cushion, in general, there is no contact of the rigid hull with the supporting surface which allows ACVs to move over any surface, i.e. ground, water, ice, swamps, etc.

The most complicated condition for ACVs is moving in the open seaway. They work well in case of the calm water, but the presence of wind or waves significantly complicate the operation. This implies the use of more advanced controller for the autopilot design. In this work we propose using the controller of the special structure, called multipurpose control law ([1]) for the task of the stabilization of the ACV's yaw angle. One of the main advantages of such structure is certain flexibility. It allows to comply with several dynamic requirements and restrictions simultaneously by decomposing the main task into simpler independent optimization subtasks. It is also possible to use only necessary parts of the controller in the current moment depending on the environmental conditions. The controller can even be applied for stabilization of some nonlinear systems ([2]).

2 Multipurpose control law

Standard stabilization problem is usually considered with respect to the linearized model of the craft's dynamics. Initial nonlinear dynamic model can be written in the following form:

$$\dot{x} = G(\boldsymbol{x}, \boldsymbol{\delta}, \boldsymbol{d}),$$

where $\boldsymbol{x} \in E^{n}$ is the plant state vector, $\boldsymbol{\delta} \in E^{m}$ – rudders deflections vector, $\boldsymbol{d} \in E^{n_d}$ – external disturbances vector.

Result of the linearization is the system of linear ordinary differential equations

$$\begin{aligned} \dot{\boldsymbol{x}} &= \mathbf{A}\boldsymbol{x} + \mathbf{B}\boldsymbol{\delta} + \mathbf{H}\boldsymbol{d}(t), \\ \boldsymbol{y} &= \mathbf{C}\boldsymbol{x}, \end{aligned} \tag{1}$$

where $\boldsymbol{x}$ is the vector of the deflections of the states from the equilibrium position, $\mathbf{A}$, $\mathbf{B}$, $\mathbf{H}$, $\mathbf{C}$ – constant matrices.

In addition to system (1) linear model of the rudder actuators should be considered in the form

$$\dot{\boldsymbol{\delta}} = \boldsymbol{u}, \tag{2}$$

where $\boldsymbol{u} \in E^{m}$ is the control signal.

The control law for the stabilization of the system (1), (2) has the following structure:

$$\begin{aligned} \dot{z} &= \mathbf{A}z + \mathbf{B}\boldsymbol{\delta} + \mathbf{G}(y - \mathbf{C}z), \\ \xi &= F(p)(y - \mathbf{C}z), p = d/dt, \\ u &= \boldsymbol{\mu}\dot{z} + \boldsymbol{\upsilon}y + \xi. \end{aligned} \tag{3}$$

Here the first equation represents the asymptotic observer. The second one plays role of the dynamic corrector, which can either provide the accurate steering ([3]) or minimize rudders deflections in case of sea waves presence ([4]). Finally, the third one is the control signal for the rudders actuators.

[a] Corresponding author : sevostyanov.ruslan@gmail.com

If we represent the dynamic filter in the normal form, then controller (3) can be written as follows:

$$\begin{aligned} \dot{z} &= Az + B\delta + G(y - Cz), \\ \dot{p} &= \alpha p + \beta(y - Cz), \\ \xi &= \gamma p, \\ u &= \mu\dot{z} + \upsilon y + \xi. \end{aligned} \tag{4}$$

In order to solve the stabilization problem, we have to find coefficients μ and υ of the control signal, matrix G of the asymptotic observer and transfer function $F(p)$ (and, therefore, coefficients α, β and γ of the normal form) of the corrector. Each of them are usually found through the solution of some optimization problem providing desired quality of the autopilot action.

3 ACV model

3.1 Nonlinear dynamics

The differential equations of the ACV motion concerning the manoeuvrability with four degrees of freedom can be written as follows [5, 6]:

$$\begin{aligned} m(\dot{V}_x + V_z\,\omega_y) &= F_{xa} + F_{xh} + T, \\ m(\dot{V}_z - V_x\,\omega_y) &= F_{za} + F_{zh} + F_{zc} + F_{zr}, \\ I_x\,\dot{\omega}_x &= M_{xa} + M_{xh} + M_\theta + M_{xr}, \\ I_y\,\dot{\omega}_y &= M_{ya} + M_{yh} + M_{yr}, \end{aligned} \tag{5}$$

where $\dot{V}_x$, $\dot{V}_z$, ω_x and ω_y are corresponding linear and angular velocities, m - craft's mass, I_x and I_y - moments of inertia. Index "a" denotes aerodynamic profile drag, "h" – hydrodynamic drag, "r" – forces and moments acting on rudders, F_{zc} – jet force produced by the air blown from the cushion in case of rolling, M_θ – restoring moment and T is the thrust. Corresponding coordinate systems are presented on Fig. 1.

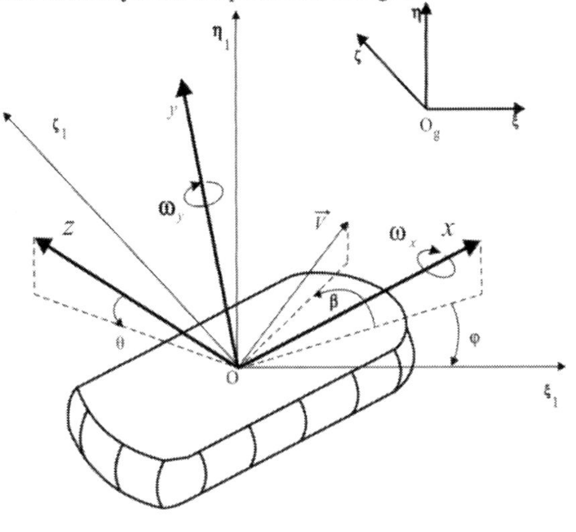

Figure 1. Coordinate systems of the model.

Aerodynamic drag has the following form:

$$\begin{aligned} F_{xa} &= 0.5C_{xa}(\beta_a)\rho_a V_0^2 S, \\ F_{za} &= 0.5C_{za}(\beta_a)\rho_a V_0^2 S, \\ M_{xa} &= 0.5F_{za}H, \\ M_{ya} &= 0.5(C_{mya}(\beta_a) + C_{mya}^{\omega_y}\frac{\omega_y L}{V_0})\rho_a V_0^2 SL, \end{aligned}$$

where β_a is aerodynamic drift angle (with respect to the wind), ρ_a – air density, V_0 – craft's velocity with respect to the wind, S – lateral surface area, H – craft's height, L – craft's length. $C_{xa}(\beta_a)$, $C_{za}(\beta_a)$, $C_{mya}(\beta_a)$, $C_{mya}^{\omega_y}$ – aerodynamic coefficients.

Hydrodynamic drag has the following form:

$$\begin{aligned} F_{xh} &= 0.5C_{xh}(Fr,\beta)\rho_w V^2 W^{2/3}, \\ F_{zh} &= 0.5C_{zh}(Fr,\beta)\rho_w V^2 W^{2/3}, \\ M_{xh} &= 0.5F_{zh}H, \\ M_{yh} &= 0.5(C_{myh}(Fr,\beta) + C_{myh}^{\omega_y}(Fr)\frac{\omega_y W^{1/3}}{V})\rho_w V^2 W, \end{aligned}$$

where β is craft's drift angle, ρ_w – water density, V – craft's velocity, W – craft's displacement. $C_{xh}(Fr,\beta)$, $C_{zh}(Fr,\beta)$, $C_{mxh}(Fr,\beta)$, $C_{myh}(Fr,\beta)$, $C_{myh}^{\omega_y}$ – hydrodynamic coefficients. Fr is the Froude's number:

$$Fr = \frac{V}{\sqrt{Lg}}$$

Forces and moments acting on rudders are:

$$\begin{aligned} F_{zr} &= C_r\,\delta\frac{\rho_a}{2}V_0^2 S, \\ M_{yr} &= F_{zr}x_p, \\ M_{xr} &= -F_{zr}y_p, \\ C_r &= C_{r1}[(1-k_r)(1+s)\frac{S_r''}{S_r} + \frac{S_r'}{S_r}], \\ k_r &= \frac{1.9\pi\lambda_{1r}s}{\lambda_r(1.9\pi + \lambda_{1r})(s+1)}, \\ s &= \sqrt{\frac{1+2.53T}{(\rho_a D^2 V_0^2)}} - 1, \end{aligned}$$

where C_r – force coefficient, δ – rudder angle, x_r and y_r – coordinates of the rudder center, C_{r1} – coefficient of the model without thrusters. S_r – rudder area, S_r', S_r'' – parts of the rudder area inside and outside of the air stream, λ_r, λ_{r1} – coorresponding parts of the rudder length, D – air fan diameter.

Finally, air jet from the cushion and restoring moment are computed as follows:

$$\begin{aligned} F_{zc} &= mgk_\theta\,\theta, \\ M_\theta &= -mgh\theta - N_\theta\,\omega_x, \end{aligned}$$

where h is metacentric height; k_θ – jet force coefficient; N_θ – restoring coefficient.

3.2 Linear model

Here we linearize system (5) in the neighbourhood of the equilibrium position $V_x = \text{const}$, $V_z = \omega_y = \theta = \delta = 0$ assuming that there are no external disturbances. Instead of lateral velocity V_z we're using drift angle β. In this case $V = V_x = \text{const}$ and $\beta = \frac{V_z}{V}$. We're also adding kinematic equation for yaw angle φ and linear model of the rudder actuator. Therefore, linear model of the lateral motion of the ACV which is used for the stabilization of the yaw angle has the following form:

$$\begin{aligned} \dot{\beta} &= a_{11}\beta + a_{12}\omega_y + b_1\delta + h_1 d(t), \\ \dot{\omega}_y &= a_{21}\beta + a_{22}\omega_y + b_2\delta + h_2 d(t), \\ \dot{\varphi} &= \omega_y, \\ \dot{\delta} &= u. \end{aligned} \tag{6}$$

For the ACV with characteristics similar to the Jinsha II-class LCAC [7] weighting 70 tons moving at the speed of 15 m/s coefficients in the right parts of the (6) have the following numerical values:

$$\begin{aligned} &a_{11} = -0.5718,\ a_{12} = -1.0, \\ &a_{12} = -0.0083,\ a_{22} = -0.2828, \\ &b_1 = -0.0134,\ b_2 = -0.0705, \\ &h_1 = 0.043, h_2 = 0.02. \end{aligned}$$

4 Control law synthesis

First of all, we derive control signal that stabilizes linear system (6):

$$u = \mu_1\dot{\beta}_1 + \mu_2\dot{\omega}_{y_2} + \mu_3\dot{\varphi}_3 + \nu\varphi + \xi,$$

where

$$\begin{aligned} &\mu_1 = -0.1318, \mu_2 = 20.3927, \\ &\mu_3 = 17.4867, \nu = 2.2361. \end{aligned}$$

Next, we construct asymptotic observer assuming that we can measure only the yaw angle:

$$\begin{aligned} \dot{z}_1 &= a_{11}z_1 + a_{12}z_2 + b_1\delta + g_1(\varphi - z_3), \\ \dot{z}_2 &= a_{21}z_1 + a_{22}z_2 + b_2\delta + g_2(\varphi - z_3), \\ \dot{z}_3 &= z_2 + g_3(\varphi - z_3), \end{aligned}$$

where

$$g_1 = 24.0296,\ g_2 = 309.9193,\ g_3 = 24.8966.$$

Finally, dynamic corrector which plays here the role of the dynamic filter that minimizes rudders deflections under the action of regular waves with frequency 0.65 has the following form:

$$\begin{aligned} \dot{p}_1 &= \alpha_{11}p_1 + \alpha_{12}p_2 + \beta_1(\varphi - z_3), \\ \dot{p}_2 &= \alpha_{21}p_1 + \alpha_{22}p_2 + \beta_2(\varphi - z_3), \\ \xi &= \gamma_1 p_1 + \gamma_2 p_2, \end{aligned}$$

where

$$\begin{aligned} &\alpha_{11} = 0.0,\ \alpha_{12} = 1.0, \\ &\alpha_{12} = -0.04,\ \alpha_{22} = -0.4, \\ &\beta_1 = -3210.8469,\ \beta_2 = -4998.4912, \\ &\gamma_1 = 0.0, \gamma_2 = 1.0. \end{aligned}$$

5 Simulation results

Fig. 2 demonstrates craft's turn on 10 degrees without action of wind or waves. In this case dynamic filter (4) is switched off.

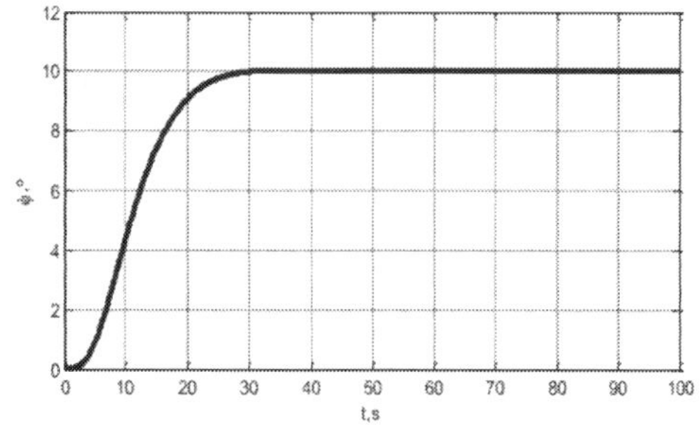

Figure 2. Yaw angle, 10 degrees turn

Fig. 3 demonstrates astatic property of the controller in case of side wind with 10 m/s velocity. It can be seen that yaw angle deflects a little more than 0.6 degrees and then converge back to zero, keeping the initial course. Here dynamic filter is also switched off.

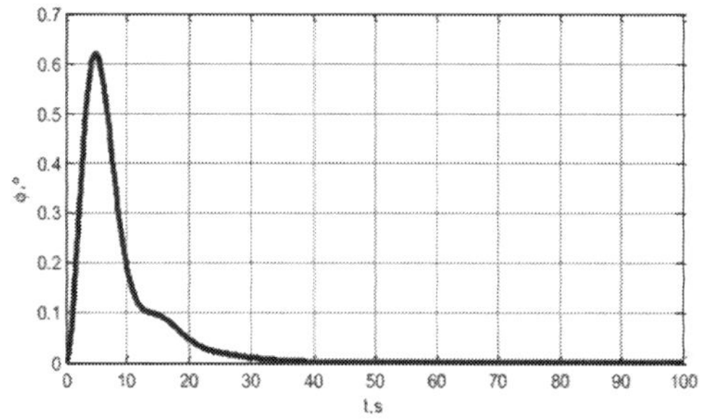

Figure 3. Yaw angle, course keeping under the action of side wind with 10 m/s velocity.

Finally, Fig. 4-5 demonstrate the craft's dynamics in case of regular side waves with 4-th number intensity on the Beaufort scale:

$$d(t) = 0.2\sin(0.65t) + 0.1\sin(0.55t) + 0.1\sin(0.75t).$$

Here the dynamic filter was switched on only after 300 seconds. It can be seen that there's no big difference in the yaw dynamics before and after switching the filter (Fig. 4), but the rudders action after 300 seconds decreases significantly (Fig. 5).

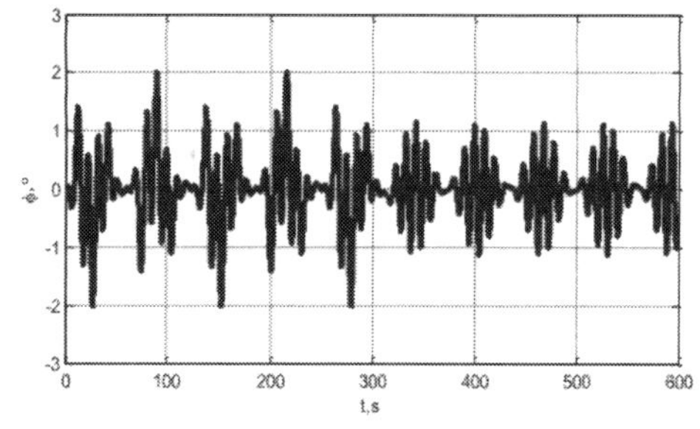

Figure 4. Yaw angle, course keeping under the action of regular side waves.

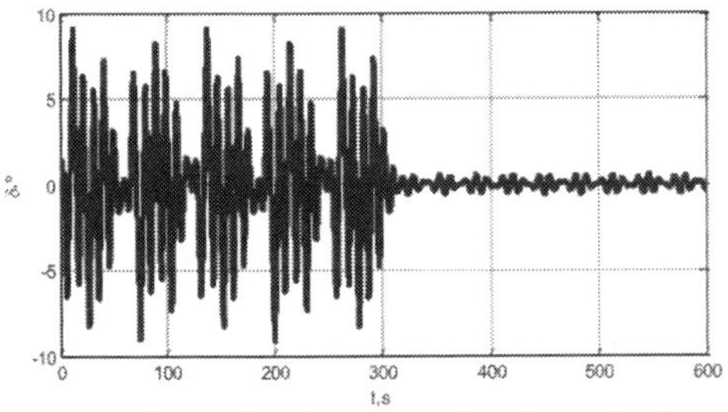

Figure 5. Rudders' deflections, course keeping under the action of regular side waves.

6 Conclusion

The goal of this work is to show the efficiency of the multipurpose control law in the task of the stabilization of the course angle of the particular type of advanced marine surface crafts such as air cushion vehicle. It can be seen from previous section that such controller actually stabilizes the course angle even in presence of the wind or waves.

Besides, the structure of the control law has certain flexibility. Each requirement for the control quality can be isolated and solved as independent task. Depending on the current environmental conditions some parts of the controller can be switched off for computational economy and overall control efficiency.

References

1. E. I. Veremey, J. Marine Sci. Appl., **13**, 127 (2014)
2. E. I. Veremey, Dynamical Correction of Positioning Control Laws, *Proceedings of 9th IFAC Conference on Maneuvering and Control of Marine Craft*, 31 (2012)
3. E. I. Veremey, M. V. Korovkin, M. V. Sotnikova, Ships' Steering in Accurate Regime Using Autopilot with Special Structure of Control Law, *IFAC-PapersOnLine*, **48 (16)**, 7 (2015)
4. E. I. Veremey, Optim. Control Appl. Meth. (2015)
5. L. Yun, A. Bliault, *Theory and Design of Air Cushion Craft*, (London: Arnolds, 2000)
6. Y. I. Voytkunskiy, *Ship Theory Manual*, **3** (Leningrad: Sudostroyeniye, 1985) (In Russian)
7. S. Saunders, *Jane's fighting ships, 2003-2004*, Coulsdon, Surrey, UK; Alexandria, (VA: Jane's Information Group, 2003)

ITM Web of Conferences 6, 01005 (2016)
DOI: 10.1051/itmconf/20160601005

Spectral H_2 optimal correction of additive fault estimation observer

Evgeny I. Veremey[1], Yaroslav V. Knyazkin[1, a]

[1]Saint-Petersburg state University, Faculty of Applied Mathematics and Control Processes, 199034 Saint-Petersburg, Russia

Abstract. This study is devoted to design of the fault estimation adaptive observer. Initial observer is modified with correction filter in order to improve robustness against external disturbance with known spectral structure. Computation of correctors parameters is based on special spectral algorithm of SISO (Single Input and Single Output) H_2 optimisation in frequency domain. Novel algorithm is proposed for practical implementation. Its effectiveness is demonstrated with example of successive additive fault estimation during marine ship yaw motion process.

1 Introduction

Due to increasing reliability demands of dynamic systems, problem of fault estimation is paid serious attention nowadays. Fast and accurate fault estimation [1-3] is necessary for effective fault tolerant control, such as described e.g. in [4]. Fault detection and fault estimation for linear time invariant (LTI) systems is well-studied area. On the other hand, most of existing methods ignore structure of external disturbance. Proposed approach can be treated as the method of observer's correction to avoid false alarms.

Most of the papers, devoted to the fault detection and fault estimation problems, use various approaches based on linear matrix inequalities. It is well known universal technique of numerical solution for control problems. On the other hand, there are many situations when the problem can be solved significantly easier with the help of the frequency domain specific approach, based on polynomial computations.

An application of this approach is demonstrated in this paper, which is organised as follows. In Section 2, structure of initial observer to be modified is presented. In Sections 3, 4 we describe spectral approach to observer correction and its practical realisation. Finally, Section 5 contains conclusion of the paper, overall results and directions for future research.

2 Problem statement

Let us consider the LTI system

$$\dot{x} = \mathbf{A}x + \mathbf{b}u + \mathbf{E}f + \mathbf{g}d,\\ y = \mathbf{C}x, \tag{1}$$

where $x \in \mathbf{R}^n$ is the system state vector; y, u, f, d are the scalar values : y is the output signal, u is the control, f represents additive fault disturbance and d is the main external disturbance. Suppose that faults are constant or slow varying, i.e. $\dot{f}(t) \approx 0$.

Adaptive fault estimation observer can be described by the following system

$$\dot{\hat{x}} = \mathbf{A}\hat{x} + \mathbf{b}u + \mathbf{E}\hat{f} + \mathbf{L}(y - \mathbf{C}z),\\ \dot{\hat{f}} = \mathbf{l}_f(y - \mathbf{C}z), \tag{2}$$

where $\hat{x} \in R^n$ is the estimated state vector, $\hat{f}$ is the estimated scalar fault, $\mathbf{L} \in R^n$ and scalar $\mathbf{l}_f$ are observer parameters to be designed. Some solutions of this problems described, e.g. in the papers [1-3].

Let us suppose that the adaptive observer (2) has already been designed for the system with no disturbance. The matter of the discussion is to propose the algorithm of its improvement with the help of corrective filter, compensating the action of regular disturbance with initially given frequency ω_0.

Generally speaking, the mentioned base observer may have more complicated structure and $\mathbf{L}, l_f$ can not be constant, but transfer functions that do not affect to the main idea. Correction of observer is given by

$$\dot{\hat{x}} = \mathbf{A}\hat{x} + \mathbf{b}u + \mathbf{E}\hat{f} + \mathbf{L}\nu,\\ \dot{\hat{f}} = \mathbf{l}_f\nu,\\ \nu(s) = W(s)(y - \mathbf{C}\hat{x}), \tag{3}$$

where $W(s)$ is a transfer function of a dynamic corrector to be computed. Let denote $e_x = x - \hat{x}$, $e_y = y - \mathbf{C}\hat{x}$, $e_f = f - \hat{f}$, $e = (e_x \;\; e_f)^{\mathrm{T}}$, $\overline{\mathbf{C}} = (\mathbf{C} \;\; 0)$, $\overline{\mathbf{L}} = -(\mathbf{L}^{\mathrm{T}} \;\; \mathbf{l}_f)^{\mathrm{T}}$, $\overline{\mathbf{g}} = (\mathbf{g} \;\; 0)^{\mathrm{T}}$, $\overline{\mathbf{A}} = \begin{pmatrix} \mathbf{A} & \mathbf{E} \\ 0 & 0 \end{pmatrix}$ and let

[a] Corresponding author : yaroslavknyazkin@gmail.com

describe an error dynamics of the corrected observer (3) with the following equations:

$$\begin{aligned} \dot{e} &= \overline{\mathbf{A}}e + \overline{\mathbf{L}}\nu + \overline{\mathbf{g}}d, \\ e_y &= \overline{\mathbf{C}}e, \\ \nu(s) &= W(s)e_y(s). \end{aligned} \quad (4)$$

It is necessary to compute a transfer function $W(s)$ of dynamic corrector (filter), providing fast and accurate fault estimation in presence of the external disturbance.

3 Spectral approach to H_2 optimisation

One of the ways to construct disturbance compensative filter is to solve mean-squire optimization problem with the functional

$$\widetilde{J} = \widetilde{J}(W) = \lim_{T\to\infty}\int_0^T \left(e_y^2 + k^2\nu^2\right)dt. \quad (5)$$

The second summand in (5) can be considered as the norm of "velocity" for estimated fault signal due to the fact that ν is proportional to its derivative.

Let us convert the system (4) to the form

$$\begin{aligned} A(s)e_y(s) &= B(s)\nu(s) + P(s)d(s), \\ \nu(s) &= W(s)e_y(s), \end{aligned} \quad (6)$$

where $A(s) = \det\left(\mathbf{I}s - \overline{\mathbf{A}}\right)$, $B(s) = A(s)\overline{\mathbf{C}}\left(\mathbf{I}s - \overline{\mathbf{A}}\right)^{-1}\overline{\mathbf{L}}$, $P(s) = A(s)\overline{\mathbf{C}}\left(\mathbf{I}s - \overline{\mathbf{A}}\right)^{-1}\overline{\mathbf{g}}$. Let suppose that the external disturbance $d(t)$ has the following spectral power density:

$$S_d(s) \equiv H(s)H(-s),$$

$$H(s) = \frac{N_d(s)}{T_d(s)} = \sqrt{\frac{4D_r\alpha}{\pi}}\frac{1}{s^2 + \alpha s + \alpha^2 + \beta^2}, \quad (7)$$

where D_r is the dispersion, β is the main frequency of the disturbance, $\alpha = s_t\beta$, s_t is the blurriness of the spectrum.

The H_2 problem solution, described in the paper [5], can be used for computing of the optimal $W(s)$. There are two main reasons to choose this approach. Firstly, it is useful, when spectral structure of external disturbance is known. Moreover, this H_2 approach is based on polynomial calculations instead of "2-Riccati" or LMI technique. This can be essentially effective, when computational resources are limited, e.g. for onboard control systems of autonomous mobile robots.

Let us consider the steps of the spectral algorithm of synthesis based on the mentioned approach:

1. Execute the factorization of the polynomials:

$$k^2A(s)A(-s) + B(s)B(-s) \equiv G(s)G(s), \quad (8)$$

$$P(s)P(-s)N_d(s)N_d(-s) \equiv N(s)N(-s), \quad (9)$$

where $N(s)$ and $G(s)$ are Hurwitz polynomials.

2. Construct the auxiliary polynomial

$$R(s) = \sum_{i=1}^{n}\frac{G(-s)}{g_i - s}\frac{B(-g_i)N(-g_i)}{A(g_i)T_d(g_i)G'(-g_i)}, \quad (10)$$

where g_i, $i = \overline{1,n}$ are the distinct roots of $G(-s)$.

3. Represent a transfer function of the optimal filter

$$\begin{aligned} W(s) = W_0(s) = \frac{W_1^0(s)}{W_2^0(s)} = \\ = \frac{\left[A(s)T_d(s)R(s) + B(-s)N(-s)\right]/G(-s)}{\left[A(s)T_d(s)R(s) - k^2A(-s)N(s)\right]/G(-s)}, \end{aligned} \quad (11)$$

where division to polynomial $G(-s)$ is done totally.

Consider transfer function $F(s)$ from external disturbance $d(s)$ to $e_f(s)$ in closed-loop system with the obtained $W(s)$. The value $|F(j\omega_0)|$ demonstrates the effectiveness of the filter. If this value is large, i.e. sensitivity of fault estimation to disturbance is too high, it is necessary to compute another filter.

Note that the function $W(s)$ must be a proper fraction to avoid numerical difficulties of implementation. Let us derive expression of degrees of the polynomials $W_1^0(s)$ and $W_2^0(s)$ from degrees of polynomials, mentioned in formulas (6),(8)-(10): $n = deg\,A(s)$, $m = deg\,B(s)$, $p = deg\,N(s)$, $q = deg\,T_d(s)$. Degrees of auxiliary polynomials $R(s)$, $G(s)$ are $deg\,R(s) = n-1$, $deg\,G(-s) = n-1$, that implies

$$\mu_1 = deg\,W_1^0(s) = \max(n+q+n-1,\ p+m) - n,$$

$$\mu_2 = deg\,W_2^0(s) = \max(m+q+n-1,\ p+n) - n.$$

There are three possible cases,

1. if $p \le m+q-1$, then

$$\begin{aligned} \mu_1 &= n+q-1, \\ \mu_2 &= m+q-1; \end{aligned} \quad (12)$$

2. if $m+q-1 \le p \le 2n-m+q-1$, then

$$\begin{aligned} \mu_1 &= n+q-1, \\ \mu_2 &= p; \end{aligned} \quad (13)$$

3. if $p \ge 2n-m+q-1$, then

$$\begin{aligned} \mu_1 &= p+m-n, \\ \mu_2 &= p. \end{aligned} \quad (14)$$

It is obvious, that order k_d of numerical derivative of output signal $e_y(t)$ can be expressed

$$k_d = \begin{cases} 0, \text{ if } \mu_1 \le \mu_2, \\ \mu_1 - \mu_2, \text{ if } \mu_1 > \mu_2. \end{cases}$$

Let us calculate k_d for every previously mentioned case (12)-(14). It's obvious that in third case $W_0(s)$ is proper fraction and, as a result,

1. if $p \le m + q - 1$, then $\mu_1 > \mu_2$ and $k_d = n - m$;
2. if $m + q - 1 \le p \le 2n - m + q - 1$, then

$$k_d = \begin{cases} n + q - 1 - p, \text{ if } m + q - 1 \le p < n + q - 1, \\ 0, \text{ if } \mu_1 \le \mu_2. \end{cases}$$

3. if $p \ge 2n - m + q - 1$, then $\mu_1 < \mu_2$ and $k_d = 0$.

These expressions imply necessary and sufficient condition of propriety of transfer function

$$p - m - q + 1 > 0. \qquad (15)$$

If condition (15) is not fulfilled, transfer function (7) must be deformed by multiplying its numerator to $n^* = n + q - p - 1$ additional terms

$$H^* = H(s)(s + h_1^2)(s + h_2^2)\ldots(s + h_{n^*}^2), \qquad (16)$$

where parameters h_i affect the effectiveness of the filter and can be also used for optimization.

Optimal solution of this problem can be treated as a tradeoff between maximization of response speed, minimization of overshoot and minimization of $|F(j\omega_0)|$. All these values are affected with parameters k and h_i, used for computations (8)-(11), (16). As a result, original problem can be reformulated as the problem to minimize of the following value:

$$J = J(W) = T_p - T_p^0 + |T_p - T_p^0| + J_p - J_p^0 + \ldots$$
$$\ldots + |J_p + J_p^0| + |F(j\omega_0)| - F_0 + \big||F(j\omega_0)| - F_0\big|, \qquad (17)$$

where T_p^0, J_p^0, F_0 are desired values of transient period, overshoot and sensitivity to a disturbance respectively. $T_p = T_p(W)$, $J_p = J_p(W)$, $F(j\omega_0)$ are their values, obtained with filter $W(s)$. It is obvious, that minimal value of functional (17) is 0, and $J(W) = 0$ implies

$$T_p \le T_p^0,\ J_p \le J_p^0,\ |F(j\omega_0)| \le F_0. \qquad (18)$$

Optimal parameters $k = k^*$ and $h_i = h_i^*$ can be computed with the following algorithm:

1. Construct the polynomials $A(s)$, $B(s)$, $P(s)$, $H(s)$. Check the condition (15) and, if necessary, calculate n^*.
2. Set initial coefficient of the intensity $k = k_0$ in the functional (5).
3. Set initial vector $h^0 = (h_1^0, h_2^0, \ldots, h_{n^*}^0)$ and deform the spectral density (16).
4. Compute transfer function (11) of the corrector $\widetilde{W}(s)$.
5. Evaluate $J = J(\widetilde{W})$ (17).
6. Minimize (17), repeating steps 3-5, with any numerical method of function minimization, e.g. Nelder-Mead method, which is implied in the simulation example, described in Section 4. Obtain vector $\widetilde{h}$ and filter $\widetilde{W}$.
7. If $J(\widetilde{W})$ is not close to zero, i.e. some of values exceed its desired values, then repeat 2-6 with new $k = \widetilde{k}$. Optimal $k = k^*$ can be searched with any numerical method of function minimization or with enumeration.
8. Replicate step 4 with optimal parameters $k = k^*$, $h = h^*$, and obtain filter, satisfying conditions (18).

4 Simulation results

Let us consider the linear time invariant system (1), describing yaw motion of marine ship and the basic fault estimation observer with parameters [6]

$$\mathbf{A} = \begin{pmatrix} -0.0936 & 0.634 & 0 \\ 0.048 & -0.0717 & 0 \\ 0 & 1 & 0 \end{pmatrix}, \mathbf{b} = \begin{pmatrix} 0.0196 \\ 0.0160 \\ 0 \end{pmatrix},$$

$$\mathbf{E} = \mathbf{b}, \mathbf{g} = \begin{pmatrix} -0.00016 \\ 0.00000246 \\ 0 \end{pmatrix}, \quad \mathbf{L} = \begin{pmatrix} 158.79 \\ 117.05 \\ 15.3 \end{pmatrix}, \quad \mathbf{l}_f = 31623.$$

Assume that the sea disturbance is $d(t) = 400\sin(0.65t)$, i.e. disturbance is regular and its frequency $\omega_0 = 0.65$. Let assume the blurriness of the spectrum $s_t = 0.01$, and the dispersion $D_r = 1$ that implies

$$H(s) = \frac{N_d(s)}{T_d(s)} = \frac{0.091}{s^2 + 0.013s + 0.423},$$

and let consider execution of algorithm, described in previous Section.

1. Base polynomials from (6) and n^*:

$$A(s) = s^4 + 0.811s^3 + 0.037s^2,$$
$$B(s) = -15.30s^3 - 129.45s^2 - 525.10s - 76.20,$$
$$P(s) = 0.0000046s^2 - 0.0000075s,\ n^* = 3.$$

2. Set initial parameters of deforming polynomial $h^0 = (0.2 \quad 2 \quad 20)$.
3. Optimal parameters $k^* = 5000$, $h^0 = (1.57 \quad 27.65 \quad 0.2)$.
4. Obtain a corrective filter with the transfer function

$$W(s) = \frac{3.97s^5 + 3.51s^4 + 1.78s^3 + 1.18s^2 + 0.046s}{s^5 + 709.7s^4 + 4178^3 + 6367s^2 + 3768s + 442.6}.$$

Figure 1 allows to compare frequency responses of the base observer and the corrected one. It can be seen that the curve $|F(j\omega)|$ has a dip in the area of ω_0, showing frequency properties of designed fault estimation observer.

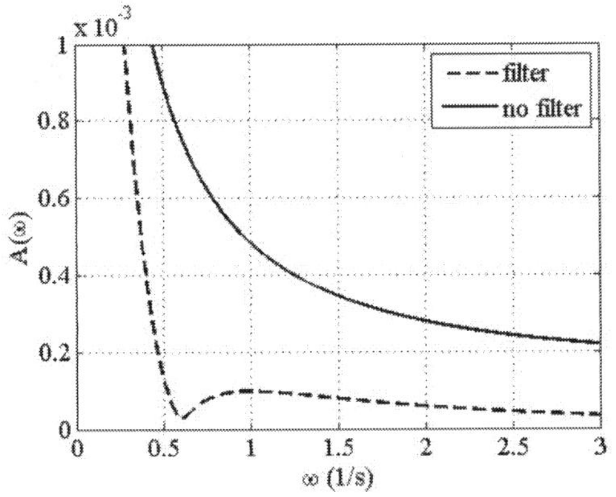

Figure 1. Comparison of frequency responses.

Figure 2 demonstrates the effectiveness of corrective filtering. It can be seen that initial observer generates signal with huge amplitude, when a fault is absent. When correction filter is switched on from the 100-th s, an error of fault estimation becomes close to zero. On the other hand, the fault at 200 s is successfully detected and estimated.

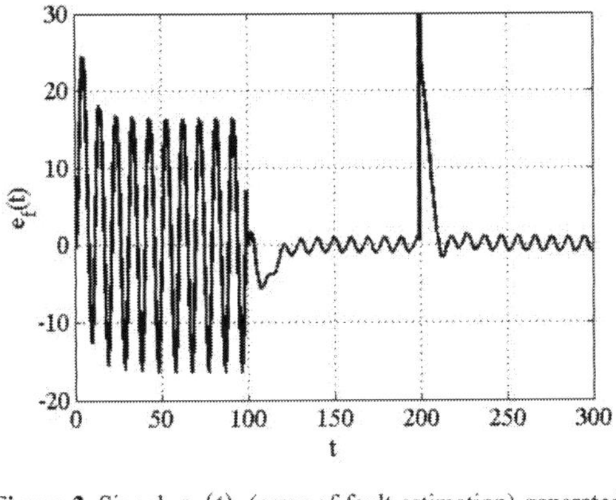

Figure 2. Signal $e_f(t)$ (error of fault estimation) generated by the basic adaptive observer (0–100 s) and corrected one with estimation of fault at 200 s.

5 Conclusion

This paper proposed a specific approach to the fault estimation in presence of external disturbances with the large amplitude. A design of the observer is realized in more extended area, than in most of the previous approaches, devoted to fault detection or estimation. It is significant that computational complexity of polynomial calculations is not very high, that may be crucial sometimes.

On the other hand, proposed approach has some disadvantages. It doesn't provide enough response speed and can't be applied to estimation of quickly varying faults. The object of future research is to overcome these problems.

References

1. K. Zhang, B. Jiang, P. Shi, *Observer-based fault estimation and accomodation for dynamic systems* (Springer 2012)
2. K. Zhang, B. Jiang, P. Shi, P., IET Control Theory & Applications, **2**, 189 (2009).
3. V. Serbak, P. Liscinsky, Advances in Electrical and Electronic Engineering, **1**, 13 (2015)
4. A Drouot, H. Noura, L. Goerig, P. Piot, IFAC-PapersOnLine, **21**, 180, (2015)
5. E. I. Veremey, Applied Mathematical Sciences, **79**, 3897, (2015).
6. E.I. Veremey. Journal of Marine Science and Application, **13**, 2, 127, (2014).

ITM Web of Conferences 6, 02001 (2016)
DOI: 10.1051/itmconf/20160602001

Using of the notion «Pareto set» for development of the forecasting models based on the modified clonal selection algorithm

Nadezhda Astakhova[1] and Liliya Demidova[1, 2, a]

[1] Ryazan State Radio Engineering University, 390005 Ryazan, Russia
[2] Moscow Technological Institute, 119334 Moscow, Russia

Abstract. The algorithm which carries out the multiobjective optimization at realization of the modified clonal selection algorithm based on the use of the notion «Pareto set» when the parental population of antibodies should be created for development of the forecasting models on the base of the strictly binary trees has been offered. Two indicators of quality of the forecasting model – the affinity indicator based on the calculation of the average forecasting error rate, and the tendencies discrepancy indicator – are applied in the role of the objective functions. The results of experimental studies which confirm the efficiency of application of the offered algorithm have been given.

1 Introduction

The key stage at the solution of the forecasting problem of time series (TS) with use of the artificial intelligence technologies is the choice's stage of the best forecasting model. In particular, in the forecasting model based on the strict binary trees (SBT) and the modified clonal selection algorithm (MCSA) [1, 2] the forecasting model is presented in the form of antibodies. The antibody is a sequence encoded by randomly selected characters. Such sequence will be transformed to the analytical dependence which represents some function. This function will be applied to obtaining the predicted values of TS.

The search of the best forecasting model occurs during process of iterative calculations. The best forecasting models must be determined at each step of this process. Such models become parents for the next generation of models at the next step [1 – 8]. Obviously, the correct selection of antibodies is the key for the effective use of the MCSA and its convergence.

The traditional approach to choose the short-term forecasting models of TS consists in the quality estimation of the forecasting models by means of the average forecasting error rate, calculated for the training set of data. Herewith the average forecasting error rate should be minimized [1 – 8].

However, the use of the average forecasting error rate as the single quality indicator of the forecasting model is not always sufficient to determine the best forecasting model. Often it is required to consider the additional quality indicators of the forecasting model, such as the compliance to the seasonal tendencies of TS, the compliance to the trend of TS, lack of emissions, complexity of the forecasting model, etc. [3].

[a] Corresponding author: liliya.demidova@rambler.ru

Usually it isn't possible to choose the single quality indicator. Therefore, the development problem of approaches to creation of the forecasting models conforming to the requirements about providing an extremum of several quality indicators is very actual.

Therefore, it is expedient to use the additional quality indicator which will allow to estimate the general tendency of values' change of the known elements of TS (for example, the tendencies discrepancy indicator) along with the average forecasting error rate [3]. Hence, it is possible to increase the efficiency of the forecasting models on the base of the SBT at the solution of the problem of medium-term forecasting.

2 Theoretical part

The average forecasting error rate $AFER$ [1, 2], which is also called the affinity indicator Aff (in the context of working with the MSCA) and used as one of the quality indicators for the forecasting models can be calculated as:

$$AFER = \frac{1}{n-r}\sum_{j=r+1}^{n} |(f^j - d^j)/d^j| \cdot 100\% , \quad (1)$$

where d^j and f^j are respectively the actual (fact) and forecasted values for the j-th element of TS (for the j-th timing); n is the number of TS elements (number of timing).

The rate of discrepancy between the tendencies of TSs (the tendencies discrepancy indicator $Tendency$) is used as other quality indicator for the forecasting models and can be calculated as:

$$Tendency = \frac{h}{n-r-1}, \quad (2)$$

where h is the number of negative multiplications $(f^{j-1}-f^{j})\cdot(d^{j-1}-d^{j})$; $j=\overline{r+2,n}$; d^{j} and f^{j} are respectively the actual (fact) and forecasted values for the j-th element of TS (for the j-th timing); n is the number of TS elements (number of timing); r is the model order; $n-r-1$ is the total number of multiplications $(f^{j-1}-f^{j})\cdot(d^{j-1}-d^{j})$.

This indicator is used for adaption of the forecasting models on the base of the SBT and MCSA for the medium-term forecasting.

Both indicators (Aff and $Tendency$) determine the similarity of the predicted values of the analyzed TS with the real ones. However, they use different principles of evaluation. The affinity indicator Aff is used in the implementation of the MCSA to define value of «adaptability» (quality) of the antibody Ab, and the tendencies discrepancy indicator $Tendency$ allows to estimate the quality of the antibody Ab taking into account the coincidence with the trend of the analyzed TS. Herewith both indicators must be minimized.

These indicators are based on various principles of the quality assessment of the forecasting model. The affinity indicator Aff estimates the similarity and difference between the predicted and actual values of the known elements of the analyzed TS. The tendencies discrepancy indicator $Tendency$ estimates the similarity and difference of the change's directions between the predicted and actual values of the known elements of the analyzed TS. This indicator helps to analyze tendencies in the TS and the presence of seasonal fluctuations.

Thus, both indicators (the affinity indicator (1) and the tendencies discrepancy indicator (2)) must be used simultaneously at the quality assessment of the forecasting models on the base of the SBT and MCSA to solve the tasks of medium-term forecasting.

Various well proved approaches can be applied to the solution of the task of the simultaneous accounting of two quality indicators for development of the forecasting models [9]. Herewith it is necessary especially to allocate approach, based on the several multiobjective optimization algorithms, including, evolutionary algorithms.

Such multiobjective optimization algorithms provide a solution of the account's problem of the several objective functions (criteria, quality indicators) at the solution of various applied tasks.

Currently the genetic algorithms (GA) have the greatest application among the evolutionary multiobjective optimization algorithms. These algorithms have such advantages as:

- lack of the restrictions imposed on nature of the optimized objective functions;
- resistance to local optimum traps;
- high speed of convergence to the decision;
- solution's possibility of the tasks' wide class (including large-scale problems of optimization);
- simplicity of realization;
- use's possibility for the tasks with the changing environment.

Nowdays the following multiobjective optimization GA are famous and widely used:

- VEGA (Vector Evaluated Genetic Algorithm);
- FFGA (Fonseca and Fleming's Genetic Algorithm);
- NPGA (Niched Pareto Genetic Algorithm);
- NSGA (Non-dominated Sorting Genetic Algorithm);
- NSGA-II (Non-dominated Sorting Genetic Algorithm-II);
- SPEA (Strength Pareto Evolutionary Algorithm).

The VEGA [10] was proposed by D. Schaffer in 1984. It belongs to the group of the selection algorithms on the base of the switching objective functions. This algorithm is based on idea that use of the parents possessing the best variations of values of various objective functions (criteria, quality indicators), i.e. with their best sum (value of «supercriterion»), as a result will allow to receive the decision which will combine the best combination of values of various criterion functions (criteria, quality indicators) in total. This algorithm is the only algorithm among the presented algorithms which doesn't use the notion «Pareto set».

The FFGA [15] was proposed by Fonseca C.M. and Fleming P.J. in 1993. It applies the simplest variant of formation of Pareto set for selection of decisions.

Set of all decisions is ranged according to success of some decision with using of all objective functions (criteria, quality indicators) in relation to other decisions. The lower the rank of the solution, the greater probability of its choice for the next step of selection. The fundamental difference of the FFGA is that all objective functions (factors, quality indicators) are considered together (as a whole) in relation to the decision. Herewith not values of the objective functions, but ranks of all solutions in the population are analyzed.

The principal difference and advantage of the NPGA [12], which was proposed by Horn J., Nafpliotis N. and Goldberg D.E. in 1994, from the other genetic multiobjective optimization algorithms is that this algorithm has a mechanism to support the diversity of the solutions' population. This algorithm carries out a combination of the principles of tournament selection and the notation of Pareto dominance. The NPGA solves the problem of convergence to a local minimum, which is one of the main problems of the GA. There are various modifications of the NPGA. They differ in the approaches to the formation of the parent population.

The NSGA [13] was proposed by Srinivas N. and Deb K. in 1994. It applies some other approach to the problem's solution of the support of a variety in the parental population. For each generation not dominating sorting is also executed, but in addition, the so-called phenotype distance for the choice of decisions for selection is calculated. If this distance to any decision in the next generation is less, than is set by means of some threshold value, the considered decision isn't added to the next generation. However, this algorithm has some shortcomings. First, the ranging of decisions becomes superfluous if the phenotype distance is used. Secondly, there is a need of determination of threshold value which sets admissible phenotype distance between the decisions.

The NSGA-II [14] was proposed by Deb K., Agrawal S., Pratap A. and Meyarivan T. in 2002. It provides correction of shortcomings of the NSGA. First, the improved sorting algorithm reduces computing complexity of calculations. Secondly, the decisions both from the modified set and from the initial set of decisions are used for formation of new population of decisions. So-called «crowding distance» is calculated for each decision. This distance allows to estimate, how some decision is close to the solutions-neighbors. Bigger mean value of «crowding distance» corresponds to the best variety of decisions in the population.

The SPEA [15] was proposed by Zitzler E. and Thiele L. in 1998. It uses the following approach. The decisions which aren't dominated by other decisions in the population are stored in the special external array. Thus the elitism mechanism which allows not to lose the good intermediate decision is realized.

The number of such selected decisions can be great. For reduction of the decisions' number which are stored in the external array, the clustering procedure is carried out. The SPEA effectively deals with the typical problem of the premature convergence which is often arising at realization of the principles of elitism. For this purpose the special mechanism of the niches' formation is used. Herewith the detection of the general suitability is carried out not on the base of distance between decisions, but on the base of the principles of Pareto dominance.

In the context of the problem's solution of development of the forecasting models on the base of the SBT and MCSA it is necessary to understand the forecasting model as the decision.

The analysis of literature devoted to the problems of multiobjective optimization with application of genetic algorithms demonstrates, that nowdays such algorithms as the SPEA, NSGA and NSGA-II find the greatest application at the solution of many applied tasks. So, for example, the NSGA and NSGA-II are successfully applied in the such problems as problem of scheduling, problem of drawing up of schedules, the travelling salesman problem [16]. Herewith the NSGA-II is significantly better than the NSGA because the NSGA-II minimizes the computing expenses.

In this regard the decision on expediency of adaptation of the ideas put in the NSGA-II at realization of the MCSA which is applied to selection of the forecasting models on the base of the SBT was made.

For confirmation of prospects of the offered transformation of the MCSA it is offered to realize the following algorithm of multiobjective optimization.

Step 1. To generate initial population of antibodies. Each antibody is coded on the base of the SBT and represents some forecasting model.

Step 2. To perform the nondominated sorting to population of antibodies on the base of two indicators of quality for the forecasting model (the affinity indicator (1) and the tendencies discrepancy indicator (2)).

Step 3. To choose the parents-antibodies for the next generation of the clones-antibodies based on the values of the rank and «crowding distance».

Step 4. To pass to step 5 if desirable values of the quality indicators are reached or the quantity of generations in the MCSA is settled. Otherwise to pass to step 2.

Step 5. To accept the antibody with the minimum value of the affinity indicator (1) in the last population as the optimum decision. To use the forecasting model corresponding to this antibody for forecasting.

As a result of application of the offered algorithm the Pareto set of the nondominated forecasting models will be received. These models provide the best combinations of values of the used quality indicators of the forecasting models for the analyzed TS.

The received forecasting models can be applied at the solution of a problem of medium-term forecasting. It will expand application scope of the forecasting models based on the SBT and MCSA.

3 Experimental studies

To confirm prospects of the offered algorithm, experimental studies on forecasting for 5 TS were conducted:

T1 (TS «The Brent crude oil price»; range of values: 15.12.2015 – 02.01.2016; unit of measure: ruble) = [46.04; 45.11; 44.46; 44.38; 44.30; 43.97; 44.70; 44.70; 44.08; 45.92; 47.08; 47.32; 47.46; 48.05; 48.84; 50.25; 48.90; 49.50];

T2 (TS «Total number of the made energy resources»; range of values: 1992 – 2012 years; unit of measure: quadrillion Btus) = [47.99; 44.69; 42.30; 41.42; 39.35; 38.74; 39.07; 40.81; 41.70; 42.63; 44.16; 47.16; 49.86; 51.05; 52.06; 52.52; 52.52; 50.01; 53.74; 54.63; 55.30];

T3 (TS «Number of Internet users per 100 people»; range of values: 1990 – 2014 years; unit of measure: percent) = [0.00000; 0.00067; 0.01345; 0.05382; 0.14815; 0.26975; 0.47296; 0.81274; 1.01899; 1.97723; 2.94437; 4.12827; 8.29886; 12.85939; 15.22667; 17.02328; 24.66000; 26.83000; 29.00000; 43.00000; 49.00000; 63.80000; 67.97000; 70.52000];

T4 (TS «Passenger traffic»; range of values: 1989 – 2012 years; unit of measure: millions passenger-kilometers) = [3669.202; 3635.441; 3305.227; 3145.413; 3087.016; 3251.615; 2714.314; 3268.434; 3743.247; 4249.406; 4468.123; 4489.569; 4651.419; 4726.832; 4986.468; 5054.200; 5482.314; 5655.296; 5129.103; 5987.268; 5933.041; 5973.308];

T5 (TS «Value added in agriculture»; range of values: 1992 – 2013 years; unit of measure: dollar) = [270112; 274000; 255000; 253200; 272475; 227102; 192117; 181200; 170300; 152900; 141042; 167100; 158000; 152900; 155573; 164272; 164262; 173699; 173411; 175800; 153500; 139028; 139842; 144612].

The chosen time series have different number of elements, the scale level of elements values, sampling points, amplitude and period. It allows to consider further conclusions universal.

Forecasting for each TS was executed with use of one (*Aff*) and two (*Aff* and *Tendency*) quality indicators of the forecasting model. The errors of forecasting are presented in Table 1.

Table 1. The erros of forecasting.

Error type	Forecasting error with use of *Aff* , %	Forecasting error with use of *Aff* and *Tendency* , %
TS #1 («The Brent crude oil price»)		
Training error (1)	3,12	1,10
Error for 1 step	1,43	0,22
Error for 2 step	0,85	0,01
Error for 3 step	0,67	0,38
Error for 4 step	1,06	0,22
Error for 5 step	0,45	0,57
Average error	0,89	0,28
TS #2 («Total number of the made energy resources»)		
Training error (1)	5,23	2,89
Error for 1 step	1,14	0,62
Error for 2 step	0,87	0,20
Error for 3 step	1,53	0,73
Error for 4 step	0,29	0,29
Error for 5 step	0,97	0,68
Average error	0,96	0,50
TS #3 («Number of Internet users per 100 people»)		
Training error (1)	5,49	3,29
Error for 1 step	1,48	0,57
Error for 2 step	3,75	0,13
Error for 3 step	7,41	0,65
Error for 4 step	5,86	0,12
Error for 5 step	9,14	0,42
Average error	5,53	0,38
TS #4 («Passenger traffic»)		
Training error (1)	5,47	2,54
Error for 1 step	1,58	1,75
Error for 2 step	2,84	1,42
Error for 3 step	3,54	1,98
Error for 4 step	3,17	1,10
Error for 5 step	3,69	1,38
Average error	2,96	1,52
TS #5 («Value added in agriculture»)		
Training error (1)	3,98	2,75
Error for 1 step	0,82	0,82
Error for 2 step	1,37	0,54
Error for 3 step	1,89	0,86
Error for 4 step	2,29	1,09
Error for 5 step	3,97	0,22
Average error	2,27	0,71

The errors of forecasting in the Table 1 are the average error values. These errors were calculated on the base of 1000 program runs for 100 generations of population. Size of population is set by 20 antibodies.

Values of the forward prediction errors (for 1 – 5 steps forward) specify that the offered approach to selection of the forecasting models is effective as for the solution of problems of short-term forecasting (for 1 – 3 step forward) as for the solution of problems of medium-term forecasting (for 4, 5 steps forward).

It should be noted that use of the additional quality indicator of the forecasting model (the indicator *Tendency*) allowed to carry out «search» of the forecasting model in the necessary (correct) direction. As a result, for all reviewed examples of time series for the small number of generations of the MCSA the smaller values of the affinity indicator *Aff* (training error (1)) and in most cases the smaller values of the forecasting errors for 1 – 5 steps forward were received (Table 1).

Results of forecasting for TS «The Brent crude oil price» have been presented in Figures 1 and 2. These results are received with use of the forecasting models on the base of one and two indicators of quality respectively.

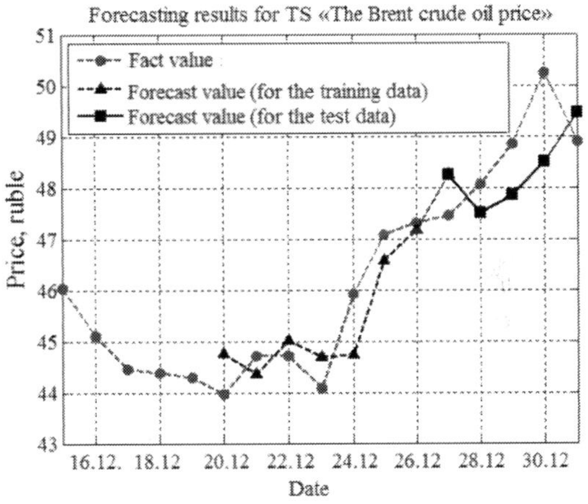

Figure 1. Forecasting of «The Brent crude oil price» (with one indicator of quality *Aff*).

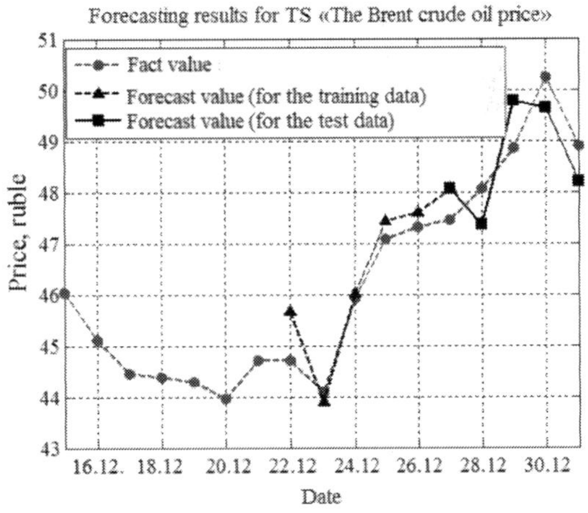

Figure 2. Forecasting of «The Brent crude oil price» (with two indicators of quality *Aff* and *Tendency*).

The presented graphic dependences show that the second model repeats the mathematical law of initial TS for the training set of data better than the first one. Moreover, this feature is kept also for the test set (when forecasting for 5 steps forward is carried out). Herewith the forecasting model on the base of two indicators of quality (*Aff* and

Tendency) demonstrates the best survival for the extended forecasting horizon than the forecasting model on the base of one indicator of quality (*Aff*). Besides this model is more effective for short-term forecasting.

These calculations allow to make the following conclusion: use of the second indicator of quality of the forecasting model provides a way to increase the life time of the forecasting model. Herewith the efficiency of the forecasting model for performing of the short-term forecasts saves that in general confirms the success of the offered approach.

4 Conclusions

Initially, the MCSA was developed for the solution of short-term forecasting problems. However, the fulfilled researches showed application's possibility of the MCSA for the solution of medium-term forecasting problems.

Apparently, application of the Pareto domination principles is the effective solution of the accounting problem of several quality indicators in the development problem of the forecasting models, which represent analytical dependences on the base of the SBT.

It should be noted that computing complexity of the MCSA, when the Pareto-optimal solutions are used, increases slightly. Herewith, it is possible to expand scope of application of the MCSA considerably.

Acknowledgment

This work is supported by Russian Federal Property Fund, 16-08-00771.

References

1. L.A. Demidova, Time series forecasting models on the base of modified clonal selection algorithm, *2014 International conference on computer technologies in physical and engineering applications (ICCTPEA)*, pp. 33–34 (2014)
2. N.N. Astakhova, *Modern informatization problems in simulation and social technologies Proceedings of the XX-th International Open Science Conference*, pp. 146–150 (2015).
3. L.A. Demidova, Cloud Sci., **1**, 202 (2014)
4. L.A. Demidova, Automation and Remote Control, **74**, 313 (2013)
5. N.N. Astakhova, L.A. Demidova and E.V. Nikulchev, Contemporary Engineering Sciences, **8**, 1659 (2015)
6. N. Astakhova, L. Demidova, E. Nikulchev and E. Pluzhnik, *16th International Symposium on Advanced Intelligent Systems*, pp. 861–873 (2015).
7. N.N. Astakhova, L.A. Demidova and E.V. Nikulchev, Applied Mathematical Sciences, **9**, 4813 (2015)
8. N. Astakhova, L. Demidova and V. Konev, The Description Problem Of The Clusters' Centroids, *2015 International Conference "Stability and Control Processes" in Memory of V.I. Zubov (SCP)* , pp. 448–451 (2015).
9. Z. Michalewicz, *Proc. of the Sixth Int. Conf. on Genetic Algorithms and their Applications, Pittsburgh, PA*, pp. 239–247 (1995)
10. D.E. Goldberg, *Genetic Algorithms in Search, Optimization, and Machine Learning* (Addison-Wesley, 1989)
11. C.M. Fonseca and P.J. Fleming, *Multiobjective optimization and multiple constraint handling with evolutionary algorithms – Part I: A unified formulation, Technical report 564* (University of Sheffield, 1995)
12. J. Horn, N. Nafpliotis and D.E. Goldberg, *Proceedings of the First IEEE Conference on Evolutionary Computation*, **1**, 82 (1994)
13. J. Knowles and D. Corne, *Proceedings of the 1999 Congress on Evolutionary Computation*, pp. 98-105 (1999)
14. K. Deb, A. Pratap, S. Agarwal and T. Meyarivan, *A Fast and Elitist Multiobjective Genetic Algorithm: NSGA II.* (Indian Institute of Technology, 2000)
15. P.J. Bentley and J.P. Wakefield, *Proceedings of the 2nd On-Line World Conference on Soft Computing in Engineering Design and Manufacturing*, pp. 126–140 (1997)
16. K. Deb, *Multi-objective Optimization using Evolutionary Algorithms* pp. 221–232 (Wiley, 2001)

ITM Web of Conferences **6**, 02002 (2016)
DOI: 10.1051/itmconf/20160602002

Cluster analysis of the bias in the SMB subsidy recipients selection

Igor Balk[1, a] and Egor Mateshuk[2]

[1]*Global Innovation Labs, USA*
[2]*Moscow Institute of Physics and Technology, Moscow, Russia*

Abstract. This paper is discussing the applicability of cluster analysis techniques to studying bias in the selection process of government SMB subsidy recipients using data from Moscow city SMB administration. Ward's Hierarchical Agglomerative Clustering Method is used to study 812 SMBs, which received subsidies in 2012-2013 from the Moscow City SMB administration. This analysis strongly demonstrates that clustering mechanisms can be used to reduce selection irregularities in government subsidy distribution.

1 Introduction

Governments around the world are making a significant effort towards stimulating various initiatives aiming to boost economic development of their countries. Naturally, this raises the question if taxpayer's money spent on such programs is achieving desired goals. Therefore, the question of effectiveness of various government projects around the world, which are designed to boost the economy, is widely discussed in the literature. One of the ways to measure this is to study treatment effects of various programs on boosting innovation and economic development as suggested by Czarnitzki [1], Hahn [2], Lechner [3] and others. The main problem when dealing with this approach is valid estimation of selection bias and correct selection of control groups. Balk [4] suggested using cluster analysis methods to properly select control groups, which provide the closest match to the group which received the treatment. In this paper we will concentrate on discussing the application of clustering algorithms to study selection bias for treatment of small and medium size businesses by Moscow Small Business Administration.

2 Overview of the clustering algorithm

In this study we have used Ward's Hierarchical Agglomerative Clustering Method, which was first introduced by Ward [5]. He suggested an agglomerative hierarchical clustering algorithm, where the criterion for choosing the pair of clusters to merge at each level is defined by the optimal value of an objective function.

We define a distance as a positive, definite, symmetric mapping of a pair of observation vectors onto the positive real, which in addition satisfies the triangular inequality. For observations i, j, k we have:

$$d(i,j) > 0, \tag{1}$$
$$d(i,j) = 0 \Leftrightarrow i = j, \tag{2}$$
$$d(i,j) = d(j,i). \tag{3}$$

For an observation set, I, with $i, j, k \in I$ we can write the distance as a mapping from the Cartesian product of the observation set into the positive real:

$$d: I \times I \to \mathbb{R}^+. \tag{4}$$

At each step of the clustering algorithm we find a pair of clusters that leads to a minimum increase in total within cluster variance after the merging, i.e. weighted squared distance between cluster centers

$$\frac{1}{|q|}\sum_{i\in q} d^2(i, q^*), \tag{5}$$

where q denote the cluster (a set) and q^* the cluster's center, which is defined as

$$q^* = \frac{1}{|q|}\sum_{i\in q} i. \tag{6}$$

Initially all clusters contain only a singe point. We can define Euclidean distance squared using norm $\|.\|$: if $i, i' \in \mathbb{R}^{|J|}$, i.e. these observations have values on attributes $j \in \{1,2,\ldots,|J|\}$, J is the attribute set, $|.|$ denotes cardinality, then

$$d^2(i,i') = \|i - i'\|^2 = \sum_j (i_j - i'_j)^2. \tag{7}$$

Suppose that clusters C_i and C_j were next to be merged. At this point all of the current pairwise cluster distances are known. The recursive formula gives the updated cluster distances following the pending merge of clusters C_i and C_j. Let

- d_{ij}, d_{ik}, and d_{jk} be the pairwise distances between clusters C_i, C_j, and C_k, respectively,
- $d_{(ij)k}$ be the distance between the new cluster $C_i \cup C_j$ and C_k.

An algorithm belongs to the Lance-Williams family if the updated cluster distance $d_{(ij)k}$ can be computed recursively by

$$d_{(ij)k} = \alpha_i d_{ik} + \alpha_j d_{jk} + \beta d_{ij} + \gamma |d_{ik} - d_{jk}|, \tag{8}$$

[a] Corresponding author: info@innovationlabs.net

where α_i, α_j, β and γ are parameters, which may depend on cluster sizes, that together with the cluster distance function determine the clustering algorithm.

3 Study of SMBs

In our study we analyzed data regarding subsidies provided by Moscow Small Business Administration in 2012 and 2013 to 810 companies. The size of the companies varies from 0 to 83 people, with the amount of cash available from 0 to 6,257,870 rubles (We must note that about half of the companies did not report any cash on hand. This probably indicates an issue with the data, rather than real information about the companies). The amount of subsidy received ranges from 123,109.68 rubles to 5,000,000.00 rubles and companies promised to create from 0 to 50 jobs for the money received. The aim of the study was to determine applicability of cluster analysis to the demonstration of the selection bias. The available data was Company ID, Company Size, Anticipated head count growth, Cash on hand, Subsidy size, Industry code, Final reporting. We applied Wards clustering algorithms to the data available and obtained 20 clusters varying in size from 1 to 187 companies (Table 1).

Table 1. Wards clustering of subsidy recipients. Cluster Sizes.

Cluster #	Cluster Size	Cluster #	Cluster Size
1	1	11	24
2	4	12	27
3	5	13	27
4	7	14	32
5	12	15	71
6	14	16	73
7	15	17	75
8	16	18	82
9	17	19	104
10	17	20	187

As we can see from the Table 1, the data forms 6 relatively large clusters (50+ entries), 10 medium size clusters (10-50 entries) and 4 small clusters (1-9 entries). For the propose of this study the latest 5 clusters form a group of a special interest as they naturally represent companies which are somehow different from the rest of the treated companies and can either demonstrate selection irregularities or some other special circumstances.

If we consider size of the treated companies and the proposed number of jobs created (Figure 1 and 2), we can see that most of the subsidy recipients have less than 20 people with two exemptions (cluster 2 and 4), and planning to create less than 20 jobs with one exemption (cluster 1). It seems to be clear that the only member of cluster 1 constitutes an irregularity, which could be attributed to the selection bias.

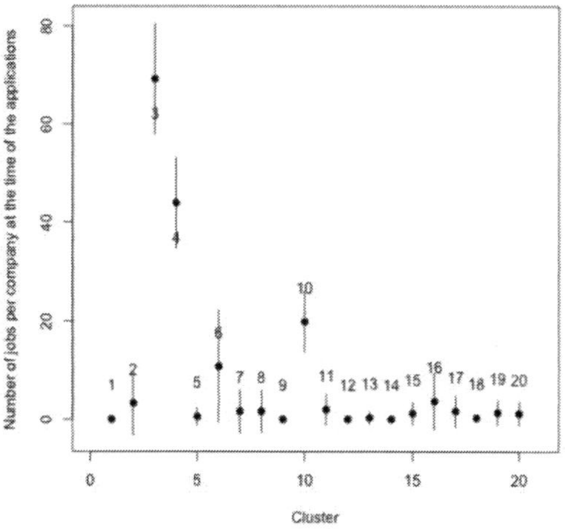

Figure 1. Number of jobs per company at the time of the applications.

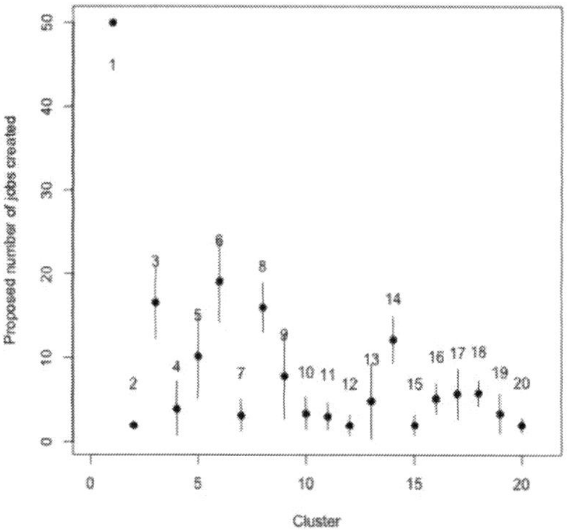

Figure 2. Proposed number of jobs created.

This conclusion becomes even clearer taken into account the amount of cash on hand at the time of application (Figure 3) and the amount of the subsidy received (Figure 4).

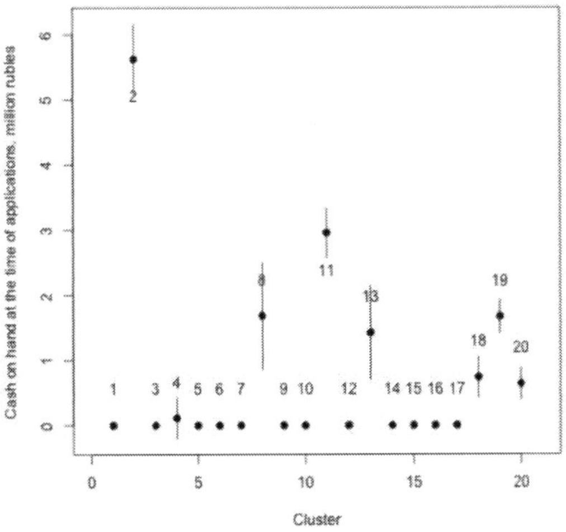

Figure 3. Cash on hand at the time of the applications.

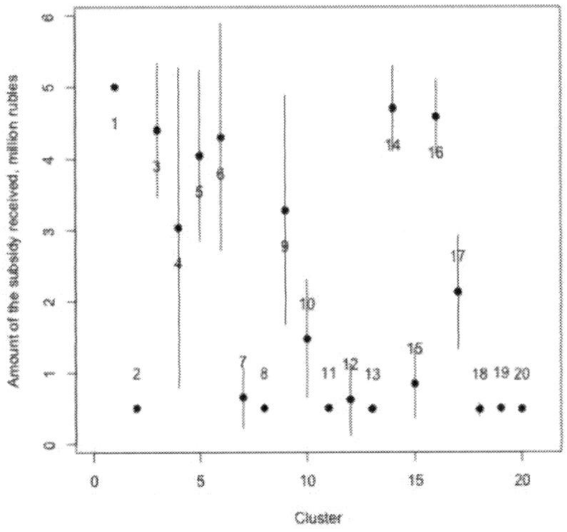

Figure 4. Subsidy received.

4 Conclusion

This paper demonstrates that even simple cluster analysis such as Ward's Hierarchical Agglomerative Clustering Method can be used to significantly reduce irregularities in selection of treatment recipients. Furthermore, we demonstrated that companies could be structured into a small number of clusters with similar properties, which later can be used to study treatment effect as suggested by Balk [4]. Unfortunately, the data available does not provide sufficient information to study treatment effect beyond proposed job creation, as data on actual job creation as well as IP creation was not part of recipients reporting at the time of this article's writing. Additionally, we have to note that data available for us is incomplete, as it did not contain industry information, and thus could not be directly used to find corresponding group of untreated companies.

References

1. D. Czarnitzki et al, ZEW Discussion Paper, *Evaluating the Impact of R&D Tax Credits on Innovation: A Microeconometric Study on Canadian Firms*, **04**, 77 (2004)
2. J. Hahn, *Identification and Estimation of Treatment Effects with Regression-Discontinuity Design*, Econometrica (2001)
3. M. Lechner, Journal of Business & Economic Statistics, *Earnings and Employment Effects of Continuous Off- the-Job Training in East Germany After Unification* (1999)
4. I. Balk, Economical Sciences, *Mathematical modeling of effectiveness of the government support of innovation using cluster modeling*, 5 (2015)
5. J.H. Ward jr., Journal of the American Statistical Association, *Hierarchical Grouping to Optimize an Objective Function*, 58 (1963)

ITM Web of Conferences 6, 02003 (2016)
DOI: 10.1051/itmconf/20160602003

Development of the SVM classifier ensemble for the classification accuracy increase

Liliya Demidova [1, 2, a] and Yulia Sokolova [2]

[1]Moscow Technological Institute, 119334 Moscow, Russia
[2]Ryazan State Radio Engineering University, 390005 Ryazan, Russia

Abstract. The problem of improving the classification accuracy using the SVM classifier ensemble has been considered. This paper defines the rules for the selection of individual SVM-classifiers used in the future for the creation of an ensemble and the strategies for the integration of ensemble members.

1 Introduction

Currently, for a wide range of classification problems in various applications the SVM algorithm (Support Vector Machines, SVM), which carries out training on precedents («supervised learning»), is successfully used and included in the group of the boundary algorithms and methods of classification [1]. It allows developing the classifiers which can be successfully used for a wide range of applications [2].

At first in the developing of the SVM classifier there is a need to implement multiple learning and testing on the basis of different randomly generated training and test sets, and then it is necessary to choose the best SVM classifier which provides the highest possible quality of classification. Assessment of classification quality can be performed using various indicators [2].

For the training of the SVM classifier it is necessary to define the internal parameters of the SVM classifier: the kernel function type, values of the kernel parameters and value of the regularization parameter. These internal parameters participate in the construction of the classifying function $f(x)$, which assign some object x to the concrete class from the set $\{-1;\ +1\}$ [2]. Therefore, the problem of the selection of parameters of the SVM-classifier is crucial for receiving exact results of classification.

In recent years, much attention is paid to a question of increase in accuracy of the models, based on the machine learning algorithms. Herewith questions of the opportunities' association of several classifiers and creation of ensembles of classifiers to increase quality of the solution of the applied tasks are investigated [3-5]. The learning of the ensemble of classifiers is a training procedure of a final set of the base (individual) classifiers, individual solutions of which are then combined to form the resulting classification decisions, based on the aggregated classifier. There are different approaches to choose the rules of combination of the individual classifiers in the ensemble and the strategies for creation of the resulting classification decision [2].

The purpose of this work is to improve the accuracy of classification decisions using the SVM classifier ensemble based on various strategies of integrating of the individual classifiers into an ensemble.

2 Theoretical part

Let the experimental data set be a set in the form of $\{(x_1,y_1),\dots,(x_n,y_n)\}$, in which each object $x_i \in X$ is assigned to the number $y_i \in Y = \{-1;\ +1\}$ having a value of -1 or $+1$ depending on the class of the object x_i. Herewith it is assumed that every object x_i is mapped to q-dimensional vector of numerical values of characteristics $x_i = (x_i^1, x_i^2, \dots, x_i^q)$ where x_i^l is a numeric value of the l-th characteristic for the i-th object ($i = \overline{1,n}$, $l = \overline{1,q}$) [3-5]. It is required with the use of special function $\kappa(x_i, x_\tau)$, which is called the kernel, to build the classifier F: $X \to Y$, comparing the class $Y = \{-1;\ +1\}$ with some object from the set X.

As the kernel function $\kappa(x_i, x_\tau)$ which allows separating the objects of different classes, typically one of the following functions is used [3]:

- linear function: $\kappa(x_i, x_\tau) = \langle x_i, x_\tau \rangle$;
- polynomial function: $\kappa(x_i, x_\tau) = (\langle x_i, x_\tau \rangle + 1)^d$;
- radial basis function:

$$\kappa(x_i, x_\tau) = exp(-\langle x_i - x_\tau, x_i - x_\tau \rangle / (2 \cdot \sigma^2));$$

- sigmoid function: $\kappa(x_i, x_\tau) = th(k_2 + k_1 \cdot \langle x_i, x_\tau \rangle)$,

where $\langle x_i, x_\tau \rangle$ is a scalar product of vectors x_i and x_τ; d [$d \in N$ (by default $d = 3$)], σ [$\sigma > 0$ (by default

[a] Corresponding author: liliya.demidova@rambler.ru

$\sigma^2 = 1$)], k_2 [$k_2 < 0$ (by default $k_2 = -1$)] and k_1 [$k_1 > 0$ (by default $k_1 = 1$)] are some parameters; th is a hyperbolic tangent.

In the training of the SVM classifier it's necessary: 1) to divide the experimental data set for training and test sets, which consist of N and $n - N$ elements respectively ($N < n$); 2) to determine the input parameters of the classifier: the kernel function type $\kappa(x_i, x_\tau)$, values of the kernel parameters and value of the regularization parameter C, which allows finding a compromise between maximizing of the gap separating the classes and minimizing of the total error; 3) to implement multiple learning and testing on different randomly generated training and test sets, with subsequent determination of the best SVM-classifier. The test set is from 1/10 to 1/3 of the experimental data set, it is not involved in the setting of the parameters of the classifier, and used to verify its accuracy. If the quality of learning and testing is acceptable, the SVM-classifier can be used to classify new objects.

As a result of training, the classification function is determined in the following form [1-3]:

$$f(x) = \sum_{i=1}^{N} \alpha_i \cdot y_i \cdot \kappa(x_i, x) + b \qquad (1)$$

The classification decision, associating the object x to the class -1 or $+1$, is adopted in accordance with the rule [1-3]:

$$F(x) = sign(f(x)) = sign\left(\sum_{i=1}^{N} \alpha_i \cdot y_i \cdot \kappa(x_i, x) + b\right) \qquad (2)$$

In (1) and (2): $\kappa(x_i, x)$ is the kernel classifier; b is the parameter determining the shortest distance from the origin to the hyperplane that separates classes; α_i is the Lagrange multiplier; $\alpha_i \geq 0$; y_i is the classification decision (-1 or $+1$) [3].

The main problem with the training of the SVM classifier, is the lack of recommendations for the choice of the regularization parameter C, the function describing the kernel $\kappa(x_i, x_\tau)$, as well as the parameters of the kernel function, for which high accuracy of data classification is achieved. This problem can be solved with the use of various optimization algorithms, in particular using the PSO algorithm [6, 7].

After training, each classifier generates its own (individual) classification decisions, the same or different from the actual results of classification. Accordingly, the different individual SVM classifiers correspond to the different classification accuracy. The quality of the received classification decisions can be improved on the base of ensembles of the SVM classifiers [2-5]. In this case, the final set of individually trained classifiers must be learned. Then the classification decisions of these classifiers are combined. The resulting solution is based on the aggregated classifier. The majority vote method and the vote method based on the degree of reliability can be used as the rules (strategies) of the definition of the aggregated solutions.

The majority vote method is one of the most common and frequently used method for combining of decisions in the ensemble of classifiers. But this method does not fully use the information about the reliability of each individual SVM classifier. For example, suppose that the SVM classifier ensemble aggregates the results of five individual SVM classifiers, where values of the function $f(x)$ of the object x obtained from the three individual SVM classifiers, are negative (class -1), but very close to the neutral position, and values of the function $f(x)$ of the other two SVM classifiers are strongly positive (class $+1$), i.e. very far away from the neutral position. Then the result of the aggregated decision of the ensemble on the basis of «one classifier – one vote» is following: the object x belongs to the negative class (majority vote), although it is obvious, that the best and more appropriate choice for the object x is a positive class. Despite the good potential of the majority vote method for combining of the group of decisions, it is recommended to use other methods to increase the accuracy of classification.

Vote method based on the degree of reliability uses value of the function $f(x)$ for the object x obtained by each individual SVM classifier. The greater the positive value of $f(x)$ in (1), returned by the SVM classifier, the more precisely the object x is determined in class $+1$, and the less negative value $f(x)$, the more precisely the object x is defined in class -1. Values «-1» and «$+1$» for $f(x)$ indicate that the object x is situated on the boundary of the negative and positive classes, respectively.

When using an ensemble of classifiers for solving classification problems the special attention should be paid to the methods of forming a set of individual classifiers, which can later be used in the development of the final SVM classifier. It is experimentally confirmed [2-5], that the ensemble of classifiers shows greater accuracy than any of its individual members, if individual classifiers are accurate and varied. Therefore, the formation of the set of the individual SVM classifiers is required: 1) to use the various kernel functions; 2) to build classifiers in the different ranges of change of the kernel parameters and regularization parameter; 3) to use various sets of training and test data. To select the appropriate members of the ensemble in the set of the trained SVM classifiers it is recommended to use the principle of maximum decorrelation. In this case the correlation between the selected classifications should be as small as possible. After training, each private j-th classifier from the k trained classifier will correspond to a certain array of errors: $e_{ij} = | y_{ij} - \tilde{y}_{ij} |$, where e_{ij} is the error of j-th classifier at i-th row of the experimental data set ($i = \overline{1,n}$; $j = \overline{1,k}$); y_{ij} is the classification decision (-1 or $+1$) of j-th classifier at i-th row of the experimental data set; $\tilde{y}_{ij}$ is the real meaning of a class (-1 or $+1$), for which the i-th object is belong to.

The SVM classifiers, not permitting an error on the experimental data set, should be excluded from further consideration, and from the remaining quantity of the SVM classifiers, it is necessary to select an appropriate number of individual SVM classifiers with maximal variety. To solve this problem, decorrelation maximization algorithm can be used. This algorithm provides a variety of individual SVM classifiers, being used in the construction of the ensemble [2]. If the correlation between the selected classifiers is small, then the decorrelation is maximum.

Let there be an error matrix E of set of individual SVM classifiers with size $n \times k$:

$$E = \begin{bmatrix} e_{11} & e_{12} & \cdots & e_{1k} \\ e_{21} & e_{22} & \cdots & e_{2k} \\ \cdots & \cdots & \cdots & \cdots \\ e_{n1} & e_{n2} & \cdots & e_{nk} \end{bmatrix}, \tag{3}$$

where e_{ij} is the error of the j-th classifier at the i-th row of the experimental data set ($i = \overline{1,n}$; $j = \overline{1,k}$).

On the basis of the error matrix E (3) the following assessments can be calculated [2]:

• mean: $\bar{e}_j = \frac{1}{n}\sum_{i=1}^{n} e_{ij}$ ($j = \overline{1,k}$); (4)

• variance: $V_{jj} = \frac{1}{n}\sum_{i=1}^{n}(e_{ij} - \bar{e}_j)^2$ ($j = \overline{1,k}$); (5)

• covariance:

$$V_{tj} = \frac{1}{n}\sum_{i=1}^{n}(e_{ij} - \bar{e}_j)\cdot(e_{it} - \bar{e}_t) \quad (j = \overline{1,k}, t = \overline{1,k}); \tag{6}$$

Then the elements r_{tj} of the correlation matrix with size $k \times k$ are calculated as:

$$r_{tj} = V_{tj} \Big/ \sqrt{V_{tt} \cdot V_{jj}}\,; \tag{7}$$

where r_{tj} is the correlation coefficient, representing the degree of correlation of t-th and j-th classifiers ($j = \overline{1,k}$; $t = \overline{1,k}$); $r_{jj} = 1$ ($j = \overline{1,k}$).

Using the correlation matrix R it is possible for each individual j-th classifier to calculate the plural-correlation coefficient ρ_j, which characterizes the degree of correlation of j-th and all other $(k-1)$ classifiers with numbers t ($t = \overline{1,k}$; $t \neq j$) [8]:

$$\rho_j = \sqrt{1 - |R| / R_{jj}} \quad (j = \overline{1,k}) \tag{8}$$

where $|R|$ is the determinant of the correlation matrix R; R_{jj} is the cofactor of the element r_{jj} of the correlation matrix R.

A quantity ρ_j^2 called the coefficient of determination. It shows the proportion of the variation of the analyzed variable, which is explained by variation of the other variables. The coefficient of determination ρ_j^2 can take values from 0 to 1. The closer the coefficient to 1, the stronger the relationship between the analyzed variables (in this case, between individual classifiers) [8]. It is believed that there is a dependency, if the coefficient of determination is not less than 0.5. If the coefficient of determination greater than 0.8, it is assumed that high dependence exists.

For selection of individual SVM classifiers for integration into the ensemble it is necessary to determine the threshold θ. Thus, the j-th individual classifier must be removed from the list of classifiers if the coefficient of determination ρ_j^2 satisfies to condition $\rho_j^2 > \theta$ ($j = \overline{1,k}$). If it is necessary to identify the most various classifiers, generating decisions with the most different arrays of errors on the experimental data set, thresholds θ, satisfying to condition $\theta < 0.7$ should be selected. Herewith the additional considerations can be also taken into account to avoid the exclusion of insufficient or excessive number of individual SVM classifiers.

The decorrelation maximization algorithm can be summarized into the following steps [2].

Step 1. To calculate the matrix V and the correlation matrix R with formulas (5), (6) and (7) respectively.

Step 2. To calculate the multiple correlation coefficients ρ_j ($j = \overline{1,k}$) with (8) for all classifiers.

Step 3. To remove classifiers, for which $\rho_j^2 > \theta$ ($j = \overline{1,k}$), from the list of classifiers.

Step 4. To repeat iteratively steps 1 – 3 for the remaining classifiers in the list until for all classifiers the condition $\rho_j^2 \le \theta$ ($j = \overline{1,k}$) will not satisfied.

As a result, the list of classifiers used to form the ensemble will consist of m ($m \le k$) individual classifiers.

For classifiers selected in the ensemble, it is necessary to carry out:

• the rationing of degrees of the reliability;

• the strategy search for the integration of members of the ensemble;

• the calculation of the aggregated decision of the ensemble.

Value of the reliability $f_j(x)$, which is defined for the object x by the j-th classifier, falls into the interval (-∞, + ∞). The main drawback of such values is that in the ensemble the individual classifiers with large absolute value are often dominated in the final decision of the ensemble. To overcome this drawback, the rationing is carried out: the transformation of values of degrees of reliability in the interval [0; 1] is fulfilled. In the case of binary classification in the rationalization for the object x the values of the reliability of its membership to positive class (labeled +1) $g_j^+(x)$ and to negative class $g_j^-(x)$ are determined. These values can be determined by the formulas [2]:

$$g_j^+(x) = \frac{1}{1+e^{-f_j(x)}} \quad (9)$$

$$g_j^-(x) = 1 - g_j^+(x) \quad (10)$$

The selected individual classifiers are combined into the ensemble using $g_j^+(x)$ and $g_j^-(x)$ ($j = \overline{1,m}$) in accordance with one of the following five strategies [2].

1. Maximum strategy:

$$A(x) = \begin{cases} 1, & \text{if} \quad \max_{j=\overline{1,m}} g_j^+(x) \geq \max_{j=\overline{1,m}} g_j^-(x), \\ -1, & \text{otherwise.} \end{cases} \quad (11)$$

2. Minimum strategy:

$$A(x) = \begin{cases} 1, & \text{if} \quad \min_{j=\overline{1,m}} g_j^+(x) \geq \min_{j=\overline{1,m}} g_j^-(x), \\ -1, & \text{otherwise.} \end{cases} \quad (12)$$

3. Median strategy:

$$A(x) = \begin{cases} 1, & \text{if} \quad \frac{1}{m}\sum_{j=1}^{m} g_j^+(x) \geq \frac{1}{m}\sum_{j=1}^{m} g_j^-(x), \\ -1, & \text{otherwise.} \end{cases} \quad (13)$$

4. Mean strategy:

$$A(x) = \begin{cases} 1, & \text{if} \quad \sum_{j=1}^{m} g_j^+(x) \geq \sum_{j=1}^{m} g_j^-(x), \\ -1, & \text{otherwise.} \end{cases} \quad (14)$$

5. Product strategy:

$$A(x) = \begin{cases} 1, & \text{if} \quad \prod_{j=1}^{m} g_j^+(x) \geq \prod_{j=1}^{m} g_j^-(x), \\ -1, & \text{otherwise.} \end{cases} \quad (15)$$

The value $A(x)$ is an aggregated measure of the reliability's value of the SVM classifier ensemble. It can be used to integrate the members of the ensemble.

The learning algorithm of the ensemble of the SVM classifiers can be summarized into the following steps.

Step 1. To divide the experimental data set into k training data sets: TR_1, ..., TR_k.

Step 2. To learn k individual SVM classifiers with the different training data sets TR_1, ..., TR_k and to obtain k individual SVM classifiers (ensemble members).

Step 3. To select m ($m \leq k$) decorrelated SVM classifiers from k classifiers using the decorrelation maximization algorithm

Step 4. To determine values of m classification functions for each selected individual SVM classifier: $f_1(x)$, ..., $f_m(x)$.

Step 5. To transform values of degrees of reliability, using (9) and (10), for the positive class $g_1^+(x)$, ..., $g_m^+(x)$ and for the negative class $g_1^-(x)$, ..., $g_m^-(x)$.

Step 6. To determine the aggregated value $A(x)$ of the reliability of the SVM classifier ensemble using (11) – (15).

This algorithm, used for the weak SVM classifiers, will provide a better quality of the classification accuracy than accuracy of any single individual classifier used for aggregation.

The problem of choosing of the threshold θ is very important. Value θ for which all five rules of classification (11) – (15) show stable improvement of quality of classification must be chosen as the threshold value θ^* ($\theta^* < 0.7$). Thus the use of each of the five rules leads to improvement of the classification quality resulting in the reduction of the number of erroneous decisions, when the smaller number of individual classifiers, corresponding to the threshold value θ^*, is applied. Herewith such stable improvement of the classification quality isn't observed for all examined values θ' (for which $\theta' > \theta^*$).

It should be noted, that the majority vote rule may be used for decisions, obtained using the classification rules (11) - (15), to determine the required threshold value θ^*.

3 Experimental studies

The feasibility of using of the SVM classifier ensembles was confirmed by test and real data.

Several individual SVM classifiers using different types of the kernel function, different values of the kernel function functions of the kernel parameters and different values of the regularization parameter were learned in the experiments for a particular data set. Herewith the different training and test sets randomly generated from the original data set used were. Then the principle of maximum decorrelation (for selection of individual classifiers, which must be included in the ensemble) and various strategies of forming of the aggregated classifier were applied for the trained classifiers. The obtained classifier should have the higher classification accuracy than the classification accuracy of any single individual classifier.

Actual data used in the experimental researches were taken from Statlog project and from UCI machine learning library. In particular, data set for credit scoring was used. The German credit data set contains 1000 instances including 700 creditworthy cases (class 1) and 300 default cases (class 2); herewith each applicant is described by 24 characteristics ($q = 24$, the source is http://archive.ics.uci.edu/ml/machine-learning-databases/statlog/german/). As a result, 18 private SVM classifiers were trained with use of various input parameters.

During testing it was found, that the individual classifiers indicate the accuracy of classification decisions from 83.1% to 93.1%, and the initial values of the determination coefficient, calculated for all 18 individual classifiers, are in the range from 0.047 to 0.563. As a result, the threshold values θ were examined from the range [0.1; 0.6] with step 0.5. Values of classification parameters corresponding to different threshold values θ are given in Table 1.

The optimal threshold value θ for the reviewed example is 0.35, since for $\theta = 0.35$ all five classification rules (11) – (15) give a stable improvement of the classification quality when the number of classifiers reduces to the number corresponding to the value $\theta = 0.35$. Herewith the final number of classifiers in the ensemble proved equal to 8. A further decrease in the number of classifiers is not feasible (due to a further sharp decrease in their number and a substantial reduction of their variety).

Table 1. Values of classification parameters at the different threshold values of the determination coefficient.

Value of classification	Strategy	The threshold value of the coefficient of determination									
		0.6	**0.55**	**0.5**	**0.45**	**0.4**	**0.35**	**0.3**	**0.25**	**0.2/ 0.15**	**0.1**
Overall accuracy (%)	Majority vote	96.00	96.00	96.00	96.00	96.00	96.00	96.00	96.00	96.00	96.00
	Maximum and minimum	81.10	81.50	82.10	83.00	83.40	83.90	84.60	91.50	92.20	92.20
	Median and sum	94.90	96.00	96.40	97.20	97.50	98.20	97.90	97.80	97.00	96.90
	Product	89.50	90.30	90.40	90.70	91.60	91.70	91.70	97.10	96.40	95.70
Sensitivity (%)	Majority vote	97.43	97.43	97.43	97.43	97.43	97.43	97.43	97.43	97.43	97.43
	Maximum and minimum	83.00	83.57	84.14	85.43	86.29	87.00	87.57	95.29	95.57	95.43
	Median and sum	95.86	96.86	97.29	98.00	97.57	98.57	98.43	98.86	98.57	97.86
	Product	90.57	91.29	91.29	91.29	91.57	91.86	91.86	98.86	97.71	97.00
Specificity (%)	Majority vote	92.67	92.67	92.67	92.67	92.67	92.67	92.67	92.67	92.67	92.67
	Maximum and minimum	76.67	76.67	77.33	77.33	76.67	76.67	77.67	82.67	84.33	86.33
	Median and sum	92.67	94.00	94.33	95.33	97.33	97.33	96.67	95.33	93.33	94.67
	Product	87.00	88.00	88.33	89.33	91.67	91.33	91.33	93.00	93.33	92.67
Number of errors of the 1-st type	Majority vote	22	22	22	22	22	22	22	22	22	22
	Maximum and minimum	70	70	68	68	70	70	67	52	47	41
	Median and sum	22	18	17	14	8	8	10	14	20	16
	Product	39	36	35	32	25	26	26	21	20	22
Number of errors of the 2-nd type	Majority vote	18	18	18	18	18	18	18	18	18	18
	Maximum and minimum	119	115	111	102	96	91	87	33	31	32
	Median and sum	29	22	19	14	17	10	11	8	10	15
	Product	66	61	61	61	59	57	57	8	16	21
Number of classifiers in the ensemble		18	16	15	11	9	8	7	5	4	3

Use of the median strategy with $\theta = 0.35$ allowed classifying correctly 98.2% of objects of the initial data set. At the same time, the maximum accuracy of one of individual SVM classifiers, used in the ensemble, was equal 93.1%, and the accuracy reached with use of the majority vote rule was equal 96%.

Thus, the use of the SVM classifier ensemble allowed increasing the classification accuracy more than 5% compared with the maximum accuracy of one of the individual classifiers.

4 Conclusions

The use of the SVM classifier ensembles allows reducing the accident classification decision received by one classifier, and helps to improve the classification accuracy. The shortcomings of some classifiers are compensated by strengths of others classifiers thanks to combination of their results. Classifiers counterbalance the results' accident of each other, finding on the basis of balance the most plausible output classification decision. It allows finding the best classification result with minimum classification error.

References

1. O. Chapelle, V. Vapnik, O. Bousquet and S. Mukherjee, Machine Learning, **46**, 131 (2002)
2. L. Yu, S. Wang, K.K. Lai and L. Zhou, *Bio-Inspired Credit Risk Analysis. Computational Intelligence with Support Vector Machines* (Springer, 2008)
3. L. Demidova, Yu. Sokolova and E. Nikulchev, International Review on Modelling and Simulations **8**, 446 (2015)
4. L. Demidova and Yu. Sokolova, *16th International Symposium on Advanced Intelligent Systems*, pp. 889-906 (2015)
5. L. Demidova and Yu. Sokolova, *International Conference «Stability and Control Processes» in Memory of V.I. Zubov*, pp. 619-622 (2015)
6. L. Demidova and Yu. Sokolova, *International Conference «Stability and Control Processes» in Memory of V.I. Zubov*, pp. 623-627 (2015)
7. L. Demidova, E. Nikulchev and Yu. Sokolova, International Journal of Advanced Computer Science and Applications, **7**, (2016)
8. S.A. Aivazian and V.S. Mkhitarian, *Applied statistics and essentials of econometrics* (Moscow, 1998)

ITM Web of Conferences 6, 02004 (2016)
DOI: 10.1051/itmconf/20160602004

Automatic approach to stabilization and control for multi robot teams by multilayer network operator

Askhat Diveev[1, 2, a] and Elizaveta Shmalko[1]

[1] Federal Research Center "Computer Science and Control" of Russian Academy of Sciences, 119333 Moscow, Russia
[2] Peoples' Friendship University of Russia, 117198 Moscow, Russia

Abstract. The paper describes a novel methodology for synthesis a high-level control of autonomous multi robot teams. The approach is based on multilayer network operator method that belongs to a symbolic regression class. Synthesis is accomplished in three steps: stabilizing robots about some given position in a state space, finding optimal trajectories of robots' motion as sets of stabilizing points and then approximating all the points of optimal trajectories by some multi-dimensional function of state variables. The feasibility and effectiveness of the proposed approach is verified on simulations of the task of control synthesis for three mobile robots parking in the constrained space.

1 Introduction

The research and development of autonomous multi robot teams become a hot topic in recent years. Multi-robot control poses crucial issues due to inter-agent communications and increased number of agents. The most standard way to design an optimal motion and coordination control for multi robot teams involves constructing stabilization system for each robot in a team about some given position in a state space and finding optimal trajectories so that robots can optimally move with regard to some criteria from any initial position to some given terminal position. The optimal trajectories herein consist of sets of points where robots are stabilized.

There are a lot of solutions to stabilization problem. Specialists apply PID-controllers [1, 2] using deviation of the state vector from the given stabilization point in a space. Potential fields [3] method has also gained popularity recently. In this method a feedback control function is synthesized in order to minimize Euclidean norm of the difference between the value of the state vector of the robot and the point of stabilization. Stabilization can also be provided through Lyapunov functions [4, 5].

Once stabilization is done, different techniques can be applied to provide optimal trajectories. But the main challenge in designing optimal trajectories for a team of robots is to take into account dynamical constraints that guarantee the absence of collisions between agents. Such constraints should be considered separatly or included into quality criteria. Collision avoidance problem can be solved by the method of receding horizon [6] when the moves of robots are computed ahead and the moments of possible collisions are detected. If the robot is going to face a static obstacle then the trajectory of movement is adjusted. If the robot is going to face with another robot then the robots are prioritized by the distance to the termination point, and the robot with the lowest priority stops or commits some manoeuvre to avoid collision.

So we apply different techniques for different parts of the synthesis problem. Another drawback of the existing methods is that they provide a set of optimal trajectories for different possible initial conditions. And in case of a wide initial domain such set of optimal trajectories can occupy a large portion of the memory.

In the present paper we propose a single method of multilayer network operator to feedback control system synthesis. The method belongs to a class of symbolic regression methods and derives from the method of network operator [7]. The method allows automatically constructing such multidimensional function of the robots' state variables that can substitute the whole set of optimal trajectories of robots moving from different initial positions. We illustrated the main features of the method on the example. Simulation results are presented for a team of three mobile robots aiming to move to a given terminal position from eight different initial conditions.

2 Problem statement of control synthesis for multi robot team

Consider a system of similar mobile robots

$$\dot{x}_i = u_{1,i}\cos(\theta_i),\ \dot{y}_i = u_{1,i}\sin(\theta_i),$$
$$\dot{\theta}_i = \frac{u_{1,i}}{L}\mathrm{tg}(u_{2,i}),\ i = 1,\dots,N, \quad (1)$$

[a] Corresponding author: aidiveev@mail.ru

where (x_i, y_i) are coordinates of the geometric center of the robot i, θ_i is an angle between the roll axis of the robot i and x-axis of the fixed coordinate system, L is an overall dimensional parameter of robot, $u_{1,i}$, $u_{2,i}$ are components of the control vector of the robot i, N is a number of robots.

Given constraints on control

$$u_1^- \le u_{1,i} \le u_1^+,\ u_2^- \le u_{2,i} \le u_2^+. \quad (2)$$

Fig.1 shows a layout view of the described mobile robot.

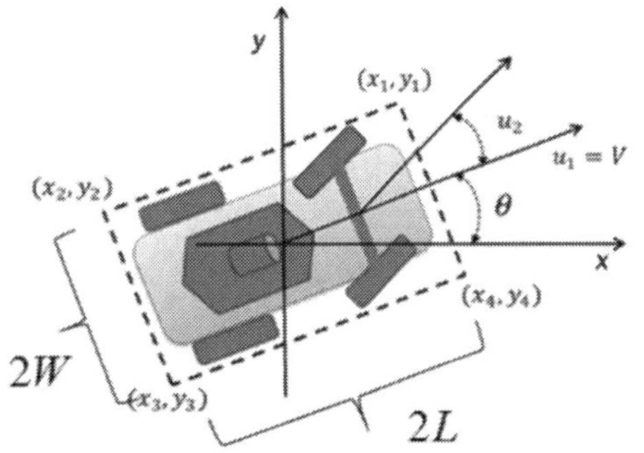

Figure 1. Overall domain of the robot and control.

Here (x_k, y_k) are coordinates of a rectangular domain of the robot, $2W$ is a width of the domain, $2L$ is a length correspondingly.

To check the absence of collisions between robots and with other static geometrical obstacles we need to know coordinates of corners of each robot. To determine the coordinates of coners of the robot i let us rotate the coordinate system by an angle θ_i. Coordinates of the geometric center of the robot i in the rotated coordinate system are defined as follows

$$\tilde{x}_i = x_i \cos(\theta_i) + y_i \sin(\theta_i),$$

$$\tilde{y}_i = -x_i \sin(\theta_i) + y_i \cos(\theta_i). \quad (3)$$

Thus calculate the coordinates of corners as

$$\tilde{x}_{k,i} = \tilde{x}_i + (-1)^{\lfloor k/2 \rfloor} L,\ \tilde{y}_{k,i} = \tilde{y}_i - (-1)^{\lfloor (k+1)/2 \rfloor} W, \quad (4)$$

$$k = 1,2,3,4.$$

To obtain coordinates of corners of the robot in a fixed coordinate system we do inverse conversion with respect to (2)

$$x_{k,i} = \tilde{x}_{k,i} \cos(\theta_i) - \tilde{y}_{k,i} \sin(\theta_i),$$

$$y_{k,i} = \tilde{x}_{k,i} \sin(\theta_i) + \tilde{y}_{k,i} \cos(\theta_i), \quad (5)$$

$$k = 1,2,3,4.$$

To check if the collision of the robot i with the robot j happens we need to determine the penetration of every corner of the robot j into the domain of the robot i, and vice versa the penetration of every corner of the robot i into the domain of the robot j. We initially calculate the coordinates of corners of the robot j in rotated by θ_i coordinate system

$$\tilde{x}_{k,j}(\theta_i) = x_{k,j} \cos(\theta_i) + y_{k,j} \sin(\theta_i),$$

$$\tilde{y}_{k,j}(\theta_i) = -x_{k,j} \sin(\theta_i) + y_{k,j} \cos(\theta_i), \quad (6)$$

$$k = 1,2,3,4.$$

The corner $(x_{k,j}, y_{k,j})$ of the robot j penetrates the domain of the robot i when the following conditions are met

$$(\tilde{x}_{k,j}(\theta_i) \le \tilde{x}_i + L) \wedge (\tilde{x}_{k,j}(\theta_i) \ge \tilde{x}_i - L) \wedge$$

$$\wedge (\tilde{y}_{k,j}(\theta_i) \le \tilde{y}_i + W) \wedge (\tilde{y}_{k,j}(\theta_i) \ge \tilde{y}_i - W), \quad (7)$$

$$k = 1,2,3,4.$$

For complete collision checking we determine as well if the corners of the robot i penetrates the domain of the robot j.

$$(\tilde{x}_{k,i}(\theta_j) \le \tilde{x}_j + L) \wedge (\tilde{x}_{k,i}(\theta_j) \ge \tilde{x}_j - L) \wedge$$

$$\wedge (\tilde{y}_{k,i}(\theta_j) \le \tilde{y}_j + W) \wedge (\tilde{y}_{k,i}(\theta_j) \ge \tilde{y}_i - W), \quad (8)$$

$$k = 1,2,3,4.$$

Conditions (7) or (8) detect the penetration of the domain of one robot by some corner of another robot.

For a team of N robots there is enough to check the collisions between pairs of robots, so the number of collision checks for the team will be equal to permutations of N things taken 2 at a time

$$A_N^2 = N(N-1).$$

Given a set of initial conditions for the team of robots

$$X_0 = \{((x_1^{0,1}, y_1^{0,1}, \theta_1^{0,1}), \ldots, (x_N^{0,1}, y_N^{0,1}, \theta_N^{0,1})), \ldots$$

$$\ldots, ((x_1^{0,M}, y_1^{0,M}, \theta_1^{0,M}), \ldots, (x_N^{0,M}, y_N^{0,M}, \theta_N^{0,M})). \quad (9)$$

Terminal conditions are also given

$$| x_k(t_f) - x_k^f | \le \varepsilon,\ | y_k(t_f) - y_k^f | \le \varepsilon,$$

$$| \theta_k(t_f) - \theta_k^f | \le \varepsilon,\ k = 1, \ldots, N, \quad (10)$$

where t_f is not given bounded above runtime of meeting terminal conditions, $t_f \le t^+$, ε is a given small positive value, t^+ is a given time limit for meeting terminal conditions.

Given a quality criterion

$$J = \sum_{i=1}^{M} \left(\sum_{k=1}^{N} \int_{0}^{t_f} f_0(x_k(t), y_k(t), \theta_k(t), u_{1,k}(t), u_{2,k}(t)) dt \right)_i \quad (11)$$

where the lower index i at brackets $(\ldots)_i$ means that the expression in brackets is calculated for initial values $((x_1^{0,i}, y_1^{0,i}, \theta_1^{0,i}), \ldots, (x_N^{0,i}, y_N^{0,i}, \theta_N^{0,i}))$, $1 \le i \le M$.

Define control as a function

$$u_{i,k} = h_{i,k}(x_1, y_1, \theta_1, \ldots, x_N, y_N, \theta_N), \quad (12)$$

$$i = 1,2, \; k = 1, \ldots, N,$$

which meets the constraints on control (2) and for any initial conditions from (9) in timeframe restricted by $t_f \le t^+$ reaches the objective (10) with minimum value of the quality criterion (11).

To solve the stated problem of control system synthesis the method of network operator can be used directly. In [8] it has been successfully applied for two mobile robot parking task. But when the number of arguments increases the direct synthesis is computationally hard and time consuming. In this case we propose to apply a three-stage synthesis algorithm. On the first stage we synthesize a stabilization system for every robot about some given point in a state space. As far as we have a group of similar robots we can synthesize a stabilizing control function for one robot and apply it for each robot in a team.

We define a point in a state space for the robot k, $(x_k^*, y_k^*, \theta_k^*)$. Deviations of the component of the state vector from the defined point are Δx_k, Δy_k, $\Delta\theta_k$ and control will be defined as

$$u_{i,k} = g_i(x_k^* - x_k, y_k^* - y_k, \theta_k^* - \theta_k), \; i = 1,2, \quad (13)$$

which provides the achievement of the termination point $(x_k^*, y_k^*, \theta_k^*)$ from any point of the domain

$$X_{0,k} = \{x_k^* \pm \Delta x_k, y_k^* \pm \Delta y_k, \theta_k^* \pm \Delta\theta_k\}. \quad (14)$$

As optimization criterion we choose a time of achieving the objective

$$J_s = \sum_{i=1}^{8} (t_1)_i \to \min, \quad (15)$$

where sum is calculated for initial conditions from (14)

$$(x_k^* + (-1)^{\lfloor (i-1)/4 \rfloor} \Delta x_k,$$

$$y_k^* + (-1)^{\lfloor (i-1)/2 \rfloor} \Delta y_k, \quad (16)$$

$$\theta_k^* + (-1)^{i-1} \Delta\theta_k), \; i = 1, \ldots, 8,$$

$$t_1 = \begin{cases} t, \text{ if } t < t^+ \text{ and} \\ \quad \max\{|x_k^* - x(t)|, |y_k^* - y(t)|, |\theta_k^* - \theta(t)|\} < \varepsilon \\ t^+ \text{ - otherwise} \end{cases} \quad (17)$$

Once the stabilization system is synthesized and the control function (13) is received the robots motion control is performed via changing the position of the stabilization points $(x_k^*, y_k^*, \theta_k^*)$. So we need to find spacial optimal trajectories made-up of the points in a state space

$$\mathrm{T}_{k,j} = ((x_{k,j,1}^*, y_{k,j,1}^*, \theta_{k,j,1}^*), \ldots,$$

$$\ldots, (x_{k,j,r}^*, y_{k,j,r_j}^*, \theta_{k,j,r_j}^*)), \quad (18)$$

$$k = 1, \ldots, N, \; j = 1, \ldots, M,$$

where the trajectories are built for each robot k moving from the initial position $(x_k^{0,k}, y_k^{0,k}, \theta_k^{0,k})$ to the terminal position

$$x_{k,j,r_j}^* = x_k^f, \; y_{k,j,r_j}^* = y_k^f, \; \theta_{k,j,r_j}^* = \theta_k^f. \quad (19)$$

The optimality of the trajectories as sets of points in the state space is defined according to the quality criterion (11) with addition of penalties in case if collisions.

Fig. 2 illustrates how the corner k of the robot j penetrates the overall domain of the robot i. The penalty value for the penetration is defined every time as minimal size of penetration

$$p(i,j,t) = \min\{|\tilde{x}_{2,i} - \tilde{x}_i - \tilde{x}_{k,j}|, |\tilde{x}_{1,i} - \tilde{x}_i - \tilde{x}_{k,j}|,$$

$$|\tilde{y}_{1,i} - \tilde{y}_i - \tilde{y}_{k,j}|, |\tilde{y}_{3,i} - \tilde{y}_i - \tilde{y}_{k,j}|\}. \quad (20)$$

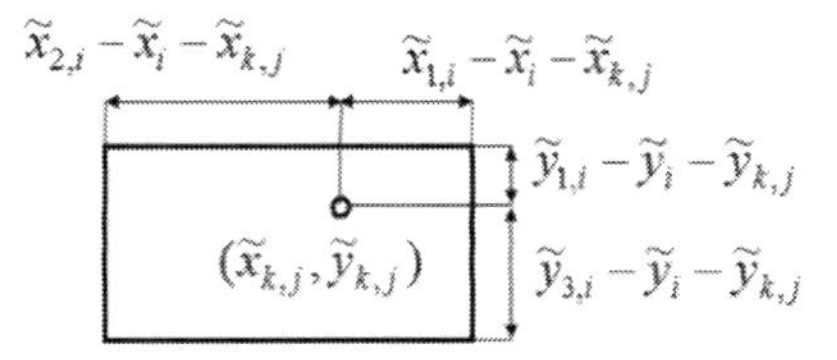

Figure 2. Penalty definition for collision.

Integrals of penalty values are computed for all M initial points and the results are summed and added to the functional (11). So the resulting quality functional is following

$$\tilde{J} = J + \sum_{l=1}^{M} \left(\int_{0}^{t_f} \sum_{i=1}^{N} \sum_{j=1}^{N} p(i,j,t) dt \right)_l \to \min. \quad (21)$$

Once the optimal trajectories as sets of points in the state space (18) are obtained we can proceed with the 3rd stage of our approach to accomolish the synthesis. On the last stage we build up a system of differentioal equations which partial solutions approximate the points of the received optimal trajectories

$$\dot{x}_k^* = g_{1,k}(x_1^f - x_1^*, \ldots, x_N^f - x_N^*,$$
$$y_1^f - y_1^*, \ldots, y_N^f - y_N^*, \theta_1^f - \theta_1^*, \ldots, \theta_N^f - \theta_N^*), \quad (22)$$
$$\dot{y}_k^* = g_{2,k}(x_1^f - x_1^*, \ldots, x_N^f - x_N^*,$$
$$y_1^f - y_1^*, \ldots, y_N^f - y_N^*, \theta_1^f - \theta_1^*, \ldots, \theta_N^f - \theta_N^*), \quad (23)$$
$$\dot{\theta}_k^* = g_{3,k}(x_1^f - x_1^*, \ldots, x_N^f - x_N^*,$$
$$y_1^f - y_1^*, \ldots, y_N^f - y_N^*, \theta_1^f - \theta_1^*, \ldots, \theta_N^f - \theta_N^*), \quad (24)$$

where right parts are the desired functions $\mathbf{R}^{3N} \to \mathbf{R}^{3N}$, $k = 1, \ldots, N$.

A block diagram of the control system of a mobile robot is presented in fig.3.

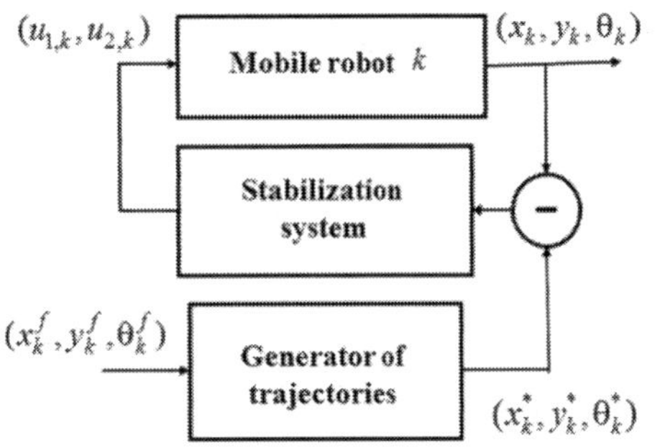

Figure 3. Control system of mobile robot.

Generator of trajectories in fig. 3 implements the solution of the system (22) - (24).

To identify a model of the generator of trajectories we use the multilayer network operator method as well.

3 Multilayer network operator

The core idea of the method of the network operator is that a mathematical expression is coded in the form of integer upper-triangular matrix. The cells of the matrix correspond by its numbers to the proper variables, parameters and mathematical operations. The search for the needed mathematical expression, which satisfies the objectives and criteria, is performed by the evolutionary algorithm on the basis of the principle of small variations of basic solution [9].

The multilayer network operator is a set of network operators connected with each other. The connections are described in a connectivity matrix of size $K \times 2I$, where K is a number of network operators or layers, I is a number of input in each layer. The outputs of the multilayer network operator are stored in an output matrix of size $M \times 2$, where M is a dimension of the vector-function described by the multilayer network operator.

Consider an example of coding a mathematical expression by multilayer network operator.

Given a vector mathematical expression

$$\begin{bmatrix} y_1 \\ y_2 \end{bmatrix} = \begin{bmatrix} \cos(x_1 + \sin(x_2 + q_2)) \\ e^{-q_1 x_1 + q_2} \cos(x_2^2 - x_1^2) \end{bmatrix}.$$

and the following sets of elementary functions

$$\mathrm{F}_0 = \{f_{0,1} = x_1, f_{0,2} = x_2, f_{0,3} = q_1, f_{0,4} = q_2\},$$

$$\mathrm{F}_1 = \{f_{1,1}(z) = z, f_{1,2}(z) = -z, f_{1,3}(z) = e^z,$$
$$f_{1,4}(z) = z^2, f_{1,5}(z) = \sin(z), f_{1,6}(z) = \sin(z)\},$$

$$\mathrm{F}_2 = \{f_{2,1}(z_1, z_2) = z_1 + z_2, f_{2,1}(z_1, z_2) = z_1 z_2\}.$$

Let us build a network operator graph of the mathematical expression according to [2]. The resulting graph is shown on fig. 4.

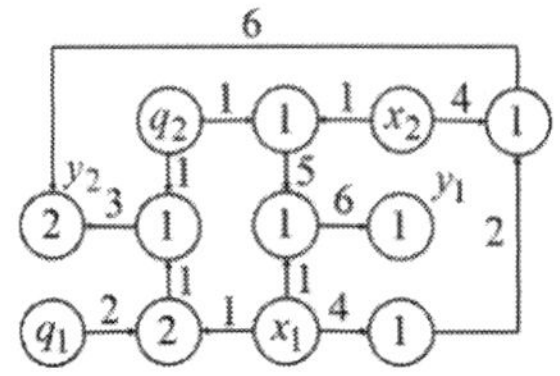

Figure 4. Network operator graph of the expression

We split the network operator graph into several subgraphs. Each subgraph is a layer. Fig.5 shows three layers of the spited graph.

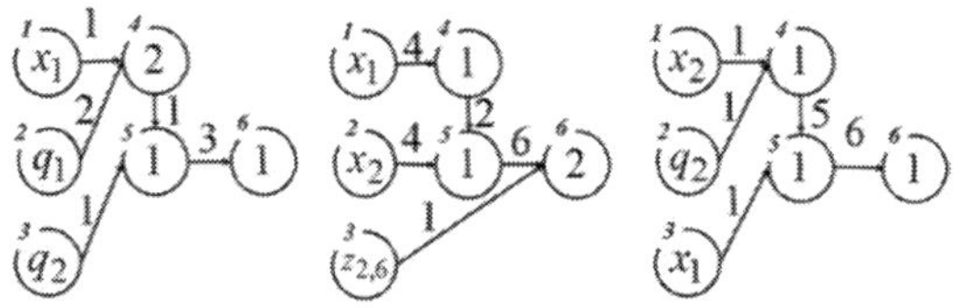

Figure 5. Layers of the network operator

The layers are described by the following matrices

$$\mathbf{\Psi}_1 = \begin{bmatrix} 0&0&0&1&0&0 \\ 0&0&0&1&0&0 \\ 0&0&0&0&1&0 \\ 0&0&0&1&5&0 \\ 0&0&0&0&1&6 \\ 0&0&0&0&0&1 \end{bmatrix}, \mathbf{\Psi}_2 = \begin{bmatrix} 0&0&0&1&0&0 \\ 0&0&0&2&0&0 \\ 0&0&0&0&1&0 \\ 0&0&0&1&1&0 \\ 0&0&0&0&1&3 \\ 0&0&0&0&0&1 \end{bmatrix}, \mathbf{\Psi}_3 = \begin{bmatrix} 0&0&0&4&0&0 \\ 0&0&0&0&4&0 \\ 0&0&0&0&0&1 \\ 0&0&0&1&2&0 \\ 0&0&0&0&1&6 \\ 0&0&0&0&0&2 \end{bmatrix}$$

and the connectivity matrix

$$\mathbf{\Sigma} = \begin{bmatrix} 0&2&0&4&0&1 \\ 0&1&0&3&0&4 \\ 0&1&0&2&2&6 \end{bmatrix}.$$

The output matrix is

$$\mathbf{\Omega} = \begin{bmatrix} 1&6 \\ 3&6 \end{bmatrix},$$

where the upper row indicates the number of layer and the bottom row contains the corresponding number of output in the indicated layer.

For backward transformations from the multilayer network operator to the mathematical expression we use the following formula

$$z_{k,r} = \begin{cases} z^0_{\sigma_{k,2r}}, \text{ if } \sigma_{k,2r-1} = 0 \\ z_{\sigma_{k,2r-1},\sigma_{k,2r}} \text{ - otherwise} \end{cases},$$

$$z_{k,j} \leftarrow \begin{cases} \chi_{\psi_{k,i,i}}\left(z_{k,j}, \rho_{\psi_{k,i,j}}(z_{k,i})\right) \text{ if } \psi_{k,i,j} \neq 0 \\ z_{k,j} \text{ - otherwise} \end{cases},$$

where $\mathbf{\Psi}_k = [\psi_{k,i,j}]$, $\mathbf{\Sigma} = [\sigma_{k,m}]$, $m = \overline{1,2I}$, k is a layer number, $k = \overline{1,N}$, r is a number of input, $r = \overline{1,I}$, i is a number of row in the network operator matrix, $i = \overline{1,L}$, j is a number of column in the network operator matrix, $j = \overline{i+1,L-2}$, $\rho_d(z)$ is a unary operation number d, $\chi_g(z_1, z_2)$ is a binary operation number g.

4 Simulations

In the simulation example three similar mobile robots are considered: $N = 3$, $L = 2$, $W = 1$. We considered 8 initial points X_0:
$\{((-10,2,0),(-10,4,0),(-10,6,0)),((10,2,0),(-10,4,0),(-10,6,0)),$
$((-10,2,0),(10,4,0),(-10,6,0)),((-10,2,0),(-10,4,0),(10,6,0)),$
$((10,2,0),(10,4,0),(-10,6,0)),((10,2,0),(-10,4,0),(10,6,0)),$
$((-10,2,0),(10,4,0),(10,6,0)),((10,2,0),(10,4,0),(10,6,0))\}$.

Terminal conditions were
$x_i - x_{i,f} = 0,\ y_i - y_{i,f} = 0,\ \theta_i - \theta_{i,f} = 0,\ i = 1,2,3,$

where $x_{1,f} = -5,\ y_{1,f} = 0,\ \theta_{1,f} = 0,\ x_{2,f} = 0,$ $y_{2,f} = 0,\ \theta_{2,f} = 0,\ x_{3,f} = 5,\ y_{3,f} = 0,\ \theta_{3,f} = 0$.

The quality functional was a total time of achiving terminal conditions

$$J = t_f \to \min,$$

where

$$t_f = \begin{cases} t, \text{ if } \max\{|x_i(t) - x_{i,f}|, |y_i(t) - y_{i,f}|, \\ \qquad |\theta_i(t) - \theta_{i,f}|, i = 1,2,3\} < \varepsilon \\ t^+ \text{ - otherwise} \end{cases},$$

$\varepsilon = 0{,}01$, $t^+ = 12$.

We set static phase constraints as two rectangular domains.

On the first stage we solved stabilization problem by the network operator. The received stabilization control allows robots stabilizing in a given point as shown in fig.6.

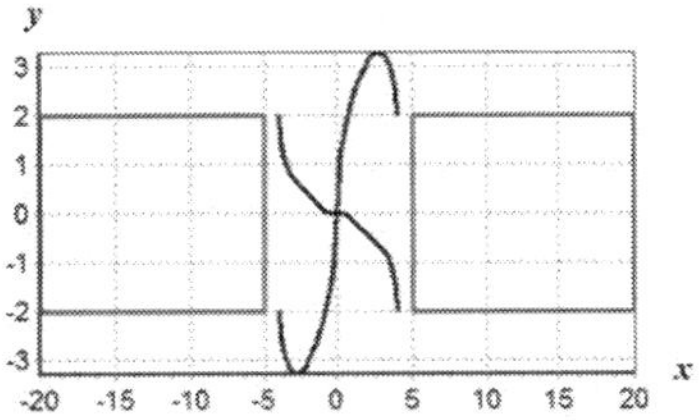

Figure 6. Stabilization of the system from initial positions (-4,-2,0), (4,2,0), (-4,2,0), (4,-2,0)

For control synthesis we used a multilayer network operator of 4 layers sized 16×16. As a result, the system of generating optimal trajectories has been received. Fig.7 illustrates the generated trajectories for one initial position.

Thus, we demonstrated a new approach for synthesis of optimal motion control of multi robot team. The received optimal trajectories allow robots achieving the terminal conditions with optimal values of functionals and not violating the phase constraints and avoiding collisions.

This work has been supported by the Russian Fund of Basic Researches (14-08-00008-a) and by the grant of the President of Russian Federation (MK-6277.2015.8).

References

1. K. Åström and T. Hägglund, *PID controllers: Theory, Design and Tuning* (1995)
2. M. Fliess and C. Join, *15th IFAC Symp. on Syst. Ident.* (2009)
3. D.P. Garg and G.K. Fricker, *iNaCoMM2013* (2013)
4. R. Bellman, SIAM J. on Cont., **1** (1962)
5. S.G. Nersesov and W. M. Haddad, IEEE Trans. on Automatic Contr., **51**, 203 (2006)
6. T. Kaviczky, F. Borelli, K. Fregene, D. Godbole and G.J.Balas, IEEE Trans. on Cont. Syst. Tech., **16**, (2008)
7. A.I. Diveev and E.A. Sofronova, *Proc. 7th Int. Conf. on Contr. and Automat. (ICCA'09)*, pp. 701-708 (2009)
8. A.I. Diveev and E.Yu. Shmalko, *Proc. of 2015 Europ. Contr. Conf.*, pp. 709-714. (2015)
9. A.I. Diveev, IFAC-PapersOnLine, **48**, 028 (2015).

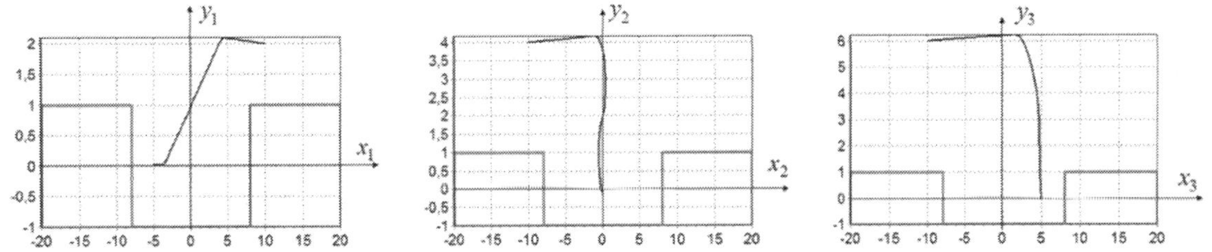

Figure 7. Optimal trajectory of the centre of the 1st, 2nd and 3rd robots from initial position $((10,2,0),(-10,4,0),(-10,6,0))$.

ITM Web of Conferences 6, 02005 (2016)
DOI: 10.1051/itmconf/20160602005

The ontological model and the hybrid expert system for products and processes quality identification involving the approach based on system analysis and quality function deployment

Aleksandr Dmitriev [1, 2] and Tatyana Mitroshkina [1, a]

[1]Samara State Aerospace University named after academician S.P. Korolev (National Research University), 443086 Samara, Russia
[2]Samara Region State Academy (Nayanova), 443010 Samara, Russia

Abstract. Discussed model of quality of identification has improved mathematical tools and allows you to use a variety of additional information. The proposed robust method is a matrix MTQFD (Matrix Technique Quality Function Deployment) allows you to determine not only the priorities but also the assessment of the target values of the product characteristics and process parameters, with the possible use of the information on the negative relationship. Designed ontological model, method and model of expert system versatile and can be used to identify the quality of services.

1 Introduction

Effective design of quality products based on the ontological approach, the requirements of the standards, the use of knowledge bases, ontology and methods of quality management is an important way to increase the competitiveness of products [1].

Design of quality products is the development of products based on consumer expectations, knowledge and parametric identification of the characteristics of quality.

The problem of quality parametric identification (identifying priorities and performance targets) on the basis of consumer expectations and the developer of knowledge is a key task [2–4]. There are difficulties in identifying the quality of new and complex products. The problem of parametric identification, in fact, is the reverse. It is necessary to determine the characteristics of the designed products or services (the cause of) satisfaction of identified (effect). The problem of parametric identification of quality products and services, as well as the majority of inverse problems is incorrect. Incorrectness is shown in a high variability of the requirements in time, the ambiguity of unspoken expectations, etc.

The aim is to improve the quality and competitiveness of products. It is proposed to design and develop products to be based on the use of various types of information (knowledge), the identification of the target values of the product characteristics and process parameters and the effective application of the QFD [5, 6].

2 System ontological approach and QFD

Modern international management system standards, including standards for quality management system ISO 9001 developed using a common approach and require a knowledge management organizations [7]. So, the new version of ISO 9001 (ISO 9001: 2015) has been developed in accordance with the Annex to the Directive ISO Annex SL (ISO / IEC Directives, Part 1 Consolidated ISO Supplement - Procedures specific to ISO). The directive establishes a new, uniform standard for management systems (based on ISO 9001, ISO 14001, ISO 50001, ISO 22000, ISO / IEC 27001, and others.), According to which all management systems standards will be given to a single structure.

Paragraph 7.1.5 ISO 9001:2015 "Knowledge" is specifies requirements for knowledge management [7]:

– The organization shall determine the knowledge necessary for the operation of the quality management system and its processes and to assure conformity of goods and services and customer satisfaction.

– This knowledge shall be maintained, protected and made available as necessary.

– Where addressing changing needs and trends the organization shall take into account its current knowledge base and determine how to acquire or access the necessary additional knowledge.

Integration with the requirements of ISO 9001 in the field of knowledge management and implementation of risk management are the main directions of the update of the standard and bring it to the modern level of management science.

Design and development of ontology (ontological engineering) - basis for the concept of knowledge management - currently the most promising approach to managing complex "content" systems. The development of knowledge management system includes several phases: accumulation, retrieval, structuring, formalization and software implementation and maintenance.

The main objective of the ontological approach - ordering of knowledge by their ordering, create a single hierarchy of concepts, harmonization of terms and rules of interpretation - has the general objective of improving

[a] Corresponding author : t.mitroshkina@gmail.com

the efficiency of product design in accordance with the requirements and expectations of customers. The methodology of ontological engineering will optimize the product design process, taking into account not only the needs and expectations of consumers, but also the knowledge base developer.

The key objective is to define the quality assurance (identification) characteristics of product quality. From this task depend on further steps of the product life cycle and, ultimately, the competitiveness of the organization. In theory, under the control of the system to understand the definition of identity structure of the system and its parameters by analyzing the inputs and outputs of the system [2, 3, 4, 8]. The structural and parametric identification of commercial products using modern methods of quality management.

Modern methods of transformation of customer requirements in the immediate characteristics of the new (or upgraded) product quality identification method is QFD. The aim of the method is the conversion request (needs and expectations) in product specifications and work instructions, visualization, documentation and planning quality. The main element of QFD is precisely the deployment of customer requirements in the production and the attainment of the relevant specifications to meet consumer expectations. That is, in this case we are talking about the pre-production to the production of new products.

In the expanded implementation of QFD process includes four levels, and each of them built a house of quality (House of Quality, HoQ).

At the consumer level I converted into technical specifications. Then the last components are converted into characteristics (level II), then - in process parameters (level III), and then performance requirements operations (IV level).

The result of the application of QFD is to set priorities and identify the product characteristics, characteristics of the components, process parameters and auxiliary operations, the greatest impact on meeting customer requirements.

Thus, the absolute value of the priority of the j-th generalized characteristics of the product by 1 level QFD is calculated using the formula:

$$ql_j = \sum_{i=1}^{n}(pl_i \cdot hl_{ij}) = pl_1 hl_{1j} + pl_2 hl_{2j} + \ldots + pl_n hl_{nj} \quad (1)$$

where hl_{ij} - the coefficient of the relationship *j-th* generalized characteristics of the product and the *i-th* requirements; pli - the relative importance of the value of the *i-th* requirements for the consumer; n - number of consumer requirements.

Methods of identifying quality evolve simultaneously with the development of the concept of "quality". At the same time a significant role in the development of QFD play mathematical approaches that are used in computer parts (matrix calculus, the solution of the inverse problem), and in terms of integration with other methods, such as a table of voice user (VOCT) [4, 5, 9], the theory of solutions Inventive Problem Solving (TRIZ) [10], analysis of the types and consequences of potential inconsistencies (FMEA) projects to improve the "Six Sigma" and others [11, 12].

The effective application of the method proposed structuring of knowledge and use of the ontological approach. The traditional approach to designing products means choosing the concept and definition of the technical characteristics of products. This is often the author of a technical project is the developer. Taken into account the knowledge base in the class "concept products" and attributes "Product Features". The ontological model of design quality on the basis of QFD, in contrast to the traditional approach to the design in the first place takes into account the class of "user requirements".

Customer requirements are determined by analyzing the voice of consumers and are described by a list of requirements (in accordance with the model N. Kano [9] consists of the basic requirements, contractual requirements and expectations of customers), the importance of the requirements (for example, on a 10-point scale) and evaluation competitiveness of products / customer satisfaction (including benchmarking data) The result of the design on the first level are the QFD concept (structure) of products and product characteristics, which are described by a list of specifications, interconnection and value characteristics. This design goal is not only the "development" or "modification" of products, and the development or modification of the product, taking into account the characteristics of the relationship and data benchmarking so as to achieve the necessary level of competitiveness. In the case of product design consisting of individual components, great care must be taken the design quality of the components, which is defined not only by their technical characteristics, but also the quality of manufacturing processes and the production conditions. The ontological model of design quality on the basis of QFD is implemented using the tool Protégé. The structure of the ontology is similar to the hierarchical directory structure.

3 Implementation of the ontological model of design quality on the basis of sustainable matrix method MTQFD

It is proposed to use the method of approximate solution of sustainable method of approximate solution of the following matrix equation (hereinafter - linear mathematical model LMM):

$$H \cdot \delta\Theta = \delta P, \quad (2)$$

where $\delta\Theta$ - n-dimensional vector of relative deviations of parameters of state (estimates of the target values of the product characteristics for level 1 QFD), δP - k-dimensional vector of relative deviations signs of state (the importance of the requirements and expectations of customers (for level 1 QFD), H - matrix of size $(k \times n)$ the coefficients of the requirements and characteristics of the relationship (for level 1 QFD).

The developed algorithm matrix method MTQFD includes both the conventional calculation of vectors of priorities, and the parametric identification of the characteristics of the products / components (1, 2 levels QFD) and parameters of technological processes and auxiliary operations (3, 4 levels QFD), is widely used in engineering sciences.

Using matrix transformations and known method of least squares (OLS) using the formula (3), we obtain not only adopted in the evaluation of QFD priorities change specifications, but other assessment areas for further improvement.

$$\delta\hat{\Theta} = (H^T PH)^{-1} H^T P \delta P \quad (3)$$

where P - is the weight matrix of error requirements and expectations.

In addition, the conditions of existence of the real possibility of serious errors in the measurements of the state of signs (for first-level error QFD marketing data can be 10..50% for small samples) use OLS requires the use of special methods of preliminary rejection of initial data [13].

It is proposed to use OLS, in limited cases, only if the number of requests is greater than the number of features / parameters involved in the model.

If the number of performance exceeds the number of claims, it is advisable to use an algorithm robust parametric identification of the mathematical model, taking into account information about the error model (matrix interconnection requirements and specifications), and features state (needs and expectations), as well as additional information about the possible values of the relative changes in the parameters state (characteristics), taking into account the risks, the characteristics of correlations ("roof» HoQ).

All sustainable scheme for estimating linear models are based on the functions of impact and sustainability assessment. Particular attention is paid to the assessment of sustainable Huber. To find a sustainable assessment Huber used an iterative procedure that converges to robust estimates for finite number of iterations [13].

Solution of the problem in this formulation allows to obtain estimates of the parameters of state (the relative change in performance), both agreed with the results of marketing research and benchmarking, and more information and knowledge about the inaccuracy of the data and the developer.

It is proposed to conduct parametric identification based on regularization theory, can reasonably take into account a wide range of different additional information. Upon receipt of regularized estimates take into account the best pilot and the additional information, the choice of the regularization parameter α carried c considering the measurement error and uncertainty factors (matrix H) LMM [1].

The developed method MTQFD regularized solution of the problem of parametric identification of the mathematical model is defined as follows:

$$\delta\hat{\Theta}^{\alpha} = \arg\min_{\delta\Theta} M^{\alpha}[\delta\Theta]$$

where (4)

$$M^{\alpha}[\delta\Theta] = \sum_{i=1}^{k} F_1(c_1, \Delta_i, p_i) + \alpha \sum_{j=1}^{n} F_2(c_2, \delta\Theta_j - \delta\Theta_j^0, q_i),$$

where F1 and F2 - function of the special form [1, 13], Δ - residual, p, q - weight discrepancy, c - setting Huber.

In the case of the quadratic norm equation (4) takes the following form:

$$M_1^{\alpha}[\delta\Theta] = \|H\delta\Theta - \delta P\|_p^2 + \alpha\left\|\delta\Theta - \delta\Theta^0\right\|_q^2,$$

where $\|\cdot\|_P = (\cdot)^T P (\cdot)$ - quadratic norm with weights. It is evident that the decision on the one hand, depends on the use of information and benchmarking LMM, prisoners in the first term $\|H\delta\Theta - \delta P\|_p^2$ smoothing functional M_I^{α}, on the other hand - on the information about the possible values of the parameters of state concluded in the second term $\|\delta\Theta - \delta\Theta^0\|_q^2$. Ratio between benchmarking and additional information is determined by the regularization parameter α.

Selecting the iteration step, which determines the desired value of the relative deviations of parameters of the state and the corresponding regularization parameter α, is carried out at the value of the regularization function $f(\alpha)$ closest to zero:

$$f(\alpha) = \left\|H\delta\hat{\Theta} - \delta P\right\|_p^2 - \alpha(\delta + h\left\|\delta\hat{\Theta}^{\alpha} - \delta\Theta^0\right\|_q)^2 \quad (5)$$

here: $\left\|\delta P - \delta\overline{P}\right\|_p \leq \delta$, $\left\|H - \overline{H}\right\| \leq h$, $\left\|\delta\hat{\Theta}^{\alpha} - \delta\Theta^0\right\|_q$ defined differently for each task.

To implement the method presented MTQFD developed a software module in the system MathCAD. To simplify the implementation of the method in the development of software module provides the use of the original data in the form of standard tables, MS Excel, which allows researchers and experts not to spend resources for technical training data and focus on the issues of "quality" of the original data and the additional information.

The purpose of the expert system of design quality on the basis of MTQFD is to improve the quality of products due to: the automated storage ways to improve product competitiveness and customer satisfaction; the development of a mathematical model of the process of identification of product quality; formalizing the knowledge representation of experts; creation modes advice, training and the acquisition of new knowledge.

Expert system is the standard structure of the knowledge base (description pro-problem areas, procedural knowledge, declarative knowledge, attributes and source data consulted) and shall take into account the experience of experts in the design of products and time-processing technology and manufacturing processes. The knowledge base in addition to the specific information requirements of consumers and characteristics of products includes models of the problem domain for components, technology and production processes, including proper description of the area and knowledge of the problem solving procedure (consultation scenario). The expert system provides a solution to problems on the basis of knowledge, including knowledge of different classifications, as well as experience experts in product design and development processes. The expert system is focused on the identification of product quality throughout the development of products, components, technology and production processes (all 4 levels QFD).

4 Discussion

The proposed objective ontology design quality is based on the ontological approach, developed in the systems management and enshrined in international standards, which, in fact, form a meta-ontology. Developed ontology MTQFD method can significantly alleviate the designers, engineers and experts to solve practical problems of identification and further planning of quality, as well as improve the accuracy and robustness of the results to the initial data errors. Ontology is implemented on the example of the problem of designing automotive wire taking into account additional information, including the results of failure mode and effect analysis (FMEA) [11]. Application of the ontological approach and method MTQFD allowed reducing design period, to improve the quality and competitiveness of automotive wire due to the calculation of new priorities, clarify product specifications and parameters of technological and manufacturing processes.

Advance understanding of the ontological paradigm and design of quality products based on parametric identification of models, customer requirements, knowledge can achieve to improve product quality and competitiveness in various industries.

References

1. A.Ya. Dmitriev and T.A. Mitroshkina. Ontology of designing, **5**, 313-327 (2015) [In Russian]
2. K.J. Astrom and P. Eykhoff, Automatica. **7**, 123 (1971)
3. L. Ljung, *System identification.Theory for the User*, (Prentice Hall, 1999)
4. E.V. Nikulchev, *2014 International Conference on Computer Technologies in Physical and Engineering Applications (ICCTPEA)*, pp. 129 (2014)
5. Y. Akao and G.H. Mazur, International Journal of Quality & Reliability Management, **20**, 20 (2003)
6. G. Mazur. *12th Symposium on QFD/6th International Symposium on QFD2000,* pp. 305-317 (2000)
7. ISO 9001:2015 (2015)
8. G.N. Rogachev, Automatic control and computer sciences, **48**, 249 (2014)
9. N. Kano, N.Seraku, F.Takahashi and S.Tsuji, Journal of Japanese Society for Quality Control, **14**, 39 (1984)
10. H. Yamashina, T. Ito and H. Kawada, International Journal of Production Research, **40**, 1031 (2002)
11. V.N. Rodionov, T.V. Popova, A.Ya. Dmitriev and T.A. Mitroshkina. Metodyi menedzhmenta kachestva. **8**, 30 (2011) [In Russian]
12. T.M. Fehlmann, Int. J. of Quality & Reliability Management, **22**, 83 (2005)
13. Peter Huber. *Robust Statistics* (Wiley, 1981)

ITM Web of Conferences 6, 02006 (2016)
DOI: 10.1051/itmconf/20160602006

Support of decision-making in the conditions of uncertainty of different types

Ha D. Doan[1,a], Alexander N. Pylkin[1], Alexander V. Kroshilin[1], Svetlana V. Kroshilina[1] and Valeriya V. Tishkina[1]

[1]Ryazan State Radio Engineering University, 390005 Ryazan, Russia

Abstract. At the present stage the solution to the problem of decision-making support in the conditions of uncertainty is seen in the application of decision-making support systems (DMSS), which are based on the theory of fuzzy sets and fuzzy logic. One of the most important stages of decision-making support in the conditions of uncertainty is the analysis of the accumulated statistical data. At present, the fuzzy algorithms, including the algorithms of fuzzy clustering of data, are successfully applied to effective research of such data. In recent years, for the effective solution to problems of fuzzy clustering, the device of fuzzy relations that is based on building fuzzy relations of data objects and their properties is widely and successfully used.

1 Introduction

The process of decision-making consists in the generation of possible alternative decisions, their assessment and the selection of the better variant. In the conditions of society informatization, support of decision-making has become the most topical. At the present stage the solution to this problem is seen in the application of decision-making support systems (DMSS).

Modern computer systems allow accumulating, storing information and managing huge volumes of data for resolving problems of processing and analysis. Unfortunately, the presence of data in itself is still not enough, as the decision-maker often needs so-called hidden information, in connection with this, it is necessary to transform available data into useful information for decision-making.

Uncertainty is an integral part of decision-making processes, as the choice of some variant of the decision demands the accounting of a large number of uncertain and inconsistent factors. In this connection, uncertainty can be classified as follows:

- the uncertainty is connected with the incompleteness of knowledge about the problem, to which the decision must be made;
- the uncertainty is connected with the impossibility of the full accounting of environment reaction to the made decisions;
- the uncertainty is connected with the wrong understanding of the purposes by the person, who makes the decision.

Inconsistency appears because of ambiguity of the assessment of situations, mistakes in the choice of priorities that, finally, strongly complicates decision-making. Researches show that the decision-makers without additional analytical support, as a rule, use simplified, sometimes inconsistent rules of decision selection.

The device of fuzzy relations that is based on the theory of fuzzy sets and fuzzy logic is widely and successfully applied to resolve above problem now. Thus the fuzziness of actions in decision-making process is presented in the form of fuzzy algorithms, on the basis of which DMSS realize formalization and processing of fuzzy information.

2 The problems of decision-making support systems

The main functions of DMSS are accumulation, storage, analysis and data processing to provide the decision-maker with useful information in the subject area, and also the ability to choose the best variant of possible decisions. Therefore, for the effective functioning of DMSS, it is necessary to provide the solution to 3 main tasks: data input; data storage and data analysis [1].

In solving the problem of data input, transaction data processing is carried out with using common database management systems (DBMS).

For data storage, modern DBMS and data warehousing concept are used.

Data analysis can be performed by the following methods:

- Information retrieval analysis of data on the basis of relational DBMS and static queries with using SQL (Structured Query Language);
- Operational data analysis with applying the technology of operative analytical data processing OLAP

[a] Corresponding author: d2h.rus@mail.ru

(Online analytical processing), which uses the concept of multi-dimensional data representation;

- Methods and algorithms of Data Mining.

DMSS do not generate the correct decision but only provide the decision-maker with tools and data for the analysis and assessment of a concrete situation in the subject area, thus for the effective use of DMSS, the decision-maker must have both the corresponding qualification and ability to use data, which are presented in the machine form.

The analysis of accumulated statistical data, which volume continuously increases, plays an important role in activity of DMSS in the conditions of uncertainty. In researching of the accumulated statistical data, there is a high probability to skip the potential helpful information, which is implicit and hidden. To effectively research the accumulated statistical information, it is necessary to apply the special methods of intellectual analysis, in which the methods of data clustering take an important place [2].

3 Fuzzy clustering of data in the decision-making support systems in the conditions of uncertainty

One of the most important stages of decision-making support in the conditions of uncertainty is the analysis of accumulated statistical data. Today for effective research of them the fuzzy algorithms that are based on the theories of fuzzy sets and fuzzy logic, including the algorithm of fuzzy clustering of data, are successfully applied [3].

Data clustering is the partitioning a set of data objects into groups of similar objects (clusters). And objects in various clusters are considerably different from each other. The main purpose of data clustering is to search the cluster structure for data understanding and information post-processing. The main feature of data clustering consists in that the number of clusters isn't known beforehand.

In the tasks of clear clustering, a row of assumptions is laid: clusters have the certain form; each data object always belongs to only one cluster; the limits among clusters are well defined and etc. In general, the form of clusters can be random, the limits among clusters can be indefinite, and some objects belong to different clusters. In practice, the obtained data has fuzzy character, which is caused by the inaccuracy, insufficiency, unreliability of information resources. They lead to the difficulty in obtaining adaptive decision.

The above-stated shortages were overcome by the ideas of fuzzy clustering: clusters are the fuzzy subsets of initial sets of data, and each data object belongs to different clusters with various belonging degrees that correspond with various values of belonging function, which can be found in the segment [0, 1].

The basic algorithm of fuzzy clustering of data Fuzzy C-Means (FCM) carries out partitioning a set X of n data объектов into m clusters by specifying the belonging matrix U of dimensions $n \times m$. In this situation, each data object x that is contained in X belongs to any cluster with a belonging degree, which is an element of belonging matrix U in the interval [0, 1]. The belonging degrees of data objects are calculated on the basis of relationships among data objects and "cluster centroids". This process is iteratively carried out until the objective function achieves the minimization value.

Besides the algorithm FCM, there is a considerable quantity of other known methods of fuzzy clustering, which are its variety, for example, the Gyustafson-Kessel's method, the K-medium methods, etc. In general, they are simple in realization and work quickly enough. However, when these methods are applied for initial information, which has a weak structure, there are some shortages: all clusters have the certain form, which is defined by the algorithm; the cluster centroids always exist, but in practice they can be missing.

In recent years, for the effective solution to problems of fuzzy clustering, the device of fuzzy relations is widely and successfully used. This approach is based on building the fuzzy relations of data objects and their properties [1].

Introduction of the concept of "the normal measure of proximity" that is based on distances between two any attributes x, y of the fuzzy set X of initial data:

$$\mu_x(y) = 1 - \frac{d(x,y)}{\max\limits_{z \in X} d(x,z)}, \qquad (1)$$

where: $x, y, z \in X$; $d(x,y)$ – the distance between x and y; $\max d(x,z)$ – the maximum distance between x and z. The distance $d(x,y)$ can be calculated by the known measures of proximity: the Euclidean distance, the Hamming distance, etc. At that time, x and y are really different from each other when $\mu_x(y) = 0$, and are absolutely close when $\mu_x(y) = 1$.

The relative measure of proximity $\mu_x(y,z)$ of two attributes y and z to the third x is defined:

$$\xi_x(y,z) = 1 - \left|\mu_x(y) - \mu_x(z)\right| \qquad (2)$$

On the whole set X the proximity measure of all attributes is built:

$$\xi(y,z) = T\left[\xi_{x_1}(y,z), \xi_{x_2}(y,z), \ldots, \xi_{x_{|X|}}(y,z)\right] \qquad (3)$$

here: $\xi_{x_i}(y,z)$ – the relative measure of proximity, $x_i \in X$, $i = \overline{1,|X|}$, T – operation *t-norm*.

T – operation *t-norm*, which answers the *min-norm* minimization according to Zadeh that is used in this case:

$$T(y,z) = \min(y,z) \qquad (4)$$

It follows from (3) and (4) that the proximity measure of two attributes on X is presented in the following type:

$$\xi(y,z) = \min\left[\xi_{x_1}(y,z), \xi_{x_2}(y,z), \ldots, \xi_{x_{|X|}}(y,z)\right] \qquad (5)$$

The relationship that receives from the expression (5) is called the fuzzy soft relationship, which transitive closure in cycle must be calculated by the following formula:

$$R_\xi^t = R_\xi^{t-1} \circ R \qquad (6)$$

where: $R_\xi = \xi(y,z)$, $t = \overline{1,|X|}$. The received result $R_\xi^{|X|}$ is the relationship of fuzzy equivalence.

Thus, the relationship gradation of fuzzy equivalence generates the family of equivalence relations in classical sense that partitions an initial set of data, which is intended for research, into classes of equivalence. The more level of relationship, the more a set X of data is partitioned in detail.

References

1. A.V. Kroshilin, A.N. Pylkin and S.V. Kroshilina, *2014 International conference on computer technologies in physical and engineering applications (ICCTPEA)*, pp. 89-90 (2014)
2. D.H. Doan, A.V. Kroshilin and S.V. Kroshilina, *The VIII International Academic Congress "Development of Countries in Asia, Africa and Europe: Past, Present and Future"* **II**, 256 (Seoul, 2015).
3. L. Demidova, E. Nikulchev and Yu. Sokolova, International Journal of Advanced Computer Science and Applications, **7** (2016)

ITM Web of Conferences **6**, 02007 (2016)
DOI: 10.1051/itmconf/20160602007

Hybrid pre training algorithm of Deep Neural Networks

I. S. Drokin[1, a]

[1] *St. Petersburg State University, Faculty of applied mathematics and control processes, 199034 St. Petersburg, Russia*

Abstract. This paper proposes a hybrid algorithm of pre training deep networks, using both marked and unmarked data. The algorithm combines and extends the ideas of Self-Taught learning and pre training of neural networks approaches on the one hand, as well as supervised learning and transfer learning on the other. Thus, the algorithm tries to integrate in itself the advantages of each approach. The article gives some examples of applying of the algorithm, as well as its comparison with the classical approach to pre training of neural networks. These examples show the effectiveness of the proposed algorithm.

1 Introduction

An application of the pre-training mechanisms for a multilayer perceptron training results in greatly improved quality and speed of the deep networks training. In this paper, we propose a way of the weights initialization using principles of supervised learning and self-taught learning approach [1]. Currently used methods for the weights initialization of a multilayer perceptron are based on restricted Boltzmann machine [2] and auto-encoders (stacked auto-encoders, SAE) [3]. There are generalizations of the auto-encoders approach for convolutional neural networks described in [4], as well as the feature extracting algorithm based on the data representations, obtained during training of stacked auto-encoders [5]. Also there is an algorithm of initialization of the network weights based on principal component analysis [6]. The article proposes an iterative algorithm of weight initialization that is based on hidden layers of neural networks weights refinement through solving the original or similar classification or regression.

2 Algorithm description

Consider the set of the pairs $\{x_i, y_i\}, i = 1 \ldots K$, where $\{x_i \in R^n, y_i \in R^m\}$, x_i – is an input sample and y_i - is a target response. It is necessary to construct such a function $f(x)$, so that $f(x_i) = y_i, i = 1 \ldots K$. A multilayer perceptron N is considered for the proposed algorithm description. Let $L = \{L_1 \ldots L_k\}$ be its hidden layers set, L_0 -is the input layer, $\{x_{i,j}\}_{i=1}^{K}$ – are the outputs of the j-th layer. Let $u(l)$ equals to numbers of the neurons in layer l, $W(L_j) = W_j$ – are neuron's weights of the j-th layer, $N(j)$ – is the j-th hidden layer of the network N. The pre-training neural network algorithm based on auto encoders can be summarized as it is showing in Algorithm 1.

For $j \leftarrow 1, k$ **Repeate**

1. Initialization of the network $\hat{N}^j$ with one hidden layer size of $u(L_j)$, an input layer size of $u(L_{j-1})$ and an output layer size of $u(L_{j-1})$. Let $\hat{W}$ were the weights of the hidden layer.
2. Training of the network $\hat{N}^j$ proceed on sample set $\{x_{i,j-1}, x_{i,j-1}\}, i = 1 \ldots K$
3. $\hat{W}_j = \hat{W}$

Result $\{\hat{W}_j\}_{j=1}^{k}$

Algorithm 1. Network pre-training with SAE application.

Applying of this algorithm allows use of the sample set $\{\hat{W}_j\}_{j=1}^{k}$ for the fairy well initialization of the hidden layer's weights of the network for the entire network training with Backpropagation method. This approach also allows to apply input data the desired response of which is not known.

This approach is proposed to be complemented as follows. Weights of the j-th hidden layer after pre-training with auto-encoder can be refined by training network with one hidden layer on the original or a similar problem, using transfer learning concept [7–9]. That means, we have to use the weights $\hat{W}$, received on the second paragraph of the j-th step of the algorithm for initialization of the network with one hidden layer, an

[a] Corresponding author : ivan.s.drokin@bk.ru

input layer size of $u(L_{j-1})$ and an output layer size of m, and train the network on $\{x_{i,j-1}, y_i\}, i = 1 \ldots K$ sample set.

Also, on the j-th iteration of the algorithm, the weight of the hidden layers from the first to j-th can be specified by training of the network with j hidden layers from the original or similar network. Weight obtained on the previous steps $\{\hat{W}_t\}_{t=1}^{j}$ are used to initialize the network with j hidden layers, an input layer size of n and an output layer size of m. The network is trained on a sample set of $\{x_i, y_i\}, i = 1 \ldots K$. This setting of parameters makes sense for all hidden layers, except of the first and the last, since this setting for the first layer is exactly the same as it was described in the above procedure from the previous paragraph, and for the last layer it is the task of the entire network training.

Thus, the original algorithm is added by two additional learning processes. The general algorithm can be described as it is showing in Algorithm 2.

For $j \leftarrow 1, k$ **Repeate**

1. Initialization of the network $\tilde{N}^j$ with one hidden layer size of $u(L_j)$, an input layer size of $u(L_{j-1})$ and an output layer size of $u(L_{j-1})$. Let $\tilde{W}$ be the weights of the hidden layer.
2. Training of the network $\tilde{N}^j$ is proceed on $\{x_{i,j-1}, x_{i,j-1}\}, i = 1 \ldots K$ sample set.
3. Initialization of the network $`N^j$ with one hidden layer size of $u(L_j)$, an input layer size of $u(L_{j-1})$ and an output layer size of m, the weights of the hidden layer are initialised as $\tilde{W}$.
4. Training of the network $`N^j$ is proceed on $\{x_{i,j-1}, y_i\}, i = 1 \ldots K$ sample set.
5. Initialization of the network $\hat{N}^j$ with j hidden layers size of $u(L_t), t = \overline{1, j}$, an input layer size of n and an output layer size of m, the weights of the hidden layers are initialised as $\{W_t\}_{t=1}^{j-1}$, $\hat{W}_j = W(`N(1))$.
6. Training of the network $\hat{N}$ is proceed on $\{x_i, y_i\}, i = 1 \ldots K$ sample set. $t = 1 \rightarrow j$ $\hat{W}_t = W(\hat{N}^j(t))$

Result $\{\hat{W}_j\}_{j=1}^{k}$

Algorithm 2. Consecutive network pre-training.

As it is evident from the description of the algorithm, the weights for the network N initialization with initial configuration will be obtained as a result of the network pre-training. The weights for $k-1$ network with fewer number of layers will be obtained on the pre-training stage just as a small additional bonus. This network can be used for further training and integration of the constructed network to a committee. Also the pre-training scheme allows to use not initial data set, but some other set which is close to the initial one. For example, if the original task is training on the CIFAR-100 data set, the set CIFAR-10 [10] for the pre-training stage can be used.

3 Experiment description

For the experiment, CIFAR-10, CIFAR-100 datasets were used. The dataset CIFAR-10 is a set of 50,000 training samples and 10,000 test samples of color images sized 32 by 32 pixels, divided into ten classes. CIFAR-100 is a set of 50,000 training samples and 10,000 test samples of color images of size 32 by 32 pixels, divided into one hundred classes. Thus, the size of the input layer of the network is 3072, the size of the output layer is 10 for CIFAR-10 and 100 for CIFAR-100 respectively. For further discussion, the network configuration will be briefly written as $n - n_1 - n_2 - \ldots - n_k - m$, where n – is the size of the input layer, $n_1, n_2 \ldots n_k$ - are the numbers of neurons in the hidden layers, m - is the size of the output layer.

A softplus activation was used for all of the hidden layers, while a softmax was used for the output layer. A categorical crossentropy was applied as an error function. A dropout with a coefficient of 0.3 was used for each hidden layer, the size of a single batch was equal to 16, a stochastic gradient descent with Nesterovsky momentum was used as an optimizer, a learning rate was 0.001, a moment was equal to 0.9. No data volume increasing techniques had been used in the experiment.

As observed parameters we have considered errors of the training process for training or testing sample depending on the epoch of learning. The proposed algorithm is suggested to compare with a classical algorithm of neural network training with pre-training through stacked autoencoders. All the parameters of multilayer perceptrons training and autoencoders in both pre-training algorithms are the same.

For the experiment with using the CIFAR-10 dataset the network configuration of 3072−2560−2048−1536−1025−512−256−10 was considered, and for the experiment with the CIFAR-100 dataset the configuration of 3072−2560−2048−1536−1025−512−256−100 was used. Similar model configuration are proposed for the experiment with pre-training on CIFAR-10 and the final training was done using CIFAR-100. The behavior of the errors during the first training epochs were investigated. The tests results for the networks are shown in Fig. 1, Fig. 2, Fig. 3.

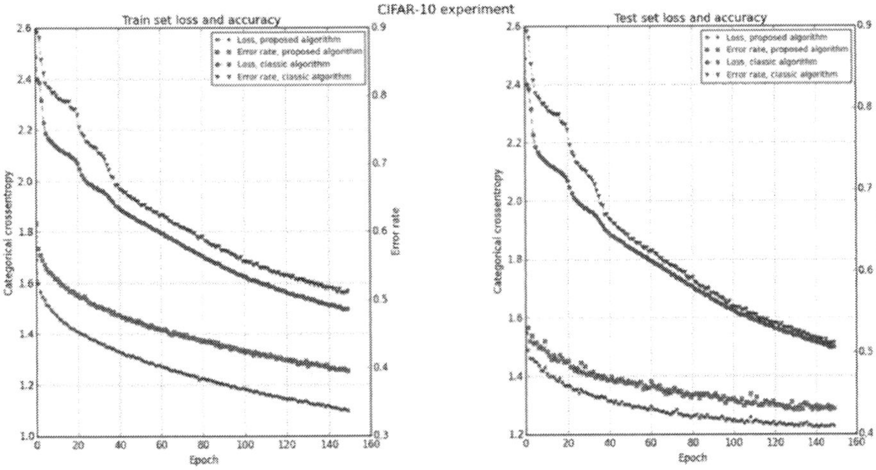

Figure 1. Errors in training and testing samples for CIFAR-10 network

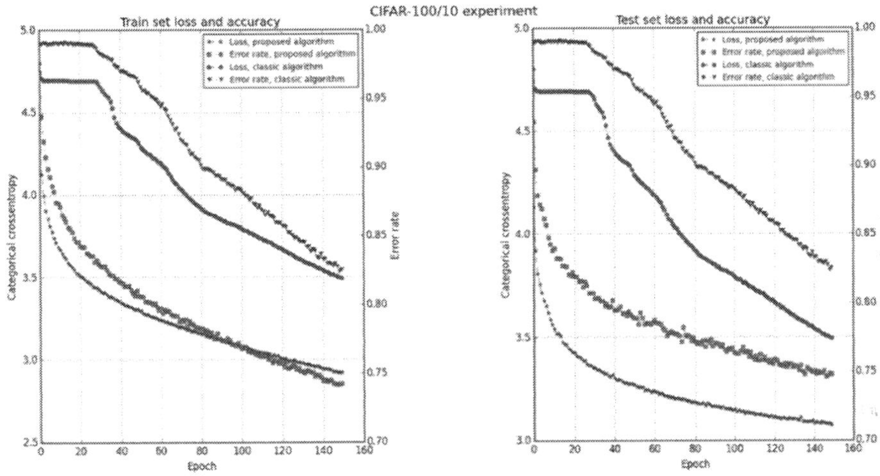

Figure 2. Errors in training and testing samples for CIFAR-100 network

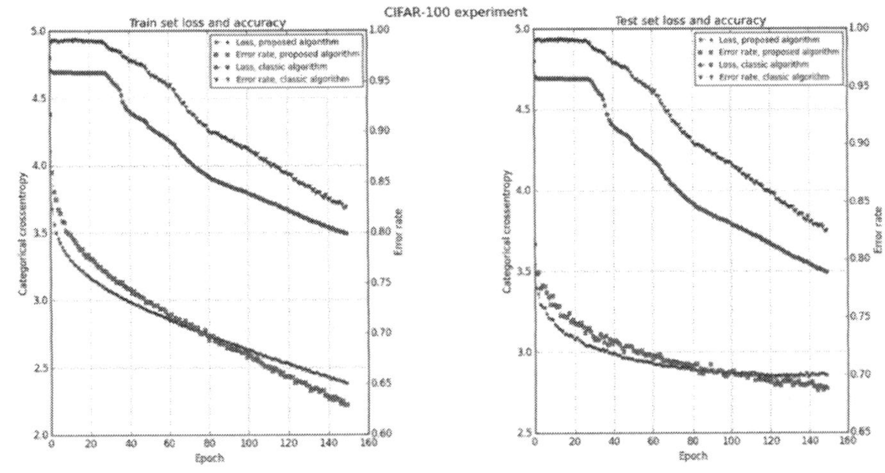

Figure 3. Errors in training and testing samples for CIFAR-100/ CIFAR-10 network

4 Results and findings

As it could be seen from the graphs, the presented method is an effective version of the multilayer perceptron weights initialization. Furthermore, efficiency of the approach is increasing with number of the hidden layers increment. However, the proposed method has a number of disadvantages. In particular, this method requires more computational resources. However, the proposed algorithm also has a number of advantages.

First of all, the algorithm allows to apply self-taught learning and transfer learning approaches. Also using the algorithm permits networks with fewer numbers of layers to be trained (or pre-trained if transfer learning is used). These networks can be used for merge in the committees using, for example, boosting algorithm. Thus, intermediate calculations would be used in the resulting classifier.

The directions for further research could include the following points:

1. In steps 3-6, one can supplement additional hidden layers
2. Steps 3-6 could be used for the first few layers only
3. Combination of the networks into general classifier obtained in steps 4 and 6

The proposal to use steps 3-6 only for the first few layers is based on the observation known as attenuation gradient [13, 14]. According to this observation, first layers of a multilayer perceptron are trained worse than others, and using stages 3-6 only for the first few layers, allows, on the one hand, to obtain the sufficient quality of the weights approximation, but, on the other hand, to save computational resources.

The proposed approach can also be used with Restricted Boltzmann machines for the multilayer perceptrons pre-training as well as with convolutional auto encoders and convolutional neural networks.

5 Conclusion

An hierarchical algorithm of a multilayer perceptron pre-training based on self-taught learning and transfer learning approaches was proposed. There were conducted some tests showing the performance of the approach in this paper. As well as the next steps and directions for further research of the algorithm and its generalizations and improvements were presented. In particular, it is proposed to conduct an analisys of the application of algorithm for convolutional neural networks, as well as for Restricted Boltzmann machines and Deep Belief Networks. The algorithm can use both marked and unmarked data for initialization and training of the neural network. Also an iterative learning process allows to apply an problem close to the original to initialize the hidden layers of the network.

References

1. UFLDL Tutorial. Available http://ufldl.stanford.edu/wiki/index.php/UFLDL_Tutorial
2. G.E. Hinton and R.R. Salakhutdinov, Science, **313**, 504 (2006)
3. P. Vincent, H. Larochelle, I. Lajoie, Y. Bengio and P.-A. Manzagol, The Journal of Machine Learning Research archive, **11**, 3371 (2010).
4. J. Masci, U. Meier, D. Ciresan and J. Schmidhuber. *21st International Conference on Artificial Neural Networks*, Part I, pp. 52-59 (2011)
5. J. Gehring, Y. Miao, F. Metze and A. Waibel, *IEEE International Conference on Acoustics, Speech and Signal Processing (ICASSP)*, pp. 3377-3381 (2013)
6. P. Baldi and K. Hornik, Neural Networks, **2**, 53 (1989)
7. R. Caruana, Machine Learning, **28**, 41 (1997)
8. R. Raina, A. Battle, H. Lee, B. Packer, and A. Y. Ng, *Proceedings of the 24th international conference on Machine learning. ACM*, pp. 759-766 (2007)
9. D.C. Ciresan, U. Meier and J. Schmidhuber, *2012 International Joint Conference on Neural Networks (IJCNN)*, pp. 1–6 (2012)
10. The CIFAR dataset. Available http://www.cs.toronto.edu/kriz/cifar.html
11. The MNIST database of handwritten digits. Available http://yann.lecun.com/exdb/mnist/
12. P. Simard, *Proc. IC-DAR*, pp. 958-962 (2003).
13. X. Glorot and Y. Bengio, *International conference on artificial intelligence and statistics*, pp. 249-256 (2010)
14. R. Pascanu, T. Mikolov and Y. Bengio, *Understanding the exploding gradient problem*. Tech. Rep. (Universite De Montreal, 2012). arXiv:arXiv:1211.5063

ITM Web of Conferences **6**, 02008 (2016)
DOI: 10.1051/itmconf/20160602008

Use of genetic algorithms for solving problems of optimal cutting

Maxim Sergievskiy[1, 2, a] and Sergey Syroezhkin[1]

[1]*National Research Nuclear University MEPhI (Moscow Engineering Physics Institute), 115409, Moscow, Russia*
[2]*Moscow Technological Institute, 119334 Moscow, Russia*

Abstract. Cutting and packing problem is one of the most common optimization problem. Even a small space or material savings allow obtaining substantial advantages on an industrial scale. This paper proposes the genetic algorithm to solve this problem. It includes multipoint operators of crossing, mutation and selection. To use these operators, the special encoding of cutting card is applied, that can be transformed to the real coordinates by using decoder. This is a block typed decoder, which substitution strategy is "first-fit". Efficiency of the solutions, obtained by the algorithm, depends on its parameters and on dimension of a task, but on average it decreases under the logarithmic law from dimension of a task. Temporary complexity of algorithm shows square dependence on the task dimension.

1 Introduction

Obtaining the effective solution of the packing rectangular objects problem in a two-dimensional container is one of the most important task of discrete optimization [1]. The necessity of finding efficient algorithms for this task is caused by its broad practical application in various branches of production. Even a small saving of resources while filling container and cutting material results in very tangible saving.

Complexity of this packing problem is caused by its belonging to a class of NP difficult problems of combinatory optimization, i.e. there are no methods and algorithms that can find the exact solution for polynomial time. The studied task is NP difficult in strong sense, because it contains NP difficult task as its subtask [2, 3].

There are many different methods for solving orthogonal packing problems: methods of mathematical programming, branch and bound methods, asymptotically exact methods, single-pass and multi-pass heuristics, metaheuristic, etc [1, 4]. Most of the methods are developed in two directions. Methods of the first direction searches for locally optimal solutions in some neighborhood of the initial acceptable solutions. They use decoders, which restore the packing map and calculate objective function value.

Another direction is development of the constructive methods. They deal with component-wise construction of the packaging, where method adds new components to the partially constructed pack while packing is not full. Offered in this paper method is the typical representative of the first class.

2 Problem statement

In this paper we consider the problem of packing rectangular objects in rectangular container (2 Dimensional Bin Packing Problem, 2DBP). Both value, the length (L) and the width (W) of the container are known. It is required to find the packing, which allows to pack the greatest number of items into one container.

Thus, the input data for the selected task is a set of values: $<W, L, m, \mathbf{w}, \mathbf{l}, e>$, where W, L – the length and width of the rectangular container; m – number of rectangular elements for packing; $\mathbf{w} = (w_1, w_2, \ldots, w_i, \ldots, w_m)$ – the vector of widths of elements; $\mathbf{l} = (l_1, l_2, \ldots, l_i, \ldots, l_m)$ – the vector of lengths of elements; ε - the sign of possibility of changing elements orientation. Let's introduce a rectangular coordinate system, where OX axis matches to horizontal edge of the object and the axis OY - to vertical. Then task's solutions can be represented as follows: $<W, L, m, \mathbf{w}, \mathbf{l}, \mathbf{X}, \mathbf{Y}, \mathbf{E}>$, where $\mathbf{X}=(x_1, x_2, \ldots, x_i, \ldots, x_m)$, $\mathbf{Y}=(y_1, y_2, \ldots y_i, \ldots, y_m)$ – vectors of the minimum coordinates of elements; $\mathbf{E}=(e_1, e_2, \ldots e_i, \ldots, e_m)$, $e_i=1$, if the element i is rotated on 90 degrees, else $e_i=0$.

The acceptability of rectangular packing (RP) means the fulfillment of the following conditions:

- orthogonal arrangement of rectangles in the packing: for (x_i, y_i), $i=1..m$ and any other vertex (x_i^k, y_i^k) of rectangle i:

$$[(x_i^k = x_i) \vee (x_i^k = x_i + l_i)] \wedge [(y_i^k = y_i) \vee (y_i^k = y_i + w_i)]$$

- not overlapping of rectangles: for $i \neq j$; $i,j=1,..,m$:

$$[(x_i \geq x_j+l_j) \vee (x_j \geq x_i+l_i)] \vee [(y_i \geq y_j+w_j) \vee (y_j \geq y_i+w_i)]$$

[a] Corresponding author: sermax@yandex.ru

- not overlapping rectangles edges by elements:
  for every $i=1..m$:

$$(x_i \geq 0) \wedge (y_i \geq 0) \wedge (y_i + w_i \leq W) \wedge (y_i + w_i \leq L)$$

An objective function can be represented as the ratio of the area occupied by the packaged objects to the area of the container:

$$Q = (\Sigma S_i)/(W \cdot L) \rightarrow 1, \text{ for } i=1..m.$$

3 Methods and algorithms

Due to the task complexity, there are no methods to check every possible solution. Therefore, all existing approaches to this problem are to limit the set of checked solutions. Genetic algorithm, which applied in this paper, also uses this approach.

Genetic algorithm is an evolutionary algorithm that includes a group of metaheuristics for finding and selecting the best solutions [5, 6]. Its core contains basic concepts of the evolution theory: inheritance, mutation, selection. The main idea is to construct some set of optimization problem's solutions (population) and by getting through some transformations obtain new solutions instead of bad fit old ones. Storing information for multiple valid solutions at each iteration creates the effect of parallel computing, and increases the chances of finding the optimum.

To evaluate the effectiveness of the obtained solutions, we should convert it to a form that would allow us to calculate the objective function value. For this purpose, a special decoder is used. There are different approaches for individual decoding, but decoders of block type are the most widespread. They use simple strategies: "the next fit" (NF), "the first fit" (FF) and "best fit" (BF) [1–3, 7–14]. Based on the complexity of the strategies, in this work we apply the FF decoder. The decoder with the strategy "Substitution of first fit" (SubFF) at each step places the first matching object (its width does not exceed the width of the residual width of the block) in a partially filled block. If a suitable object is not found, it generates a free position of the next block and places there the first suitable object. Such algorithm (Sub(FF)) requires $O(m^2 \log m)$ of time.

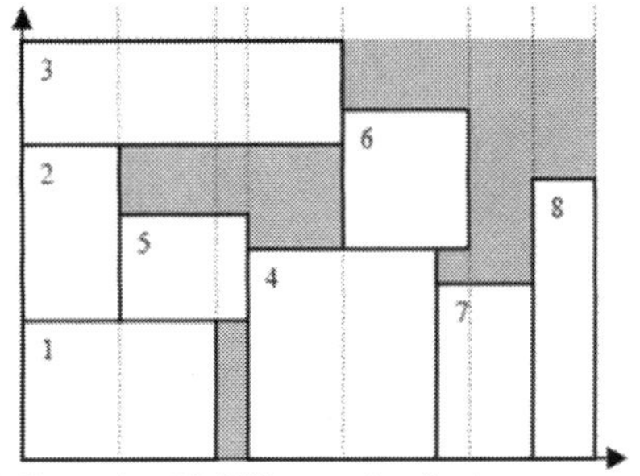

Figure 1. Example of SubFF executing for the sequence: {1,2,3,4,5,6,7,8}.

Decoder gets the priority list (replacement) of elements through input parameters and returns the packing - list of element's minimum coordinates. Unlike most of the existing block decoders, which use packing block structure for encoding rectangular, and based on already compiled pair of block structures (one packing) calculate the coordinates of the packing elements, our decoder operates differently. It fills a container in accordance with the priority sequence of rectangular objects, thus it operates like tiered decoders, however in the search for solutions it uses the classic division into blocks. This decoder was developed to combine the advantages of the both decoder types: blocked and tiered. Generally, the block type decoder uses spatial resources more effectively, while a decoder of tiered type has less temporal complexity because it uses just the identifications sequence for filling container instead of block structures.

In operation, the decoder stores information about free sections of the container, and when the element is installed in such section (it is installed to the lower left corner of the section), the decoder stores the coordinates of the lower left point of the element, and "forget" about the portion of the container, which was occupied. This is implemented through the list of block-levels. Block-level is a structure consisting of three coordinates: X_{Left}, Y_{Begin}, Y_{End}. X_{Left} – the coordinate of the left edge of the block level (the same as the coordinate of the left edge of the block); Y_{Begin} – coordinate of the lower edge of the block-level (the same as the y-coordinate of the lower boundary of the free area in the block); Y_{End} – coordinate of the top edge of the block-level (the same as the y-coordinate of the upper boundary of the free area in the block). Figure 2 shows decoder's algorithm in more detail.

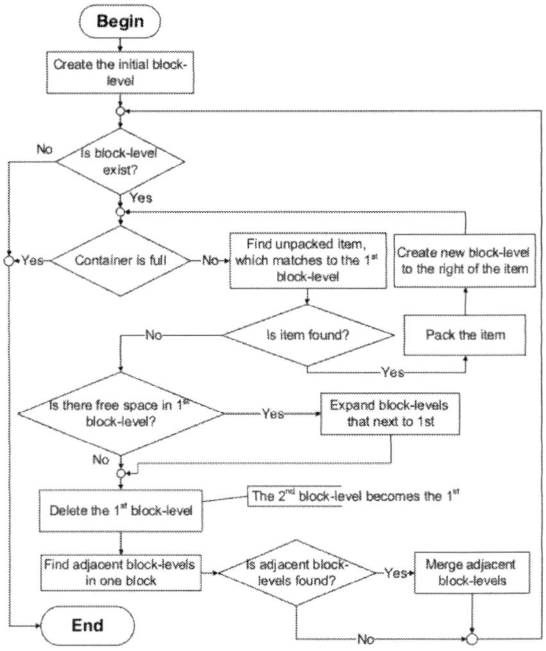

Figure.2. Block diagram of decoder

The solution in the population is a numerical sequence of object identifier for the package. The negative value of the element's identifier in the solution means the element's rotation. Solution may contain several identical identifiers; it means that the packaging contains several identical elements. The number of repetitions of the elements is specified in the input parameters of the algorithm.

In the beginning, the algorithm randomly generates the initial population, that is, each solution in the population is created as a sequence of random numbers. Further, operators of crossing, mutation and selection change solutions at each iteration.

Crossover operator crosses pairs of solutions with a given probability. If task's dimension is large, solutions may contain long sequences of numbers. Single-point crossover operator is not effective in this case. For these circumstances, n-point crossover operator was developed.

By default, the crossing points are selected uniformly: the solution breaks into *n* length-equal ranges (where *n* – number of crossing points), and each crossing point gets out of the range corresponding to it. If crossing operator forms solution, in which the number of an element occurrences exceeds the maximum permissible value, operator will replace redundant elements with any other remained ones.

The developed crossing operator has several operating modes:

1) classic *n*-point. The number of crossing points *n* is specified by the user. In this mode, each solution in the list of new solutions formed by the crossing of two old solutions at *n* points.

2) gradually increasing number of crossing points. In this mode, after each crossing of two solutions, obtained solutions are stored in the list of new solutions. Thus, if the number of crossing point is *n*, the list of new solutions will contain new solutions formed by crossing of two old solutions in *1,2,3, ...,* and *n* points. This mode allows you to get more different solutions, and it should increase the probability of finding more effective packing, however, this mode has a higher time complexity.

3) mixed mode with the specified ratio (default is 30%). This mode combines the first two modes, so you can get an expanded set of solutions by using the second mode, but only with a given probability, to reduce the computation time.

Obviously, to get a better solution, you need to check more different solutions. Therefore, the crossover operator has a special mode in which the count of crossing points is selected randomly and closer to the top of the solutions. Experimentally it was found that the crossing points located at the beginning of the solution, allow to obtain the better solutions. Probably, the reason is that the first packaged elements mainly define the configuration of the entire package.

Mutation operator makes random changes in solution, allowing you to avoid "getting stuck" in a local extremum. Implemented operator consists of two parts. The first part carries out a swap of the elements within solution, the second part performs rotation of elements by 90 degrees about its center in the plane of the container. For the same reasons as in the crossing operator, here we use multi-points mutation.

Selection operator is probably the most important part of genetic algorithm. It performs analysis of solutions, calculation of the objective function and the formation of a new population. It is formed on the basis of all individuals existing on the current iteration: solutions concluded in the current population and a set of the new solutions obtained after operators of crossing and a mutation. Every individual can take its place in a new population with sufficiently high probability P_{sel}. To ensure the impact of individuals, which are not included in the new population, replacement is made: *n* solutions with the smallest value of the objective function of the new population is replaced by *n* solutions with the smallest value of the objective function of the entire set of solutions to the current iteration (the most "bad" solutions). *n* is a small number equal to about 10% of the number of solutions in the population.

At the end of the algorithm, the decoder restores the packaging by using a solution with the highest value of the objective function, and the algorithm terminates.

4 Results

In this paper, the dimension of the source data is a number of rectangular objects to be packed. This approach is most suitable for the tested algorithm, since just the number of rectangular objects has the value for it, not the sizes of objects. To assess the effectiveness of the genetic algorithm, experiments were performed on a special sets of input data. Their peculiarity lies in the fact that for each of them there is at least one solution with objective function value of 100%.

Based on recommendations from a variety of sources [12–14] and on the results of our experiments the "default values" for genetic algorithm parameters were set:

- the population size – 20
- number of iterations - 1000
- probability of the crossing operator performing - 30%
- probability of performing of the swap operation- 10%
- probability of performing of the turn operation - 50%.

For the given parameters values the algorithm showed the better results in most cases. To see this, here are some graphs (Figs. 3.1-3.4), which show different dependencies obtained in experiments.

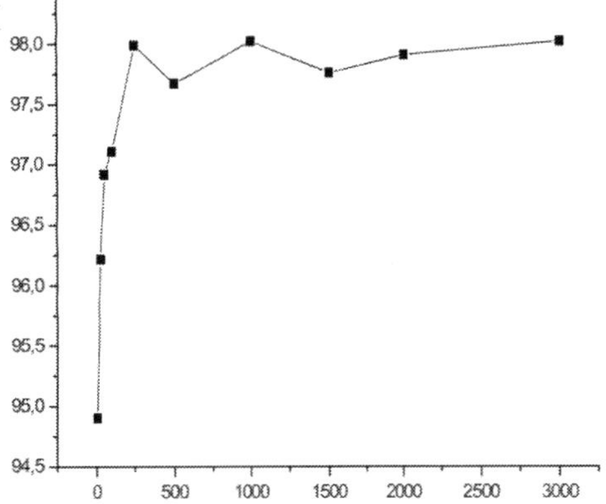

Figure. 3.1. The average value of the objective function on the iterations number

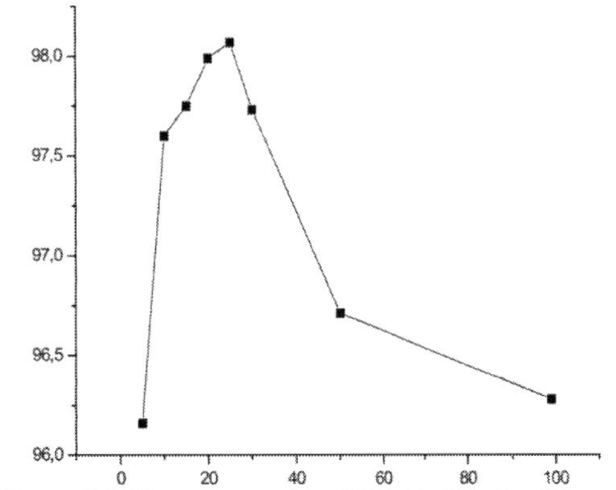

Figure. 3.2. The average value of the objective function on the size of the population

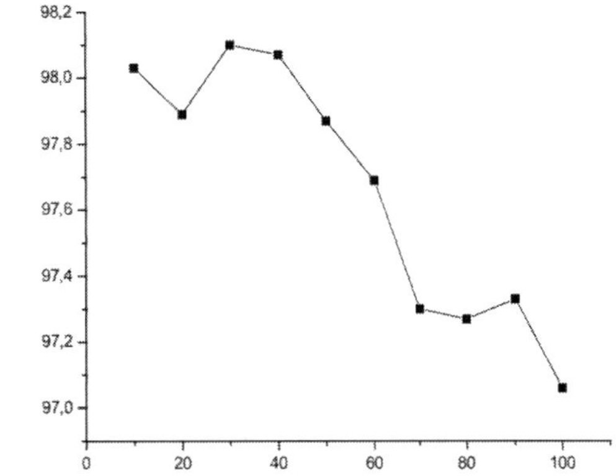

Figure.3.3. The average value of the objective function on swap probability

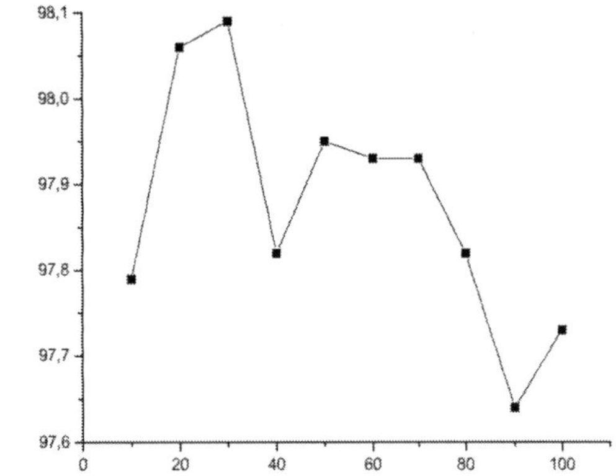

Figure.3.4. The average value of the objective function on crossing probability

Assessments of the solution's quality and searching time were carried out for two classes of containers: wide and long. Wide container is container with ratio of length to width is less than three, in other case container is long. Such division of containers into categories was required to test flexibility of algorithm. Figures 4.1–4.2 show results of experiments.

The average value of the objective function falls under the law of the natural logarithm with increasing of dimension of the problem, which corresponds to the theory. Also the results demonstrate the difference in the quality of the solutions obtained for the two categories of containers. The algorithm provides a slightly better solution for long containers than for the wide. Most likely, the reason of this result is decoder. Average search time of solution increases according to the law of n^2 with increasing of problem's dimension. This result is also close to theory, which states that genetic algorithms using the block decoder with FF strategies have a time complexity $O(m^2 \log m) \sim O(m^{2,5} \log m)$. As expected, the category of the container does not have a significant effect on the solution search time.

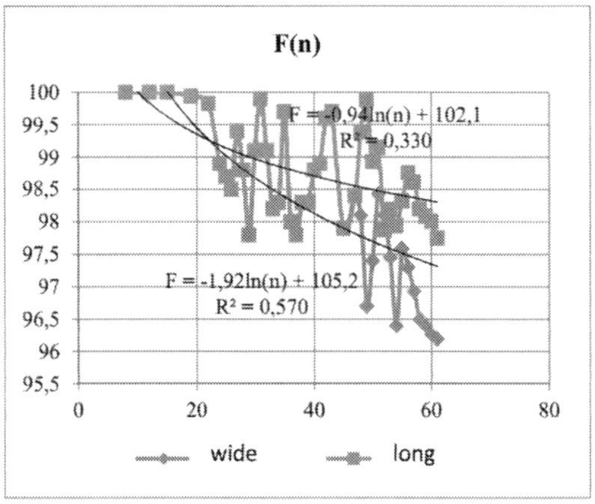

Figure. 4.1. Dependency of average value of the objective function on task dimension

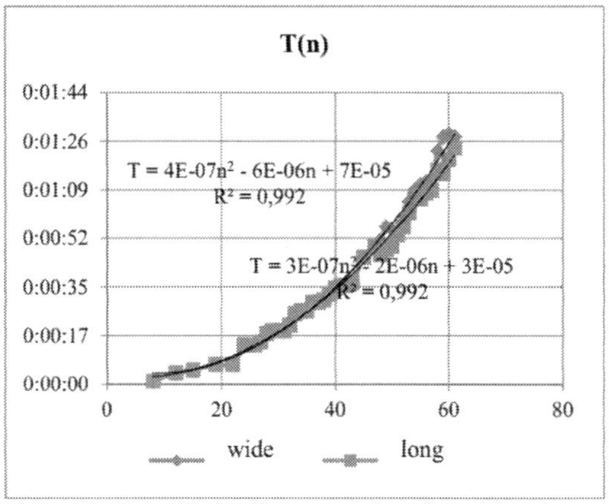

Figure. 4.2. Dependency of average value of searching time on task dimension

The developed algorithm uses multi-point crossover and mutation operators, as well as several other heuristics, the purpose of which is to increase a variety of solutions in the population. It would be interesting to determine their impact on the results. To do this, every used heuristic has been turned off, and the number of points of crossover and mutation set to *1*. To compare the performance of these two configurations of genetic algorithms: modified (multipoint and with heuristics) and simple (single-point), we construct the following dependencies:

- a graph of the difference between the average values of the objective functions, that we obtained by the first and second algorithms on the task dimension (figure 5,1). The graph shows that the average value of the objective function increase will be 2,5%, if we use the modified algorithm.

- a graph of the difference between the average of searching time values on the task dimension (figure 5,2). The graph shows that the searching time is greatly higher in the case of modified algorithm.

The performance improvement, obtained by using modified genetic algorithm, may seem too insignificant in comparison with the increased time cost, and, as a result, the use of this algorithm may seem unjustified. But do not forget that graphs show the average value of the objective function. When using the modified algorithm globally-optimal solution were obtained in 91% of experiments, but in case of simple algorithm only in 56%.

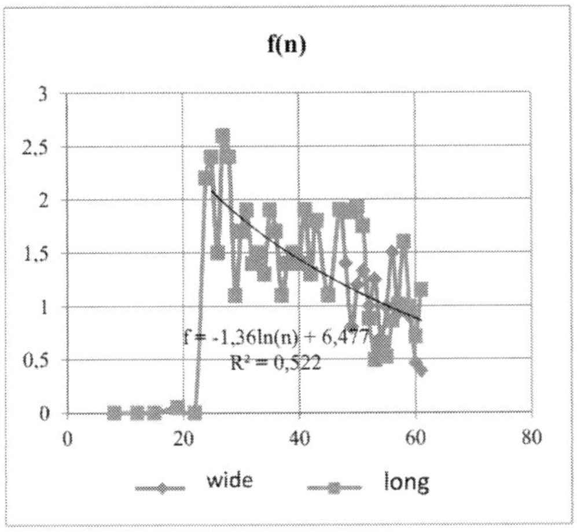

Figure. 5.1. Dependency of difference of average values of the objective function on task dimension

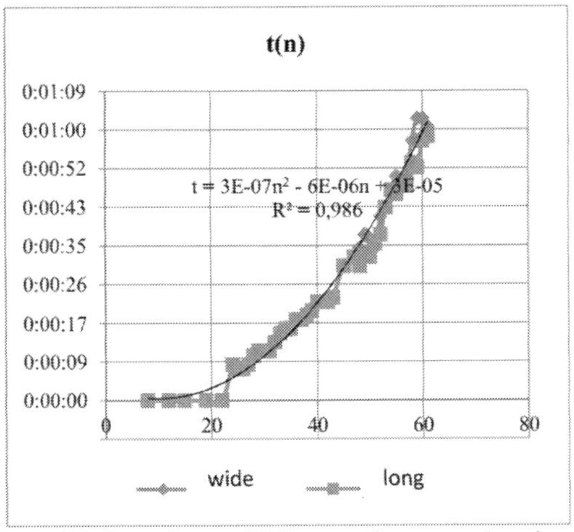

Figure. 5.2. Dependency of difference of average value of searching time on task dimension

5 Conclusion

Genetic algorithms show good results in solving problems of optimal cutting. With their help it is possible to obtain effective solutions in a short time, looking less than 1% of the total possible combinations of solutions.

The tests have confirmed that the use of multi-point crossover and mutation operators in the modified algorithm allows us to find the solution with the better objective function value and find globally-optimal solution in many cases. However, when choosing an algorithm for solving a specific problem, it also important take into account the available time resources.

References

1. A.S. Philippova, *Methods of the solution of orthogonal packing problems on the basis of block structures technology* (Ufa, 2007) [In Rus]
2. R.I. Phayzrahmanov *Optimization of process of cutting of industrial materials by criterion of a minimum of material losses in the presence of technological restrictions* (Ufa, 2011) [In Rus]
3. A.I. Lipovetskiy, *Automatic design in mechanical engineering BSSR AN ITK*, **80** (1985) [In Rus]
4. A.Ph. Valeeva, *Constructive methods for solving orthogonal packing and cutting task* (Ufa, 2006) [In Rus]
5. L.A. Gladkov, V.V. Kureychik and V.M. Kureychik *Genetic algorithms* (Moscow, 2006) [In Rus]
6. V.V. Emelyianov, V.V. Kureychik and V. M. Kureychik, *Theory and practice of evolutionary modeling* (Moscow, 2003) [In Rus]
7. E. Hopper and B. Turton, European Journal of Operational Research, **128**, 34 (2001)
8. A.A. Petunin, E.A. Muhacheva and A.S. Philipova, Information technology, **1**, 28 (2008) [In Rus]
9. V.D. Avakumov. Information technology, **5**, 31 (2009) [In Rus]
10. E.A. Muhacheva, A.S. Muhacheva and A.V. Chiglincev, Information technology, **11**, 13 (1999) [In Rus]
11. N.N. Kuzyurin and A.I. Pospelov Diskr. Mat., **18**, 76 (2006)
12. A.A. Petunin, E.A. Muhacheva and A.S. Philippova, Information technology, **1**, 28 (2008) [In Rus]
13. D. Rutkovskaya, M. Pilinskiy and L. Rutkovskiy, *Neural networks, genetic algorithms and fuzzy systems* (Moscow, 2006)
14. A.S. Muhacheva, S.H. Kurelenkov, M.A. Smagin, R.R. Shirgazin, Information technology, **10**, 26 (2002) [In Rus]

ITM Web of Conferences 6, 02009 (2016)
DOI: 10.1051/itmconf/20160602009

Analytical estimates of efficiency of attractor neural networks with inborn connections

Ksenia Solovyeva[1, 2, 3], Iakov Karandashev[1, 2] and Witali Dunin-Barkowski[1, 2]

[1]*Moscow Institute of Physics and Technology, Dolgoprudny, Moscow Region, 141700, Russia*
[2]*Scientific Research Institute for System Analysis, RAS, Moscow, Nakhimovskiy Prospect 36, b.1, 117218, Russia*
[3]*Moscow Technological Institute, Moscow, Leninskii Prospect 38a, 119334, Russia*

Abstract. The analysis is restricted to the features of neural networks endowed to the latter by the inborn (not learned) connections. We study attractor neural networks in which for almost all operation time the activity resides in close vicinity of a relatively small number of attractor states. The number of the latter, *M*, is proportional to the number of neurons in the neural network, *N*, while the total number of the states in it is 2^N. The unified procedure of growth/fabrication of neural networks with sets of all attractor states with dimensionality d=0 and d=1, based on model molecular markers, is studied in detail. The specificity of the networks (d=0 or d=1) depends on topology (i.e., the set of distances between elements) which can be provided to the set of molecular markers by their physical nature. The neural networks parameters estimates and trade-offs for them in attractor neural networks are calculated analytically. The proposed mechanisms reveal simple and efficient ways of implementation in artificial as well as in natural neural networks of multiplexity, i.e. of using activity of single neurons in representation of multiple values of the variables, which are operated by the neural systems. It is discussed how the neuronal multiplexity provides efficient and reliable ways of performing functional operations in the neural systems.

1 Introduction

The analysis and multiple applications of neural networks are currently on a steep rise. Among the recent achievements in this field are: human-like recognition of images, human-level spoken words identification, machine translation between multiple images [1]. There emerges general understanding that constructing the neuromorphic devices might present the easiest way to obtain smart informational technologies (deep learning and related methods). These impressive results increased visibility of and attracted tens of thousands of scientists to the neural network research, both modern and classical. In this novel atmosphere of research of particular importance become the topics of computational neuroscience, which have not yet been included into modern neural network toolkit. Potentially, they can improve particular aspects of neural network functioning.

In present work, we complement computer simulations of [2] with a thorough mathematical analysis, which enables us to make analytical estimates of the network operational parameters.

The structure of the present note is following.

First, we consider a notion of neural attractors and their types. In this work, we restrict the analysis with stationary attractors, i.e. stable in time states of activities of neural networks. Our attention is focused on relations between these states: the distances between the states in configurational space of the neural networks and properties of the set of attractor states of a neural network. Our contribution to the field is in an analysis of the preformed, inborn connections between the neurons in the network. Most of previous works, following John Hopfield, considered networks, in which the connections were established, using the Hebb rules [3]. That means that the connections were formed, depending on coincidence of activities of the neurons, which are to be connected. We deal with the connections, established by the mechanism, which does not depend on the neural activity. Unlike previous works, which simply postulated the existence of inborn connections with needed properties [4], we introduce in Section 2 biologically realistic details of connection setting mechanism, the method of model molecular markers. The gains, obtained with this method are analyzed in detail throughout our work.

Section 3, consisting of four subsections, presents details of the analysis. The first two subsections are devoted to the networks with $d = 0$, the last two – to the networks with $d = 1$.

The subsection 3.1 deals with evaluation of the number of attractor states for $d = 0$. The number to find is determined by the condition that every 'theoretical' or predetermined by the connection formation process

[a] Corresponding author: kasya726@gmail.com

attractor state is stable. The analysis yields a relation between the number of the stable theoretical attractor states and the number of neurons in the network. The analytical estimates are compared to the results of computational experiments [2].

Section 3.2 continues the analysis to get the trade-off relations for the numbers of attractor states, the number of neurons in the network and the number of active neurons in each attractor state. The results are compared with the computational experiments data [2], which are presented in Figs. 1 and 2.

In section 3.3 the important property of d=1 attractors is evaluated. The overall structure of these attractors is described by the 'snake-in-a-box' metaphor [3]. In this presentation, the points of attractor are supposed to make the axis of a snake, which is put into the box[1]. In this case, the points at the snake axis, which are at a large distance from each other along the snake axis, in the configurational space of the neural network, cannot be closer to each other than some positive value, which is dubbed the 'snake thickness'. The dependence of the distance between the points at the snake axis in configurational space on the distance between these points along the snake axis is effectively calculated in this section. The calculations are performed for the algorithm of obtaining d=1 attractors, described in section 2. Again, the results are compared to computational experiments showing a good agreement.

Section 3.4 treats the problem of the upper limit of the length (the size) of a continuous 1-d attractor in the network. The estimate is in accordance with the computational experiments.

As it is argued in Conclusion, the most important results of this work are: (1) a formulation of an algorithm for forming neural networks, which specificity is determined by topology model molecular markers and (2) the finding that the number of attractor points in neural networks of biologically realistic size can exceed the number of neurons in 100-1000 times.

2 Inborn attractors

We consider neural networks, which contain N neurons. The behavior of the i-th $(i=1,...,N)$ neuron is described by its phase function, $\varphi_i(t)$. There are two constants: the duration of excitation, w, and the duration of refractoriness, r. If $\varphi_i(t) \geq r$ and $\left(\sum_{j=1}^{N}(w_{ji} \cdot x_j(t)) - \theta_i\right) \geq 0$, then $\varphi_i(t+1)=0$, otherwise $\varphi_i(t+1)=\varphi_i(t)+1$. The output of the neuron $x_i(t)=1$, if $\varphi_i(t)<w$, otherwise $x_i(t)=0$. Usually, $w=1$ and $r=0$.

In computational experiments [2] we have explored the methods for making inter-neuronal connections, which enable the neural networks to have attractor states (states which are transformed into themselves under the specified above rules of neural dynamics). The states of the neural network are N-dimensional vectors of ones (neuron is excited) and zeros (neuron is quiet). Our approach is based on using model molecular markers, which we first distribute randomly between neurons. Then connections between the neurons are established, depending on properties of markers, which the neurons receive at the previous stage. The set of all attractor states (SAAS) of the network can be characterized by pairwise distances between the states and properties of the whole set of the attractor states. Two cases are of particular importance: (1) when all attractor states are at large distances from each other. We say that these SAAS have dimensionality d equal to zero (d=0); (2) each attractor state has two other attractor states close to it and all states compose a closed chain, in which each state has immediate neighbor, then neighbor of neighbor, etc. The distance to neighbors grows linear with the degree of neighboring relations until some limit, beyond which the distances do not systematically increase and fluctuate around some value, which is about the same as average distances between states in SAAS with $d=0$. If the set of attractor states has these properties, we say that the SAAS of the neural network has dimensionality $d=1$.

Let M be the total number of molecular markers. To obtain a neural network having SAAS with $d=0$ we divide the markers in $n = M/L$ [2] groups. Inside a group, the distance between markers is zero; between the groups, it is "very large", say that it is close to N.

To obtain a neural network having SAAS with $d=1$ we endow the markers with the other metrics. We consider that all M markers are placed equidistantly on a ring. The distance between any two markers is defined as the minimum number of other markers, which are located between the selected ones.

Ones the distances between markers are established, the further procedures, leading to formation of neural networks with the desirable properties of the SAAS do not depend on the type of SAAS. The markers are distributed between N neurons randomly subject to only one restriction: the distance between markers inside one neuron should exceed some pre-determined value, Δ. As soon as the markers are distributed between the neurons, the latter are connected with excitatory synapses. The connections are symmetric and are set between two neurons, if they have markers, the distance between which is less, than another pre-determined value, δ. Computational experiments have demonstrated that the two types of metrics marks, described above, yield the neural networks with the SAAS with $d=0$ and the SAAS with $d=1$, when the same for both cases conditions for marker distribution and connection setting have been used [2].

3 Parameters estimation

In this section we obtain parameters estimation for both types of attractors, which have been described in Section 2.

[1] To avoid complications, connected to boundary conditions, "the snake" is considered to be a closed elastic ring, like the bike wheel inner tube.

[2] When applicable in this paper, the ratio expressions are considered to yield integer values. Generalization to the non-integer values is not difficult, but is not treated here.

3.1 Number of inborn attractor states for d=0

Consider T_{ij}, the neurons interconnections matrix $N \times N$, with values 1, at i and j, where excitatory connections are formed as described, and values 0 otherwise. The mean value of matrix elements is:

$$\gamma = \overline{T_{ij}} = \Pr\{T_{ij}=1\} = 1 - \Pr\{T_{ij}=0\} = 1 - \left(1 - \frac{L^2}{N^2}\right)^n \quad (1)$$

We suppose that n is proportional to N^2/L^2, i.e. $n = q \cdot (N^2/L^2)$. As $n \to \infty$, we have:

$$\gamma = 1 - (1 - q/n)^n = 1 - e^{-q} \quad (2)$$

Now, let the network have at the input one of its theoretical attractor patterns. Then, the probability, that a 'foreign' neuron have L excitatory inputs is:

$$P\{h_i = L\} = \gamma^L .$$

So, the probability that at least one of (N-L) foreign neurons will get L units of excitation is:

$$P_{err} = P\{\exists i_{inactive} : h_i = L\} = 1 - (1-\gamma^L)^{N-L} \approx 1 - (1-\gamma^L)^N$$

Taking $P_{err} = 1/N$, we have:

$$1 - (1-\gamma^L)^N = 1/N ,$$

and, after non-complicated transformations, leaving only first order terms (by $1/N$), we have:

$$\gamma = N^{-2/L} . \quad (3)$$

Comparison of (2) and (3) finally yields:

$$q = -\ln\left(1 - N^{-2/L}\right) . \quad (4)$$

Table 1 gives numerical values of q for a set of N values at L=20. Although computational estimates of q give the constant value $q = 1$, one can see that the analytical reasoning does not diverge too far from the computational experiments estimate.

Table 1. Computational estimates of q

N	100	500	1000	2000	3000	5000
q	1.0	0.77	0.69	0.63	0.6	0.56

3.2 Trade-off relations for attractors with d=0

For neural network applications, it is important to know how the network behaves depending on the values of its parameters. In particular, it is important to know if the attractor states are stable, *i.e.* after small perturbations the states of the system returns to the original attractor state. Fig. 1 shows the "error" in states, as a function of N, n at $L = 20$, obtained in Monte Carlo computational experiments. The synchronous L winners dynamics of the network was used [5] and the "error" was considered to be the Hamming distance between the experimentally obtained stable state and the "theoretical" attractor point which served as the initial condition. It can be seen that the error grows with n. For n less than a critical value, n_{cr}, the "theoretical" attractor points are stable.

Fig. 2 shows dependence of $\alpha_{cr} = n_{cr}/N$ on N. The linear empirical approximation shows that with increasing N, the value of n_{cr} increases $\approx N^2$ (when L is constant): $n_{cr} \approx (N/L)^2$. The mean value of matrix elements is

$$\overline{T_{ij}} \cong ML^2/N^2 . \quad (5)$$

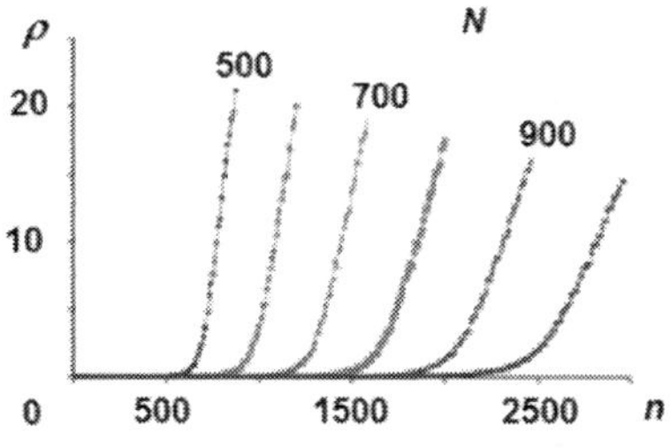

Figure 1. The "error" in neural network stable states. N and n are the numbers of neurons and markers, correspondingly. The number of excited elements, L = 20. In each case, plotted are values, averaged over all attractor points.

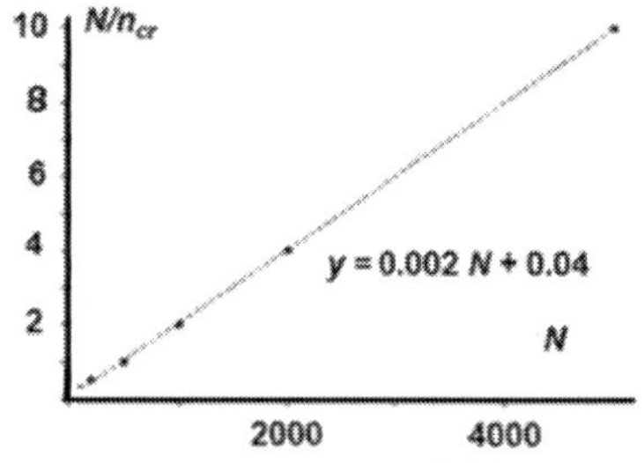

Fig. 2. The critical values of ratio n_{cr}/N as a function of N. Computational experiments (dots); broken line is the least square regression; L=20.

When the network resides at attractor state, S^m, the L neurons which are active get the following inputs:

$$h_{act} = \sum_{j=1, j\neq i}^{N} \mathbf{T}_{ij} S_j^m = L - 1 . \quad (6)$$

Input to the rest ($N - L$) of the neurons is approximately:

$$h_{inact} = L \cdot \overline{\mathbf{T}_{ij}} . \quad (7)$$

Here $\overline{\mathbf{T}_{ij}}$ is the average value of matrix element of $\mathbf{T}$. The distinction between the right parts of (6) and (7) enables the neural network discriminate between attractor and non-attractor states. Thus, we obtain the trade-off relation $n_{cr} \approx (N/L)^2$ for the number of attractor states, n ($n<n_{cr}$), the number of neurons in the network, N, and the number of active neurons in each attractor state L. Besides, we get an analytical reasoning, which qualitatively explains the data of computational experiments, displayed in Figs. 1 and 2.

3.3 Distances between attractor states in 1 d continuous attractor obtained with help of model molecular markers

Fig. 3 presents a fragment of the layout of all neurons in order of the order numbers of the markers, which they contain (as each neuron has k markers, each neuron is presented k times in this layout). The neurons become excited in the same order, while the activity propagates over the attractor[3]. We now consider the distance between an initial state, X_0 and states which are following it, $X_1, X_2, X_3, ... X_t$, (t=1, 2, ... M).

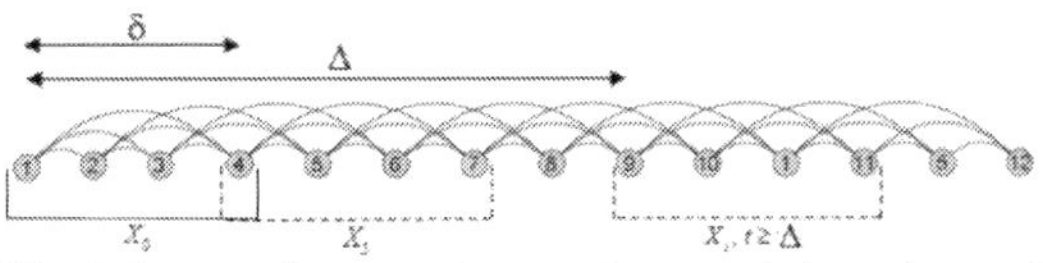

Fig. 3. Layout of neurons in accordance to their markers order number

Fig. 4 shows the inner product (X_0, X_t) of two states plotted against t. It is obvious that in the beginning, the intersection between X_0 and X_t decreases linearly from L to 0. Then, it stays equal to 0 up to $t = \Delta$. For $t > \Delta$, the intersection is random. Its mean value can be obtained as follows. Each neuron of the first state takes later part in (k-1) states That means that for any neuron which is excited in X_0, the probability to be excited in X_t (for large t) is

$$p = \frac{(k-1)L}{M-L}$$

That means that the average intersection between X_0 and X_t will be $pL \approx (k-1)L^2 / M$. The Hamming distance between the states is connected an intersection of them according to the relation $H(X_t, X_0) = 2(L - (X_t, X_0))$, where from we get for $t \geq \Delta$:

$$\underline{D} \approx 2L\left(1 - \frac{(k-1)L}{M}\right)$$

With L=15, k=3, M=900, we have $\underline{D} \approx 29$, which coincides with the results of the computational experiments [2].

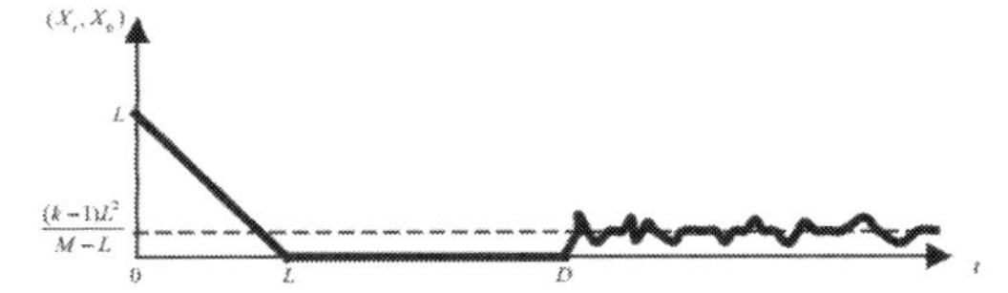

Fig. 4. Schematic plot of the scalar product (X_0, X_t)

3.4 Evaluation of kc in one-dimensional continuous attractors

As each neuron takes part in k attractor states, each line of the matrix **T** contains about $2\delta k$ positive (equal to 1) matrix elements. The probability of positive matrix element is $2\delta k / N$. That means that the probability of firing of one excessive neuron, which is not active in X_0, is $(2\delta k / N)^L$. On the contrary, the probability that this will not happen for any of the remaining $N - L$ neurons is $[1 - (2\delta k / N)^L]^{N-L}$. In computational experiments, the critical value k_c was defined as the value of k, such that five random networks with a given k show perfect cycles. Thus, for k_c we obtain an equation:

$$1 - \left[1 - (2\delta k_c / N)^L\right]^{N-L} < 1/5 .$$

And finally, for the critical value of k, we have:

$$k_c < N / \left(2\delta \sqrt[L]{5N}\right) . \tag{8}$$

Factor $\sqrt[L]{5N}$ is of the order of 1 and changes very slowly with N. So, (8) yields practically linear dependence of k_c on N.

In particular, we have:

at L = 15, N = 300, $\sqrt[15]{5 \cdot 300} \approx 1.62$, k = 7.7 (in experiment, k = 5);

at L = 15, N = 1200, $\sqrt[15]{5 \cdot 1200} \approx 1.79$, k = 28 (in experiment, k = 21).

Thus, we have obtained analytical justification of results of computational experiments [2].

4. Conclusion

This work belongs to the series of analytical and computational studies of data formats in neuronal systems [2, 5, 6]. In this series we explore neural networks properties, which can be provided by the mechanisms of inborn connection formation. Here we for the first time explicitly state that using a single mechanism for connection formation we obtain two different important classes of neural networks SAAS, i.e. the attractor neural networks with d=0 and the attractor neural networks with d=1. The particular class of neural network depends on the properties of the set of molecular markers. If this set is endowed with continuously changing distance function, we obtain d=1. In the discrete case, we get d=0. The model molecular markers, postulated in our approach, can be actually implemented (naturally or artificially) with bio-molecular techniques (as discussed in [2]).

Further, we have demonstrated the workability of one of the important principles of the work of natural multi-component systems – the multiple using of single elements. Thus, one can see from Fig. 2 that in attractor neural network with d = 0, each neuron can take part in up to 10 isolated points of the neural attractor. When extrapolated to the higher possible sizes of elementary neural ensembles (10^5 elements) this figure may be increased up to 200. This fact has a practical value as it is well-known that in neural systems meaningful objects are represented with activities of many neurons (appropriate citations are given in [2]). If so, then the number of represented objects would be severely restricted to a number, small compared to the number of neurons in the neural system. Our simulations and analytical

[3] To study the structure of attractors with d=1, the artificial neural network dynamics has been used in [2]. In this case, the neuron threshold increases, when the neuron is active for a long time. Due to this modification of the neuron model, the activity of the network with 1d 'snake-in-a-box' attractor, can run for indefinite time over the ring of the attractor states.

calculations demonstrate that the number of attractor points in neural system can substantially exceed the number of neurons, by a factor of up to 100.

A slightly different and also important in practice is the fact that the number of attractor points in continuous neural attractors can exceed the number of neurons in the neural network. In this case the "multiplexing" factor attains the values of 21 for the number of neurons N = 1200. When, again, extrapolated to the largest possible natural neural networks we come to the factor of 900. On one side, this is natural, that representation of single values of continuous variables demands less resources than representation of discrete variables (cf. figures 900, here and 100, above). On the other side, the large number of d=1 attractor states enable precise representation of the external world in neural systems.

Another important principle, demonstrated analytically and computationally in our work is the exceptional role of the random structural codes in neural systems. This principle was first revealed (based on heuristic approximate reasoning) by Sir Giles Brindley, F.R.S. [7]. Recently, results of [7] were thoroughly checked in thorough computational experiments [8].

This principle appeals to well-known high efficiency of random codes in systems of noise-resistant communications [9]. In few words, the communicational randomized systems become "large" and demonstrate "asymptotic" noise-tolerant deterministic features when the number of constituent elements is measured by hundreds and thousands (like in neural systems) and not by 10^{20}, as in statistical physics.

We hope that our work might be helpful in understanding natural neural systems – brains and also can be used for synthesis of artificial neural constructions.

The work was supported by the Russian Foundation of Basic Research grant # 16-07-01059.

References

1. Y. LeCunn, Y. Bengio and G.Hinton, Nature, **521**, 436 (2015)
2. K. Solovyeva, I. Karandashev and W. Dunin-Barkowski, Front. Syst. Neurosci., **9**, 178 (2016)
3. W. Dunin-Barkowski and N. Osovets, Neural Processing Letters, **2**, 28 (1995)
4. S. Romani and M. Tsodyks, PLoS Comput Biol, **6**, e1000869 (2010)
5. I. Karandashev, *Proc. XV Conf. "Neuroinformatics 2013"*, part 2, p. 125 (Moscow, 2013)
6. K. Solovyeva, *Proc. XVI Conf. "Neuroinformatics 2014"*, part 1, p. 155 (Moscow, 2014)
7. G. Brindley, Proc. Roy. Soc. Lond. B, **174**, 173 (1969)
8. I. Karandashev and W. Dunin-Barkowski, Optical Memory and Neural Networks, **24**, 8 (2015)
9. G. Battail, Lecture Notes in Computer Science, **1133**, 76 (1996)

ITM Web of Conferences **6**, 02010 (2016)
DOI: 10.1051/itmconf/20160602010

Structural equation modeling in the genetically informative study of the covariation of intelligence, working memory and planning

I. Voronin[1,a], V. Ismatullina[1] I. Zakharov[1], G. Vasin[1] and S. Malykh[1]

[1]*Psychological Institute of Russian Academy of Education, Laboratory of developmental behaviour genetics, 125009 Moscow, Russia*

Abstract. Structural equation modelling (SEM) has become an important tool in behaviour genetic research. The application of SEM for multivariate twin analysis allows revealing the structure of genetic and environmental factors underlying individual differences in human traits. We outline the framework of twin method and SEM, describe SEM implementation of a multivariate twin model and provide an example of a multivariate twin study. The study included 901 adolescent twin pairs from Russia. We measured general cognitive ability and characteristics of working memory and planning. The individual differences in working memory and planning were explained mostly by person-specific environment. The variability of intelligence is related to genes, family environment, and person specific environment. Moderate and weak associations between intelligence, working memory, and planning were entirely explained by shared environmental effects.

1 Introduction

Behavioural genetic research aims to disentangle the genetic and environmental influences on the individual differences in behavioural traits. The information about exact genetic code of a person is still hardly accessible and the exact mechanisms of gene-environment interplay are mostly unknown. However the methods of behaviour genetics provide indirect estimates of the variance accounted for genetic and environmental factors. Such methods compare family members with known genetic relatedness. Twin method is most used among them.

The combination of twin method and structural equation modelling allows addressing complex research questions: the role of genes and environment in the relationship between several traits, the sources of stability and change of certain trait in time etc. This paper provides an example of the application of structural equation modelling for multivariate twin research.

2 Twin method

Twin method compares two groups of twins to disentangle genetic and environmental effects on the measured trait (phenotype). **Monozygotic** (MZ) twins develop from the same egg and have similar genetic code. **Dizygotic** (DZ) twins develop from two different eggs fertilized at the same time, so they share 50% of genetic variation [1]. Twin method consider following sources of individual differences:

- Additive genetic effects (A) represent the additive effects of many genetic variants which influence the trait.
- Non-additive genetic effects (D) represent the interaction between alleles (dominance and epistasis).
- Environmental effects shared by the members of the same family (C): socioeconomic status, parenting style etc.
- Individual experience of family members (person-specific environmental effects, E), and also measurement error.

The similarity of twins within pair sources from shared genes and shared family environment. MZ twins share genetic effects and family environment to the full extent. DZ twins share 50% of additive genetic effects, 25% of non-additive genetic effects, and 100% of family environment. MZ twins differ because of person-specific environment, DZ twins – because of unique environment and genes. This set of assumptions defines the set of equations:

$$\begin{gathered} r_{MZ} = A + D + C \\ r_{DZ} = 0.5A + 0.25D + C \\ 1 = A + D + C + E \end{gathered} \qquad (1)$$

The set of three equations (1) allows computing three components at the same time: A, C, and E, or A, D, and E:

$$\begin{gathered} E = 1 - r_{MZ} \\ A = 2(r_{MZ} - r_{DZ}) \\ C = 2r_{DZ} - r_{MZ} \end{gathered} \qquad (2)$$

$$\begin{gathered} E = 1 - r_{MZ} \\ A = 4r_{DZ} - r_{MZ} \\ D = 2(r_{MZ} - 2r_{DZ}) \end{gathered} \qquad (3)$$

[a] Corresponding author: ivan.voronin@pirao.ru

Twin method provides reliable evidence about genetic and environmental effects under following assumptions:

- The twins do not differ from general population in terms of a certain phenotype.
- MZ and DZ twins share their environments to the same extent.
- There are no gene-environment correlations or interactions.
- The mating in population is random.

3 Structural equation modelling

3.1 Basic principles of structural equation modelling

Structural equation modeling (SEM) is a set of methods which allows checking the hypotheses about the structure of relationships between observed and unobserved (latent) variables [2].

The model is usually represented by path diagram which include variables and linear relationships between them. On such a diagram circles are latent variables, squares are observed variables, single-headed arrows are one-way (causal) relationships, and double-headed arrows are two-way relationships (covariances). Figure 1 provides an example of a path diagram.

Path coefficients (the values of causal effects and covariances) constitute the set of model parameters. The estimation is possible only when the number of estimated parameters is less or equal than number of available data (number of observed variances and covariances). The difference between the two is known as number of degrees of freedom of the model (*df*).

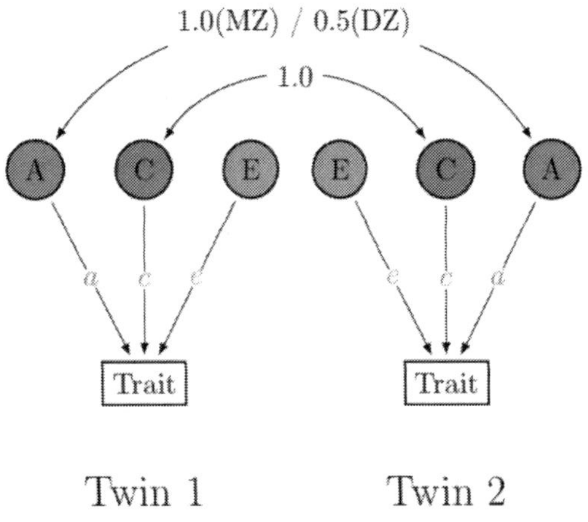

Figure 1: Path diagram for the univariate twin model

The expected covariance between two variables is computed as a sum of the covariances accounted for all possible paths between these variables. Such path must not go through the same variable twice, and must go first through one-way paths backwards, then through the one two-way path, then through one-way paths forward. The value of covariance accounted for the path is the product of path coefficients along this path.

The model can include several sub-models. For example, any twin model comprises separate sub-models for MZ and DZ twins. The models use same set of parameters but fit on different datasets (Figure 1).

The difference between actual and expected covariance matrices indexes general fit of a model: the model with better fit explains the covariance structure more accurately. The programs for structural equation modeling estimate model parameters by minimizing the difference between actual and expected covariance matrices. Least squares and maximum likelihood are the most used methods of estimation. Least squares suggest minimizing sum of the squared differences between actual and expected data. Maximum likelihood estimation maximizes the likelihood of the data given the model with certain parameters). For twin analysis the full information maximum likelihood estimation is most appropriate as it uses each single data point to compute the likelihood. Likelihood-based fit statistics can also be used for the estimation of parameters' confidence intervals.

The main measure of general model fit is the difference between the model likelihood and the likelihood of perfectly fitting (Saturated) model. This difference distributed as χ^2 with *df* equal the difference in *df* between two models. χ^2 test shows if the model fits the data well. A statistically significant p-value ($p < 0.05$) means that expected and observed covariance matrices differ significantly, so the model does not fit the data. The opposite means that the model explains data well.

χ^2 test can also be used to compare the nested models – when the set of parameters of one model is the subset of the parameters of another. The model with fewer parameters (more parsimonious) is preferable when two models have similar goodness-of-fit. The comparison of nested models is often used to exclude non-significant parameters.

3.2 Application of structural equation modelling in twin research

Although SEM is a useful tool in a univariate twin study, it provides even more opportunities for the study of genetic and environmental effects underlying the variance shared by several phenotypes. This approach is based on the comparison of cross-trait cross-twin correlations (correlations between one trait in one twin and another trait in another twin) in MZ and DZ twins. The discrepancy between the correlations indexes genetic effects which affect both phenotypes.

Basic multivariate twin model can be defined via Cholesky decomposition (Figure 2) [3]. The advantage of Cholesky decomposition is that each component of the covariance matrix has a compact representation as matrix algebra:

$$A = \begin{pmatrix} a_1 & 0 \\ x & a_2 \end{pmatrix} \times \begin{pmatrix} a_1 & x \\ 0 & a_2 \end{pmatrix}$$
$$C = \begin{pmatrix} c_1 & 0 \\ y & c_2 \end{pmatrix} \times \begin{pmatrix} c_1 & y \\ 0 & c_2 \end{pmatrix} \quad (4)$$
$$E = \begin{pmatrix} e_1 & 0 \\ z & e_2 \end{pmatrix} \times \begin{pmatrix} e_1 & z \\ 0 & e_2 \end{pmatrix}$$

This allows computing cross-twin covariance matrices in matrix algebra form as well:

$$cov(MZ) = \begin{pmatrix} A+C+E & A+C \\ A+C & A+C+E \end{pmatrix}$$
$$cov(DZ) = \begin{pmatrix} A+C+E & 0.5A+C \\ 0.5A+C & A+C+E \end{pmatrix} \quad (5)$$

The correlations between genetic and environmental factors affecting phenotypic variables can be computed upon the parameters of the Cholesky model.

4 The study of genetic and environmental factors of the relationships between intelligence, working memory, and planning

4.1 Introduction

Intelligence (general cognitive ability) is a stable cognitive ability which explains individual differences in a broad range of intellectual activities. Working memory is a cognitive system aimed to concurrently maintain access to information relevant to a task. The strong relationship between intelligence and working memory has been established in many studies [4, 5] and raised the discussion about the nature of their covariance. At the same time intelligence is assessed by means of complex multi-step tasks which require the elaboration of plan and strategy. Indeed, the study of Gilhooly et al. [6] demonstrates the relationships between individual differences in intelligence, working memory, and planning ability.

The current study investigates genetic and environmental sources of phenotypic relationships between planning intelligence, working memory, and planning ability in Russian adolescents.

4.2 Sample and methods

The sample included 377 MZ and 524 DZ pairs of Russian twins (mean age 12.9 years, SD=3.0 years, 45% of twins were female).

General cognitive ability was assessed by means of Raven's Standard Progressive Matrices. The test comprises 5 sub-scales (12 items each) of increasing difficulty. Each task requires to choose an element which completes the pattern (matrix). The sum of correct responses was used as an index of intelligence.

Working memory and planning ability were measured by means of Spatial Working Memory (SWM) and Stocking of Cambridge (SOC) tests from the automated neuropsychological test battery CANTAB. SWM test includes the series of trials where a participant has to collect the tokens searching for them in the boxes on the screen. Within a trial each box contains the token once, so efficient strategy of the search assumes opening the boxes which have not been opened within this search. For twin analysis we used the index of working memory productivity which takes into account both number of errors and response time.

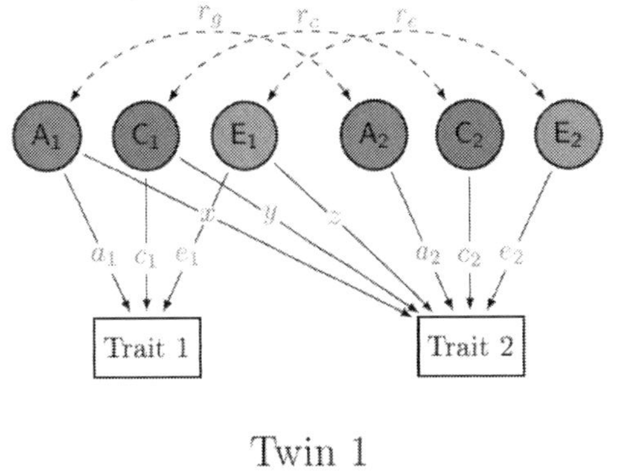

Figure 2: Path diagram for the bivariate twin model (one twin, dashed paths are computed upon other parameters)

SOC test include the tasks which require repeating the pattern shown in the bottom part of the panel by moving balls from one 'sock' in minimum number of moves. The participant is encouraged to plan the moves beforehand. For twin analysis we used the index of planning efficiency which takes into account number of problems solved in minimum moves and the time of initial planning.

As a first step we computed phenotypic Pearson correlations between intelligence, working memory, and planning ability measures. The correlations were computed on the sample of one twin selected randomly from each twin pair. We fit three univariate twin models to estimate genetic and environmental effects separately for each measure. Then we fit a trivariate twin model with correlated factors (Figure 3) to find out whether genetic or environmental factors explain phenotypic correlations between the measures. We constrained the correlations between genetic and environmental components to be positive as previous research gave no evidence that they could be negative.

Before performing twin analyses we adjusted phenotypic variables for the effects of sex and age to avoid possible confounds [7] and standardized them.

4.3 Results

The measure of intelligence showed moderate correlation with SWM score $(0.231, p = 0.006)$ and small correlation with SOC score $(0.127, p = 0.105)$. Working memory and planning ability measures correlated weakly $(0.105, p = 0.166)$.

The univariate twin analysis showed that the variability of Raven's score was associated with genes, family environment, and person-specific environment $(A = 30\%, C = 46\%, E = 24\%)$. The individual differences in SOC score was explained by environmental factors $(A = 7\%, C = 30\%, E = 63\%)$. The variance of SWM score was explained by genes and person-specific environment $(A = 34\%, C = 8\%, E = 58\%)$. The results of the univariate twin analysis

Table 1. The estimates of genetic and environmental correlations across intelligence, working memory, and planning ability measures and their impact to phenotypic correlations (with 95% confidence intervals).

	A	C	E	Phenotypic*	A (%)	C (%)	E (%)
Raven ↔ SOC	0.00 [0.00, 1.00]	0.77 [0.43, 1.00]	0.00 [0.00, 0.08]	0.29 [0.17, 0.38]	0% [0%, 32%]	100% [69%, 100%]	0% [0%, 11%]
Raven ↔ SWM	0.06 [0.00, 1.00]	0.77 [0.09, 1.00]	0.00 [0.00, 0.20]	0.24 [0.12, 0.36]	0% [0%, 93%]	94% [7%, 100%]	0% [0%, 31%]
SOC ↔ SWM	0.02 [0.00, 1.00]	0.17 [0.00, 1.00]	0.14 [0.00, 0.29]	0.13 [0.03, 0.24]	2% [0%, 100%]	33% [0%, 100%]	65% [0%, 100%]

* *Estimated phenotypic correlation*

suggests that the phenotypic correlation between intelligence and working memory can be explained by common genetic effects, as genes has effect on both phenotypes. Another possible source is person-specific environment; however, the factors of person-specific environment of intelligence usually represent measurement error which is independent for different assessment tools.

The results of the trivariate twin modelling are shown on Figure 3 and Table 1. The estimates for the individual impact of genetic and environmental factors to the variation of Raven's, SOC, and SWM scores differ from ones obtained from the univariate analysis. The reason for this is that in multivariate twin analysis the estimation of the effects of genes and environment on individual phenotypic variables takes into account cross-twin cross-trait correlations as well as cross-twin within-trait correlations. It should also be noted that the estimates of the phenotypic correlations obtained from the trivariate model are higher and all statistically significant according to the 95% confidence intervals (Table 1). The reason for this is that these estimates are computed upon the model's parameters and take into account larger amount of data (both twins).

The correlations across genetic and person-specific environmental components of intelligence, planning ability, and working memory measures are small and non-significant. There are statistically significant relationships of size 0.77 between family environmental components of Raven's and SOC, and Raven's and SWM. These relationships explain the corresponding phenotypic correlations entirely.

4.4 Discussion

The multivariate twin study shows that intelligence, working memory, and planning ability in Russian adolescent twins show different structure of phenotypic variability. Individual differences in planning ability and working memory are explained mostly by unique environment, but also to some extent by family environment (planning ability) and genes (working

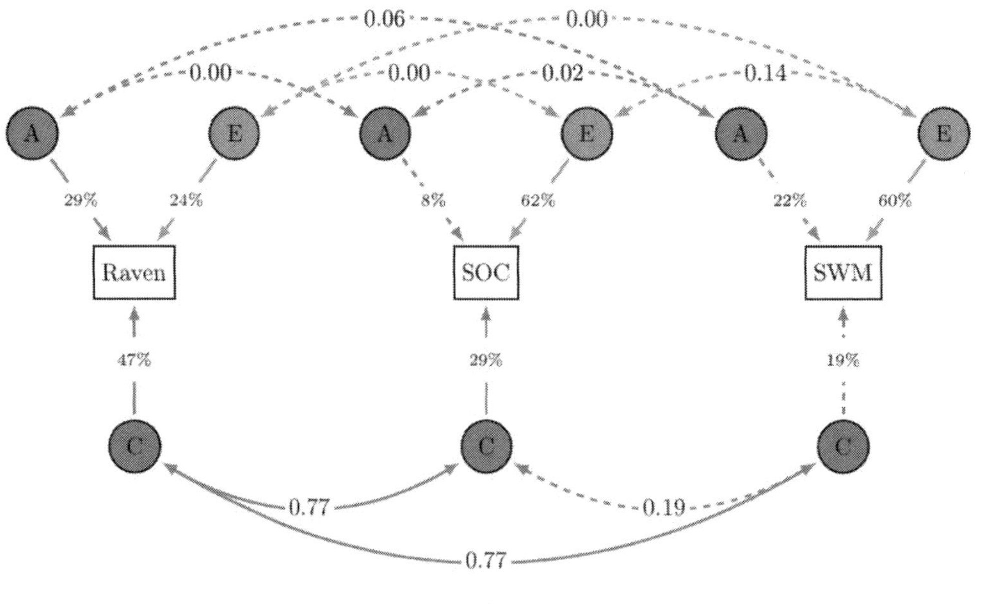

Figure 3: Trivariate twin model with correlated factors (one twin). Non-significant relatioships are dashed.

memory). The variability of intelligence is accounted for all three sources of individual differences. The relationships between the phenotypes are explained by shared environmental correlations.

Previous research generally shows higher genetic effects on general and specific cognitive abilities and functions. The large twin study of intelligence performed by [8] gives the estimate of heritability of intelligence 55%. In the study of Ando, Ono, and Wright [9] genes explained 43-49% of individual differences in working memory characteristics.

In our study we observe high impact of person-specific environmental factors to individual differences in cognitive measures (working memory and planning ability). Person-specific environmental factors include measurement error, so low reliability of composite indices can explain unexpectedly high impact of E and low impact of A.

Another possible reason of the discrepancy is age of participants and cross-cultural differences across studies. The increase of heritability of intelligence through the lifespan is a well-established fact [10]. The possible explanation for this is gene-environment correlation which amplifies genetic effects in favourable environments [11]. This effect manifests both in the increase of heritability through the lifespan and in the variability of estimates of heritability in twin studies.

The study of genetic covariance among measures of general cognitive ability and working memory shows that the covariance between two phenotypes can be explained by shared genetic effects [12] However, the authors used AE model which included genetic and person-specific effects only. In our study genetic effects are moderate or low, so they cannot explain substantial amount of the relationships between intelligence, working memory, and planning ability.

Further research is required to make firm conclusion about aetiology of relationships between intelligence, working memory, and planning ability because the study of moderate or small phenotypic relationships requires large sample size. Another possible option is to use other measures of the phenotypes to reduce measurement error.

5 General discussion

We aimed to outline the application of structural equation modelling in twin study and to provide an example of multivariate twin study.

Multivariate twin study allows to reveal the structure of generic and environmental factors which underlie the variability of several phenotypes. One of the prominent results of multivariate twin study is the hypothesis of generalist genes for cognitive abilities [13, 14]. Cholesky decomposition was used to show that various cognitive processes are associated with same genetic factors.

The flexibility of structural equation modelling tools allows to verify the wide range of hypotheses in twin study. However, the methods are demanding in terms of sample size and the reliability of measures, especially when phenotypic relationships are moderate or weak.

Acknowledgement

The research was supported by the grant from Russian Foundation for Basic Research No.15-36-20902.

References

1. F.V. Rijsdijk, P.C. Sham, Brief. Bioinform. **3**, 119 (2002)
2. J.C. Loehlin, *Latent variable models: An introduction to factor, path, and structural equation analysis* (Psychology Press, 2004).
3. J.C. Loehlin, Behav. Genet. **26**, 65 (1996)
4. M.J. Kane, D.Z. Hambrick and A.R. Conway, Psuchol. Bull. **131**, 66 (2005)
5. K. Oberauer, R. Schulze, O. Wilhelm and H.M. Süß, Psychol. Bull., **131**, 61 (2005)
6. K.J. Gilhooly, V. Wynn, L.H. Phillips, R.H. Logie and S.D. Sala, Think. Rreasoning, **8**, 165 (2002)
7. M. McGue, T.J. Bouchard and Jr, Behav. Genet., **14**, 325 (1984)
8. C.M.A. Haworth, M.J. Wright, M. Luciano, N.G. Martin, E.J.C. De Geus, C.E.M. Van Beijsterveldt, ... Y. Kovas, Mol. Psychiatr. **15**, 1112 (2010)
9. J. Ando, Y. Ono, M.J. Wright, Behav. genet., **31**, 615 (2001)
10. T.J. Bouchard, Twin Res. Hum. Genet., **16**, 923 (2013)
11. E.M. Tucker-Drob, D.A. Briley and K.P. Harden, Curr. Dir. Psychol. Sci., **22**, 349 (2013)
12. M. Luciano, M.J. Wright, G.A. Smith, G.M. Geffen, L.B. Geffen and N.G. Martin, Behav. Genet. **31**, 581 (2001)
13. Y. Kovas and R. Plomin, Trends Cogn. Sci. **10**, 198 (2006)
14. Y. Kovas, C.M. Haworth, P.S. Dale, R. Plomin, R.A. Weinberg, J.M. Thomson and K.W. Fischer, Monogr. Soc. Res. Child., **72**, (2007)

ITM Web of Conferences **6**, 03001 (2016)
DOI: 10.1051/itmconf/20160603001

Mobility support in publish/subscribe systems

Vladimir Antipov[1, a], Oleg Antipov[1] and Aleksander Pylkin[1]

[1] *Ryazan State Radioengineering University, Department of Computational and Applied Mathematics, 390005, Ryazan, Russia*

Abstract. Publish/subscribe (pub/sub) is considered as a valuable middleware architecture that proliferates loose coupling and leverages reconfigurability and evolution. Up to now, existing pub/sub middleware was optimized for static systems where users as well as the underlying system structure were rather fixed. We explore the question whether existing pub/sub middleware can be extended to support mobile and location-dependent applications. We first analyze the requirements of such applications and distinguish two orthogonal forms of mobility: the system-centric physical mobility and an application-centric logical mobility (where users are aware that they are changing location). We introduce location-dependent subscriptions as a suitable means to exploit the power of the event-based paradigm in mobile applications.

1 Introduction

Publish/subscribe (pub/sub) is considered as a valuable middleware architecture that proliferates loose coupling and leverages reconfigurability and evolution. Up to now, existing pub/sub middleware was optimized for static systems where users as well as the underlying system structure were rather fixed. We explore the question whether existing pub/sub middleware can be extended to support mobile and location-dependent applications.

2 Mobility issues in publish/subscribe middleware

Mobile clients have many characteristics, among them the need to disconnect from the network by different reasons. Be it by geographical, administrative, or power saving reasons, connection to the same broker all the time is no longer possible. Hence, we have to take into *account* that clients will disconnect from their border broker once in a while. The middleware has to deal with moving clients and the possibility that a disconnected client will reconnect to the same or to a different broker later. A first step towards mobility is to enhance existing pub/sub middleware to allow for roaming clients so that existing applications can be used in mobile environments.

This means that the interfaces for accessing the middleware and the top level applications are not required for changing. More importantly, the quality of service offered by the middleware must not degrade substantially. The resulting location transparency is necessary to make existing applications mobile, e.g., stock quote monitoring seamlessly transferred from PCs to PDAs. On the other hand, future applications do not require complete transparency, but rely on awareness of mobility. More specifically, mobility support should blend out unwanted phenomena, like disconnectedness, and enforce wanted behavior, like the location awareness in location-based services. Consequently, extending the interface of the pub/sub middleware to facilitate location awareness is a promising open issue, since most existing works are concentrated on the transparency only.

When roaming, clients change (at least some portion of) the context they are operating in, and they might want to react to these changes, e.g., to adapt their subscriptions. However, an appropriate infrastructure support has to relieve the application from having to react "manually" to all changes. The middleware should rather offer an automated adaptation to context changes, i.e., facilitating location dependency. This leads to a different notion of mobility and we distinguish:

Physical mobility: a client that is physically mobile disconnects for certain periods of time and has different border brokers along its itinerary through the infrastructure. The main concern of physical mobility is location transparency.

Logical mobility: a client that is logically mobile is aware of its location changes. In order to relieve the client from adapting manually to new locations, the main concern of logical mobility is automated location awareness within the pub/sub middleware.

Physical and logical mobility are two orthogonal aspects of mobility. Since the physical layout of a pub/sub system is usually fixed and its layout does not usually correspond to geographical realities, it seems reasonable to separate the two notions of mobility. In this paper, we assume logical mobility to be a refinement of physical mobility in that a client remains connected to the same broker when is roaming logically. The two notions

[a] Corresponding author : s_titov@mti.edu.ru

have different quality of service requirements and therefore different solutions are developed to match both.

3 Physical mobility

Physical mobility is similar to what in the area of mobile computing is called terminal mobility or roaming. A client accesses the system through a certain number of access points (GSM base stations, WLAN access points, or border brokers). When moving physically, the client may get out of reaching of one access point and move into the reaching of a second access point which are not necessarily overlapping. In general we cannot expect to have seamless access to the broker network but more a sequence of phases of connectedness, e.g., on the daily route between home and office. In this setting we analyze the quality of service requirements from the viewpoint of roaming clients:

Interface. Obviously, the interface to the pub/sub system must not be changed as the legacy applications have not an aware of mobility.

Completeness. Despite intermittent disconnects, the pub/sub middleware delivers all notifications for a client eventually. This is the core requirement for transparency.

Ordering. The sender orders notifications on first come (FIFO).

Responsiveness. The delay of relocating a roaming client should be minimal to maximize the responsiveness of the system. This has to be taken into account when designing a relocation protocol.

4 Possible solutions

One solution would be to rely on Mobile IP [1] for connecting clients to border brokers, hiding physically mobility in the network layer. The drawback, however, is that the communication is also hidden from the pub/sub middleware, which is then not able to draw from any notification delivery localities or routing optimizations, thereby possibly violating the requirement of responsiveness. Such an approach might only be feasible if the physical and logical layouts of a given system are completely orthogonal.

A different, solution to implement physical mobility would be to use sequences of sub-unsub-sub calls to register a client at a new broker. When a client moves from border broker B1 to B2, it simply unsubscribes at B1 and (re-) subscribes at B2, without any support in the middleware. But a client may not detect leaving the range of a broker and in this case is not able to unsubscribe at its old location. Even more severely, during its time of disconnectedness, the client might miss several notifications or get duplicates, even if notifications are flooded in the network and the location change is instantaneous. This problem is depicted in Figure 1. Hence, this solution is not complete [2].

While physical mobility is a rather technical issue invisible to the application, logical mobility involves location awareness. An example for logical mobility is when clients move around a house or building that is served by only one border broker. In this case, the user might be interested to receive just those notifications that refer to the room he is currently located in. Note that a client can be both logically and physically mobile at the same time.

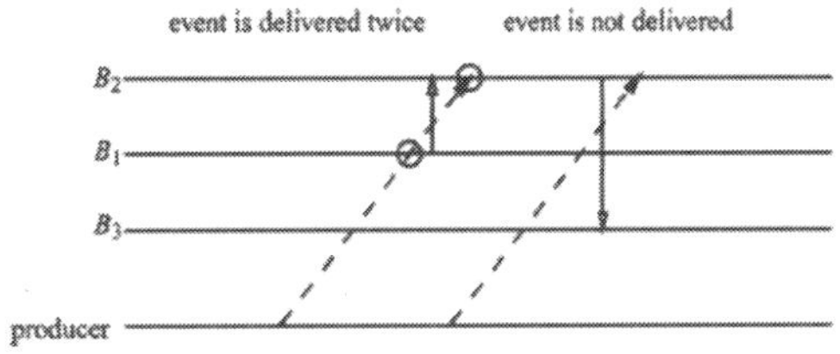

Figure 1. Missing notifications in a flooding scenario

A logically mobile client moving from one location to another, e.g., from one room to the other in a company building, will expect a frictionless change of location explicitly without a notable setup time after having changed from its own office to the conference room next door. The adaptation of some location dependent subscription should take place "instantaneously". Intuitively, we would like to experience the notion of being subscribed to "everything, everywhere, all the time" and increase the reactivity of the system to moving clients.

5 Location-dependent filters

A pub/sub system that offers location-dependent filters has the same interface as a regular pub/sub system (i.e., it offers the pub, sub, unsub, notify primitives). However, in specifying subscription filters for name/value pairs referring to "location" it supports a new primitive to specify things like "all notifications where the attribute location equals my current location". More precisely, we postulate a specific marker myloc that can be used in a subscription. The marker consists of a specific set of locations that depend on the current location of the client. For example, a client could issue a subscription for all free parking spaces in the vicinity of his current location as follows: (service = "parking"), (location $\in$ myloc), (car-type $\geq$ "compact").

The set of locations associated with the marker is taken from a particular range L of locations. This set is application dependent and can, for instance, contain all the different rooms of a building, all the streets of a town, or all the geographical coordinates given by a GPS system up to a certain granularity.

Given a notification with the attribute location, the subscription (location $\in$ myloc) will evaluate to true for a particular client at location y if and only if $x \in$ myloc(y) where myloc(y) is the specific set of locations associated with y. In this case we say that the notification matches the location-dependent filter. The simplest form of myloc(y) is simply the set$\{y\}$. In this case a notification matches the subscription if $x = y$. But in the car example, the car driver looking for a parking space might want to specify: (location = "at most two blocks away from myloc"). In this case, myloc corresponds to all elements of L that satisfy this requirement.

A Tentative but Incomplete Solution for Logical Mobility. While location-dependent filters are not directly supported by current pub/sub middleware, one might argue that it is not very difficult to emulate them on top of currently available systems in this case. The idea would be to build a wrapper around an existing system that follows the location changes of the users and transparently unsubscribes to the old location and subscribes to the new one when the user moves. However, depending on the internal routing strategy of the event system, it may lead to unexpected results. The routing strategies deployed in many existing content-based event systems such as Siena [3], Elvin [4], and Rebeca [5] lead to blackout periods where no notifications are delivered. The problem is that it usually takes an unnegligible time delay to process a new subscription. After subscribing to a filter, it takes some time td until the subscription is propagated to a potential source. Then it takes at least another td time until a notification reaches the subscriber. This phenomenon is depicted in Figure 2a. (Note that the delay t_d may be different for different notification sources and may change over time.) If the client remains at any new location less than $2t_d$ time, then the subscriber will "starve", i.e., it will receive only few or no notifications.

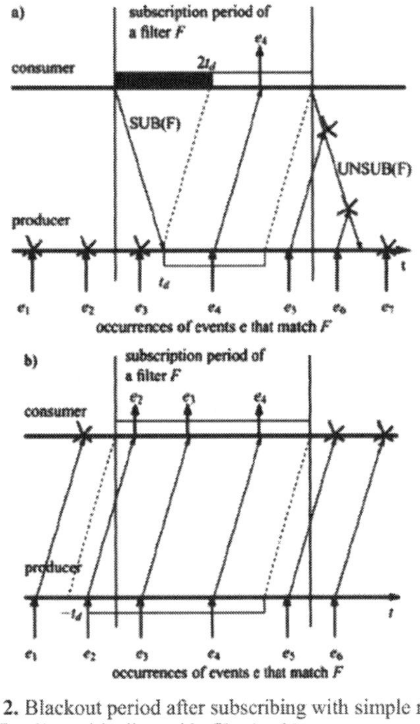

Figure 2. Blackout period after subscribing with simple routing a) and flooding with client-side filtering b).

An Intuitive but Inefficient Solution. Another basic solution that can be immediately built using existing technology is again based on flooding. The local broker can then decide to deliver a notification to a client depending on the client's current location (Figure 2b). Obviously, flooding prevents the blackout periods, which were present in the previous solution, but it should be equally clear that flooding is a very expensive routing strategy especially for large pub/sub systems [6].

Quality of Service of Logical Mobility. Interestingly, while flooding is very expensive and therefore not desirable, it comes very close to the quality of service that we would like to achieve for logical mobility, namely to the notion of being subscribed to "everything, everywhere, all the time". The problem is that it is hard to precisely define the behavior of flooding without reverting to some unpleasantly theoretical constructions of operational semantics.

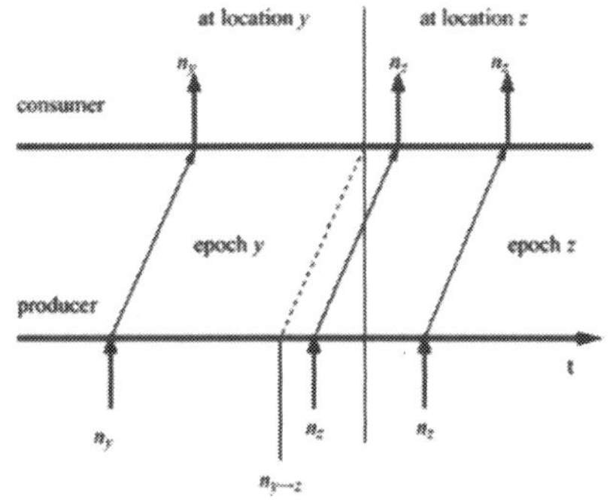

Figure 3. Defining the quality of service for logical mobility using virtual notifications $ny \rightarrow z$ that arrives at the consumer just at the time of the location change from y to z.

With logical mobility there is, however, no danger of receiving a notification twice because the consumer remains attached to the same "delivery path". The quality of service we require for logical mobility therefore is simply stated as follows: On change of location from x to y, all notifications should be delivered to the consumer "as if" flooding were used as underlying routing strategy. This statement is made a little more concrete in Figure 3 where the sequence of notifications generated by any consumer is divided into epochs that correspond to when the notification actually arrives at the consumer (the epoch borders between location y and z are drawn as a virtual notification $ny \rightarrow z$). We require that all notifications matching the current location-dependent subscription from every such epoch must be delivered. Intuitively, the epochs define the semantics of flooding.

6 Conclusion

This paper has presented an approach to support mobility in existing publish/subscribe middleware. We have analyzed the problem of mobility from the viewpoint of the event-based paradigm and have identified two separate types of mobility. While physical mobility is tied to the notion of rebinding a client to different brokers and can be implemented transparently, logical mobility refers to a certain form of location awareness offering a client a fine-grained control over notification delivery in the form of location-dependent filters.

References

1. D. Johnson. Wireless Networks, **1**, 311 (1995).
2. Zeidler and L. Fiege, *Proceedings of the 23rd International Conference on Distributed Computing*

Systems Workshop on Mobile Computing Middleware, (2003).
3. W. Segall and D. Arnold, *Proceedings of the 1997 Australian UNIX Users Group*, (Brisbane, 1997).
4. A. Carzaniga, D.S. Rosenblum, and A.L. Wolf. ACM Transactions on Computer Systems, **19**, 332 (2001)
5. L. Fiege and G. Mühl, *Rebeca Event-Based Electronic Commerce Architecture* (2000)
6. G. Mühl, L. Fiege, F.C. Gärtner, and A.P. Buchmann. *Tenth IEEE/ACM International Symposium on Modeling, Analysis and Simulation of Computer and Telecommunication Systems (MASCOTS 2002)* (2002).

ITM Web of Conferences **6**, 03002 (2016)
DOI: 10.1051/itmconf/20160603002

Capability maturity models in engineering companies: case study analysis

Sergei Titov[1,a], Gregory Bubnov[1], Maria Guseva[2], Alexei Lyalin[2] and Irina Brikoshina[2]

[1]*Moscow Technological Institute, 119334 Moscow, Russia*
[2]*State University of Management, 109542 Moscow, Russia*

Abstract. In the conditions of the current economic downturn engineering companies in Russia and worldwide are searching for new approaches and frameworks to improve their strategic position, increase the efficiency of the internal business processes and enhance the quality of the final products. Capability maturity models are well-known tools used by many foreign engineering companies to assess the productivity of the processes, to elaborate the program of business process improvement and to prioritize the efforts to optimize the whole company performance. The impact of capability maturity model implementation on cost and time are documented and analyzed in the existing research. However, the potential of maturity models as tools of quality management is less known. The article attempts to analyze the impact of CMM implementation on the quality issues. The research is based on a case study methodology and investigates the real life situation in a Russian engineering company.

1 Introduction

Engineering companies in Russia and worldwide facing a number of challenges generated by the current economic downturn are eagerly searching for managerial frameworks and tools which promise them higher effectiveness of business processes, higher quality of products and solutions and better adaptability for change [1, 2]. More and more engineering companies in Russia and other countries are turning to various capability maturity models (CMMs) that help them improve their processes and practices.

Capability maturity models help engineering organizations to assess and position the company's internal processes and resources, to define the current level of maturity and to elaborate the evolution path to improve the processes and resources [3]. There are dozens of different maturity models [4]. However, a typical maturity model consists of a sequence of maturity levels for all or the most important processes of an engineering company [5]. The lowest level stands for the initial state with the poorest performance of the business processes. The top maturity level is characterized by the best practices and the highest performance. With the help of the capability maturity models the management of the engineering companies can define the areas of processes that need to be improved, prioritize all the improvement efforts, develop the strategy of the business process optimization across the whole company, assess the results of the efforts [6].

Since the 1900s when the first maturity models were introduced in the practice of engineering companies they became extremely popular due to the ability to bring about real improvements. There is the documented evidence that CMMs can lead to significant cost and time reduction, improvements in budget performance and timeliness of engineering projects [7–9]. However, the improvements in the quality of engineering solutions and products is widely declared in the theory of CMMs, but is investigated rather sketchily. This article attempts to analyze the impact of CMM implementation in a Russian company on the quality issues.

2 Capability maturity models and their application in engineering companies

The first capability maturity model was developed by Software Engineering Institute in Carnegie-Mellon University in 1991 [10]. In the development of the first version of the capability maturity model many specialists in the engineering of computer, electronic, electrical and mechanical systems participated. The main contribution was made by the specialists from Department of Defence and Systems Engineering Committee of the National Defence Industrial Association of the United States.

Initially, the CMM was developed for new software development projects and programs. However, the model became quickly very popular among not only software companies, but also engineering companies engaged in the various system engineering and development projects and programs initiated for the military and civil purposes. The initial CMM helped companies to streamline and optimize the internal processes of system design, development and technical maintenance.

[a] Corresponding author: parfant@rambler.ru

After the successful implementation of the CMM in many companies the model went through the stages of the further developments and improvement. On the basis of the first CMM the second version was elaborated. It was called Systems Engineering Capability Model [11]. At the same time, the more specialized version of the model was created for the software systems – Software Engineering Capability Model. The idea was to offer two types of models – one for the broad spectrum of companies and projects dealing with engineering of the systems of the various purposes and natures and another one specifically for software system engineering. However, the specialized capability maturity models did not prove to be very popular and after some time SEI developed integrated model – Integrated Product and Process Engineering Capability Maturity Model (IPD-CMM) which allowed streamlining the activities connected not only with the new product development and also with the process development, deployment and optimization [5].

The successes of the different versions of CMM inspired specialists in other industries and professional spheres to create similar capability maturity models. For example, there was an attempt to develop the specialized model for human resources management process – People Capability Maturity Model [12]. The concept of organizational maturity became very popular and productive in the field of project management. The dozens of different capability maturity models were developed in various organizations by different specialists. One of the first project management maturity models was the model developed by Ibbs and Kwak [13]. As the original capability maturity model it consisted of five levels of maturity of processes, different characteristics of processes and key distinguishing capabilities on each maturity level. Another well known project management maturity model was elaborated by Kerzner [14]. Even more detailed model was based on PRINCE2 standard of project management and was called P3M3 (Portfolio, Programme and Project Management Maturity Model) [15]. The distinguishing feature of this model was that it included not only the processes of project management, but also the processes of portfolio and program management. The same approach was used by Project Management Institute in their own project management maturity model – OPM3 (Organizational Project Management Maturity Model) [16]. As P3M3, it was based on the family of international standards of portfolio, program and project management [17–19]. Up to now, OPM3 is the most sophisticated and widely known project management maturity model.

Engineering companies initially showed high interest in project management maturity models. However, after a while the popularity of project management and other specialized maturity models decreased significantly [20]. The reasons for this were:

- Project management maturity models and other specialized models somehow duplicated the approach embodied in the traditional capability maturity models created by SEI,
- They covered only a part of the whole system of processes in engineering companies, whereas CMM was more holistic in nature,
- They were less elaborated and less detailed than CMM.

Today some researchers are highlighting that the classic CMM (in its latest version – CMMI [5]) can be considered as much more popular and useful than any other modification of this model, including project management maturity models [21].

There is some body of research on the results of CMM implementation [7; 8]. Many researchers agree upon the fact that CMM implementation can lead to higher performance in terms of cost and time reduction. However, the effect of CMM on quality is not so clear. The article attempts to fill the gap in the current research and describes the findings of the empirical case study research in the area of CMM implementation results for quality management.

3 Research methodology

The research presented in this article is based on the case study methodology. The reasons for this research design decision are:

- The implementation of the managerial frameworks and optimization models in each organization affects different parts of the organization. In one company CMM can be applied to one process area and in another company to quite different group of processes.
- As result, CMM implementation brings different results which are difficult to generalize and compare within the empirical study based on the surveys.

There are two main perspectives of the case study methodology. One perspective emphasizes the crucial role of the case or the object of study. According to Stake (1998) the most important is not the methods of research, but the object of study itself: "As a form of research, case study is defined by interest in individual cases, not by the methods of inquiry used" [22]. Other perspective, presented by such researchers as Yin (1994), places more emphasis on the tools and techniques of investigation [23]. The authors of this article not denying the importance of research tools and techniques agree more with Stake and consider as one of the most important decisions pertaining to case study research methodology is the selection of the appropriate case.

4 Description of the company

The object of study in the case study methodology should be a complex contemporary functioning unit investigated in its natural context [24]. In order to investigate the results of the CMM implementation and the possibilities of the combined application of CMM and other management optimization approaches we needed to find an engineering companies that already implement CMM and other tools which was ready to share the results of this implementation.

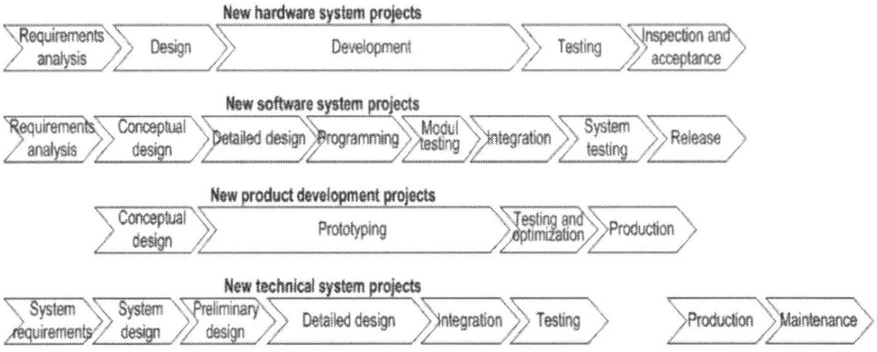

Figure 1. Life cycles of the project in four different business streams of the company

As the case in this article we selected a Russian company engaged in the engineering of radio stations and radio systems for military use. The company is one of the leaders in its industry on the territory of Russia and countries of the former Soviet Union. The business of the company can be considered as four main project streams. The life cycles of the projects from each stream are shown in Figure 1.

In early 2013 the company started the implementation of CMMI. This endeavor was initiated as a part of the strategic program of the internal business processes optimization. The program included the following strategic directions:

- Adaptation of CMMI with the strategic targets of the company,
- Identification of the best practices in process management and dissemination of them across the company,
- Organization of a corporate project office responsible for the coordination of all company projects,
- Identification of the interfaces between internal business process and business processes of contractors and vendors, optimization of these interfaces.

5 Findings of research

The assessment of the current state of business process was undertaken with the help of external consultants and representatives of partners. It was defined that the majority of business process had the third level of maturity. As a result, management of the company decided to upgrade the processes to the fourth level of maturity. At the beginning of 2014 the assessment showed that this aim was achieved and almost all business processes reached the fourth level of maturity. After that it was decided to continue the optimization efforts according to the recommendations from CMMI, and in 2015 the bulk of the processes obtained the fifth level of maturity.

The following analysis is based on the comparison of the situations at the beginning of 2013 and at the beginning of 2015. In other words we analyzed the performance indicators at the third level of maturity and at the fifth level of maturity.

In the area of project management performance it was detected that as the result of CMMI implementation the schedule performance index improved from 0,78 to 0,93. The timeliness of project completion improved by 4,9%. The cost performance index in all company projects increased from 0,88 to 0,96. The indirect costs were cut on average by 7,3%. The product development costs decreased by 28%.

In the area of quality management the improvement were even more notable. The time wasted on defects detection and correction decreased by 6,35 times. The reduction of time wasted on defects detection and correction through different stages of the project life cycles is depicted on Figure 2.

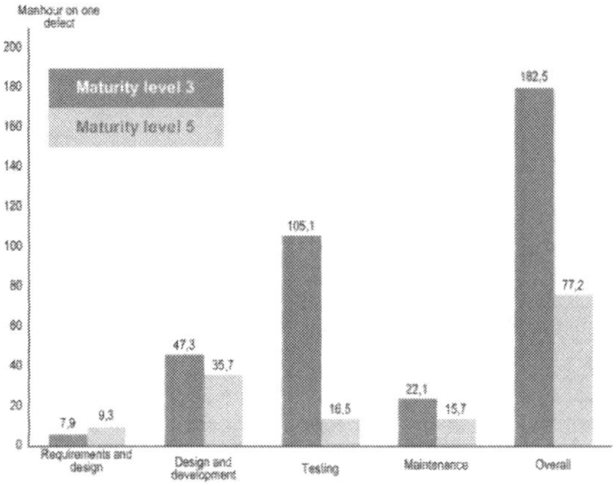

Figure 2. Reduction of time wasted on defects detection and correction on different project stages

From Fig. 2 it is clear that the overall number of defects decreased significantly. But the most outstanding improvements were achieved at the stage of testing.

The costs of defects detection and correction were cut on 22%. The number of critical defects dropped on 62,5%. The index of defect containment (the measure of how many defects were detected and corrected at the place where they were made) improved on 240%.

6 Conclusion

In accordance with the previous research [7–9, 21] the findings suggest that CMM implementation can bring about serious improvements in processes of engineering

[a] Corresponding author: parfant@rambler.ru

companies in terms of cost and time reductions. The transition of the process of the company from the third level of maturity to the fifth was accompanied by the prominent improvement of time and budget performance indexes. At the same time, the research shows that CMM implementation significantly improved the engineering project performance in terms of the quality management. The cost of and time on defects detection and correction reduced notably. The number of defects dropped dramatically as well. Therefore, capability maturity models can be considered not only as a tool of process optimization, but also as an instrument of quality improvement.

References

1. G. Bubnov, S. Titov, B. Titarenko and R. Titarenko, Contemporary Engineering Sciences, **8**, 991 (2015)
2. B. Titarenko, S. Titov and R. Titarenko, PM World Journal, **4**, 1 (2015)
3. M. Röglinger, J. Pöppelbuß and J. Becker, BPMJ, **18**, 328 (2012)
4. T. De Bruin and M. Rosemann, *Proceedings of the Thriteenth European Conference on Information Systems, ECIS* (2005)
5. Software Engineering Institute, *CMMI® for Development, v1.3.* (Carnegie Mellon University, 2010)
6. B. Curtis, J. Alden and C.V. Weber, *The Use of Process Maturity Models in Business Process Management* (Borland Software Corporation, 2004)
7. M. Aubakirov and E. Nikulchev, International Journal of Advanced Computer Science and Applications, **7** (2016)
8. I.V. Osipov, E. Nikulchev, A.A. Volinsky and A.Y. Prasikova, International Journal of Advanced Computer Science and Applications, **6**, 71 (2015)
9. M. Scott, PM World Today, **11**, 23 (2009)
10. Software Engineering Institute, *The Capability Maturity Model: Guidelines for Improving the Software Process* (Addison-Wesley, 1995)
11. Software Engineering Institute, *A Systems Engineering Capability Maturity Model. v1.1* (Addison-Wesley, 1995)
12. B. Curtis, B. Hefley and S. Miller, *People Capability Maturity Model (P-CMM) Version 2.0* (Carnegie-Mellon University, 2009)
13. Y.H. Kwak and W. Ibbs, J Manage Eng, **18**, 150 (2002)
14. H. Kerzner, *Strategic Planning for Project Management Using a Project Management Maturity Model* (Wiley, 2001)
15. R. Sowden, D. Hinley, & S. Clarke, *Portfolio, Programme and Project Management Maturity Model, v2.1* (2010)
16. Project Management Institute, *Organizational Project Management Maturity Model (OPM3). Knowledge Foundation* (2003)
17. Project Management Institute, *A Guide to the Project Management Body of Knowledge* (2010)
18. Project Management Institute, *The Standard for Portfolio Management* (2013)
19. Project Management Institute, *The Standard for Program Management* (2013)
20. L. O'Brian, B. Britt, *Microsoft's OPM3 Implementation*, (2010) available at http://www.opmexperts.com/microsoft_opm3_case_study.html
21. Software Engineering Institute, *Benefits of CMMI within the defense industry* (Carnegie Mellon University, 2010)
22. R. Stake, *Case Studies* (N. Denzin & Y. Lincoln. (eds.), Strategies of Qualitative Inquiry, Sage, 2010)
23. R. Yin, *Case Study Research: Design and Methods* (Sage, 1994)
24. B. Gillham, *Case Study Research Methods* (2001).

ITM Web of Conferences **6**, 03003 (2016)
DOI: 10.1051/itmconf/20160603003

Improving the structural quality of UML class diagrams with the genetic algorithm

Olga Deryugina[1,a]

[1]*Moscow Technological University (MIREA), Institute of Integrated Security and Special Instrument Engineering, 119454 Moscow, Russia*

Abstract. The problem of improving the structural quality of UML class diagrams can be formulated as an optimization problem. The Genetic algorithm is concerned to be able to solve such problems. This paper focuses on the ways in which the Genetic algorithm can be applied to the problem of improving structural quality of UML class diagrams. It develops the theme of semantically equivalent transformations of UML class diagrams during the evolutionary search. This paper suggests the structural semantics of the UML class diagrams. It also formulates the problem of improving the structural quality of a UML class diagram during the evolutionary search and proposes a solution of the problem based on the Genetic algorithm. The paper presents the results of the computational experiment aimed at improving of the structural quality of the UML class diagram with the help of the Genetic algorithm and identifies issues for future work.

1 Introduction

Recent advances in SBSE (Search Based Software Engineering) have provided the possibility of applying evolutionary algorithms to the problems of software engineering, many of which can be formulated as the optimization problems.

The evolutionary algorithm is a bio-inspired algorithm, which iteratively searches for a solution of the problem. The evolutionary algorithms include the genetic algorithm [1], genetic programming [2], simulated annealing [3], swarm intellect [4], bio-geographic algorithm [5], etc.

The Genetic algorithm (GA) is an evolutionary algorithm based on a natural selection mechanism.

A number of studies have investigated different ways of object-oriented software architecture design based on evolutionary algorithms and UML diagram transformations. For example, in [6] hierarchical decomposition of the system has been performed. In [7] pattern based evolutionary transformations have been performed. In [8] authors solve the class responsibility assignment problem with the help of the Genetic algorithm. However, to date it remains unclear which transformations (design patterns, for example) can be automatically performed on the architecture design stage and whether these transformations are semantically equivalent.

The aim of this work is to formalize structural semantics of UML class diagrams and to suggest an algorithm of UML class diagram evolutionary transformation aimed at the improving the diagram structural quality.

The evolutionary transformation of UML diagrams is significant because it allows implementing automatic refactoring of software architecture.

The primary contributions of this paper are:

1. To propose the structural semantics of the UML class diagrams to be able to check equivalence of two UML diagrams.
2. To formalize the problem of improving the structural quality of a UML class diagram during the evolutionary search.
3. To propose a solution of the problem based on the GA.
4. To present the results of the computational experiment aimed at the improving of the structural quality of the UML class diagrams.

2 Structural semantics of the UML class diagrams

In paper [9], the structural semantics of UML class diagrams was suggested. This semantics provides a formal way of describing UML diagram transformations (interface insertion, Façade pattern applying).

Let d be a UML class diagram $d = \{C, I, R\}$, where C is a set of classes $C = \{c_0, c_1, \dots c_n\}$; I is a set of interfaces $I = \{i_1, i_2, \dots i_k\}$, R is a set of relations $R = \{r_1, r_2 \dots r_m\}$.

Then c_i is a class $c_i = \{A^i, M^i, F^i\}$, where A_i is a set of attributes $A_i = \{a_0^i, a_1^i \dots a_n^i\}$, M_i is a set of methods $M_i = \{m_0^i, m_1^i \dots m_m^i\}$, F_i is a set of features $F_i = \{st_i, v_i, abs_i\}$, st_i is an isStatic feature st_i $\{0,1\}$, v_i is a visibility

[a] Corresponding author : o.a.derugina@yandex.ru

parameter $v_i \in$ {*public, private, protected*}, abs_i is an isAbstract feature $abs_i \in \{0,1\}$.

In addition, i_i is an interface $i_i = \{m_0^i, m_1^i ... m_m^i\}$ characterized by a set of methods $\{m_0^i, m_1^i ... m_m^i\}$.

The following kinds of relations r_i are possible between classes: association ($c_1 \xrightarrow{assoc} c_2$), generalization ($c_1 \xrightarrow{gener} c_2$), aggregation ($c_1 \xrightarrow{aggreg} c_2$), composition ($c_1 \xrightarrow{comp} c_2$), and dependency ($c_1 \xrightarrow{dep} c_2$), where $\{p_1, p_2\}$ is a power of a relation.

Moreover, the following relations r_i are possible between a class and an interface: realization ($c_1 \xrightarrow{real} i_1$) and dependency ($c_1 \xrightarrow{dep} i_1$).

Now we assume that the structural semantics S_i of the UML class diagram d_i can be described as follows:

$$S_i = \{\{c_1^i=\{...\}, c_2^i = \{...\}, ... \; c_k^i = \{...\}\}, \{i_1^i = \{...\}, i_2^i = \{...\}, ... \; i_l^i = \{...\}\}, \{r_1^i, r_2^i, ... \; r_m^i\}\}, \quad (1)$$

where S_i is a semantic value of the class diagram d_i; $c_1^i...c_k^i \in d_i$ are the classes of the class diagram d_i; $i_1^i...i_l^i \in d_i$ are the interfaces of the class diagram d_i; $r_1^i...r_m^i \in d_i$ are the relations of the class diagram d_i.

Assume that we are given a UML class diagram $d_1 = \{C_1, I_1, R_1\}$, where C_1 – a set of classes $C_1 = \{c_0^1 ... c_k^1\}$, I_1 is a set of interfaces $I_1 = \{i_0^1 ... i_l^1\}$, R_1 is a set of relations $R_1 = \{r_0^1 ... r_g^1\}$, and the semantic value of d_1 is denoted as S_1.

Moreover, there is a function $f(d_1)$ evaluating a structural quality of the UML class diagram d_1.

In addition, we are given a set of semantically equivalent transformations $T = \{t_0, t_1...t_N\}$. An example of such transformation (Interface insertion) is given at Figure 1:

$$S[\{c_1,c_2\},\{i_1\},\{c_2 \xrightarrow{dep} i_1; c_1 \xrightarrow{real} i_1\}] \cong \cong S[\{c_1,c_2\},\{\varnothing\},\{c_2 \xrightarrow{dep} c_1\}], \quad (2)$$

where S is a semantic value of the class diagram d; c_1, $c_2 \in d$ are the classes of the class diagram d; $i_1 \in d$ is an interface of the class diagram d.

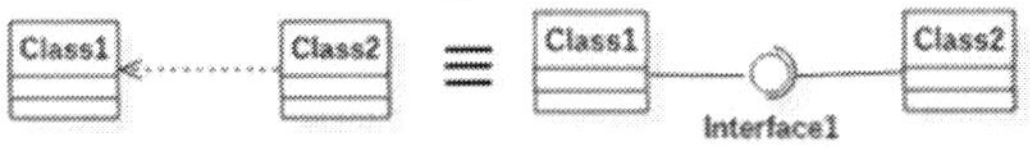

Figure 1. The Interface insertion transformation

Then we can formulate the problem of improving the structural quality of a UML class diagram during the evolutionary search as follows:

It is required to find such a diagram d_2 for n generations with m individuals that:

$$\{d_2 \mid S_{d_1} \cong S_{d_2}; f(d_2) = \min_{d_i} f(d_i)\} \quad (3)$$

In other words, it is required to find such a set of transformations $T^* \in T$, which transfers the d_1 into the d_2, $d_1 \xrightarrow{T^*} d_2$ that:

$$\{T^* \mid S_{d_1} \cong S_{d_2}; f(d_2) = \min_{d_i} f(d_i)\} \quad (4)$$

3 Solution of the problem based on the GA

In order to use GA, the UML class diagram d_i can be considered as an individual, which corresponds to a chromosome consisting of genes, number of which is equal to the number of classes $C^i \in d_i$. Each of genes stores an information about whether or not the transformation $t_k \in T$ has been applied to a class c_m^i.

This approach is similar to that proposed in [7], where the authors applied design patterns to classes, but our transformation approach includes the essential check of semantic equivalence of the transformation.

Individual mutation occurs by adding/deleting a random transformation to/from a gene.

In order to simplify the representation of UML class diagrams in RAM to process them with the GA, the abstract data structure (ADS) UML Map was proposed [10]. UML Map is based on hash maps; therefore, the evaluation of search complexity is $O(1)$.

A scheme of applying the GA in order to improve the structural quality of the UML class diagram is showed at Figure 2.

Let us formulate $f(d_i)$ in accordance with the Low Coupling principle. For example, we can use a CBO (Coupling Between Objects) metric:

$$CBO_i = \frac{1}{n}\sum_{j=0}^{n} CBO_{ij} \quad , \quad (5)$$

where CBO_i is an average CBO value of a class diagram d_i with n classes c_j, $j \in 0..n$, which reflects a degree of dependence between the components of the system; CBO_{ij} is a CBO value of the class $c_j \in d_i$, a number of classes connected with c_j except from the dependency relation; n is a number of classes located at the diagram d_i.

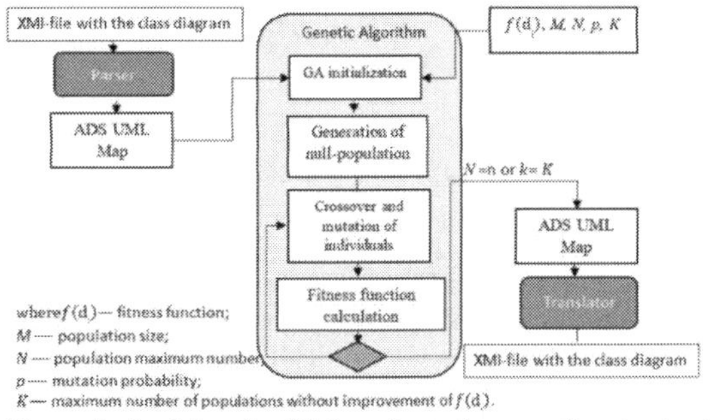

Figure 2. Applying the GA in order to improve the structural quality of the UML class diagram

4 Conducting a computational experiment

Suppose we are given a UML class diagram 'E-commerce' d_1, which is showed at Figure 3. Its semantic value S_1 is as follows:

$$S_1=\{\{c_1,\ldots,c_{17}\},\{\varnothing\},\{c_{17}\overset{aggreg}{\rightarrow}c_8;c_2,c_5,c_6\overset{comp}{\rightarrow}c_1;\ c_{11}\overset{comp}{\rightarrow}c_3;c_{12}\overset{comp}{\rightarrow}c_7;c_{17}\overset{comp}{\rightarrow}c_{10};c_{16}\overset{comp}{\rightarrow}c_{14};\ c_2,c_5,c_6,c_{13}\overset{gener}{\rightarrow}c_9;c_2,c_7,c_8,c_{10},c_{14}\overset{gener}{\rightarrow}c_4;\ c_{11},c_{12},c_{16},c_{17}\overset{gener}{\rightarrow}c_{15};c_2,c_5\overset{dep}{\rightarrow}c_3;c_6,c_8,c_{13}\overset{dep}{\rightarrow}c_7;\ c_{13}\overset{dep}{\rightarrow}c_8;c_9\overset{dep}{\rightarrow}c_{10};c_5,c_9\overset{dep}{\rightarrow}c_{14}\}\} \quad (6)$$

A computational experiment has been conducted with the number of individuals in population = 200, the probability of mutation = 0.5, the percentage of crossover participants = 25%. The attained dynamics of $f(d_1)$ is showed at Figure 5.

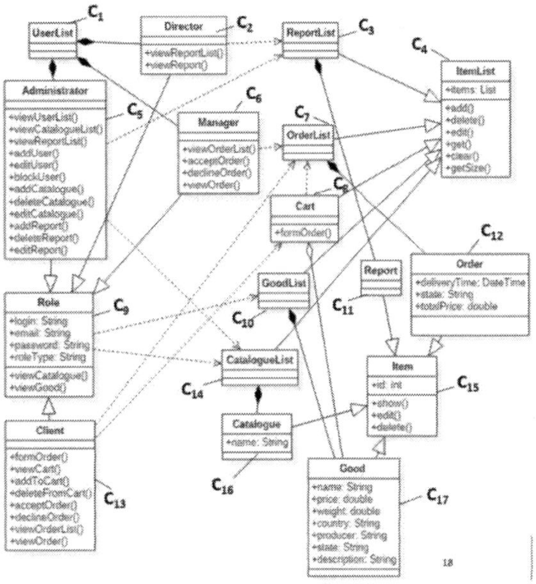

Figure 3. The null-diagram d_1 'E-commerce'

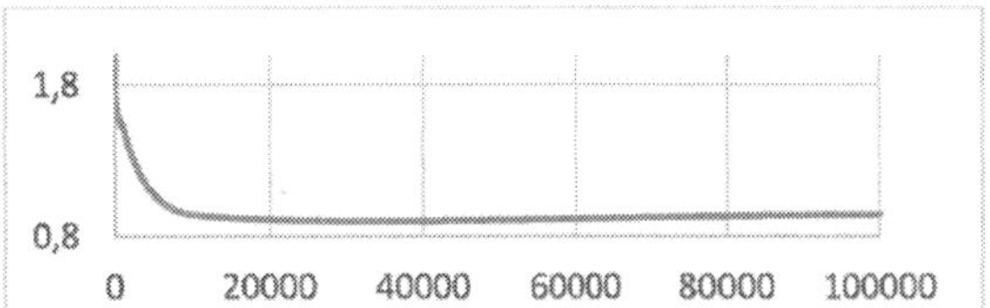

Figure 4. The dependence of $f(d_1)$ values from the iterations count

On the 100 000th iteration has been achieved an individual d_2 with the lowest value of CBO=0.941, which is showed at Figure 5. The semantic value S_2 of the d_2 is as follows:

$$S_2=\{\{c_1,\ldots,c_{17}\},\{i_1,\ldots,i_4\},\{c_{17}\overset{aggreg}{\rightarrow}c_8;c_2,c_5,c_6\overset{comp}{\rightarrow}c_1;\ c_{11}\overset{comp}{\rightarrow}c_3;c_{12}\overset{comp}{\rightarrow}c_7;c_{17}\overset{comp}{\rightarrow}c_{10};c_{16}\overset{comp}{\rightarrow}c_{14};\ c_2,c_5,c_6,c_{13}\overset{gener}{\rightarrow}c_9;c_2,c_7,c_8,c_{10},c_{14}\overset{gener}{\rightarrow}c_4;\ c_{11},c_{12},c_{16},c_{17}\overset{gener}{\rightarrow}c_{15};c_2,c_5\overset{dep}{\rightarrow}i_1;c_6,c_8,c_{13}\overset{dep}{\rightarrow}i_2;\ c_{13}\overset{dep}{\rightarrow}i_3;c_9\overset{dep}{\rightarrow}c_{10};c_5,c_9\overset{dep}{\rightarrow}i_4;c_3\overset{real}{\rightarrow}i_1;c_7\overset{real}{\rightarrow}i_2;c_8\overset{real}{\rightarrow}i_3;\ c_{14}\overset{real}{\rightarrow}i_4\}\} \quad (7)$$

Applying the rule (2) to the expression (7), we attain:

$$S_2=\{\{c_1,\ldots,c_{17}\},\{\varnothing\},\{c_{17}\overset{aggreg}{\rightarrow}c_8;c_2,c_5,c_6\overset{comp}{\rightarrow}c_1;\ c_{11}\overset{comp}{\rightarrow}c_3;c_{12}\overset{comp}{\rightarrow}c_7;c_{17}\overset{comp}{\rightarrow}c_{10};c_{16}\overset{comp}{\rightarrow}c_{14};\ c_2,c_5,c_6,c_{13}\overset{gener}{\rightarrow}c_9;c_2,c_7,c_8,c_{10},c_{14}\overset{gener}{\rightarrow}c_4;\ c_{11},c_{12},c_{16},c_{17}\overset{gener}{\rightarrow}c_{15};c_2,c_5\overset{dep}{\rightarrow}c_3;c_6,c_8,c_{13}\overset{dep}{\rightarrow}c_7;\ c_{13}\overset{dep}{\rightarrow}c_8;c_9\overset{dep}{\rightarrow}c_{10};c_5,c_9\overset{dep}{\rightarrow}c_{14}\}\} \quad (8)$$

From (8) it follows that $S_1 \cong S_2$, so the obtained diagram d_2 is semantically equivalent to the diagram d_1.

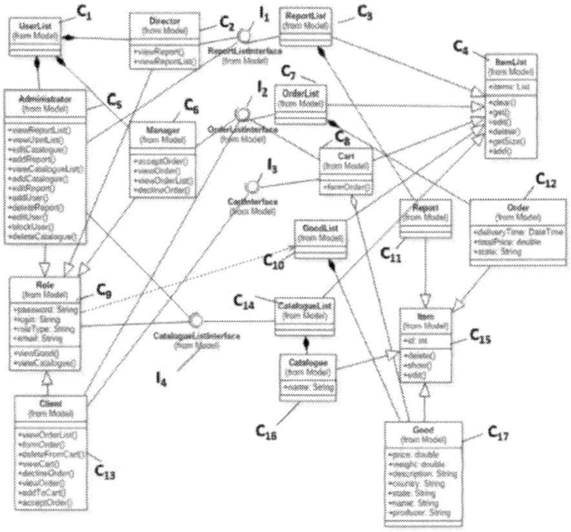

Figure 5. The diagram d_2 attained on the 100 000th iteration

5 Discussion

The results presented here demonstrate that GA has a potential to conduct automatic refactoring of UML class diagrams, but further studies are needed.

The limitation of the present research is that the only one type of transformations has been applied. The rate of the convergence might have decreased if the experiment had been carried out with a significantly larger set of transformations T^* and it would be beneficial to investigate this further [11].

In addition, the current study did not investigate the qualitative effect of different transformations on the values of various structure quality parameters.

6 Conclusions

In this work, we have formalized the structural semantics of UML class diagrams and the semantically equivalent transformations. In addition, we have formalized the problem of improving the UML class diagram structural quality.

We have proposed a solution of the problem based on the GA and on the UML Map data structure.

The study indicates that it is possible to perform automatic refactoring of UML class diagrams using semantically equivalent transformations. The results of this research can serve as a basis for further studies into evolutionary UML diagram transformations.

References

1. D.E. Goldberg, *Algorithms in Search, Optimization and Machine Learning* (1989)
2. J. Koza, *Genetic Programming: On the Programming of Computers by Means of Natural Selection* (1992)
3. S. Kirkpatrick, C. Gelatt and M. Vecchi, Science, **220**, 671 (1983)
4. R. Eberhart and J. Kennedy, *International Symposium on Micro Machine and Human Science*, 39 (1995)
5. D. Simon, IEEE Trans. Evol. Comput, **12**, 702 (2008)
6. Lutz R., JSA, **47**, 613 (2001)
7. O. Räihä, *Genetic Synthesis of Software Architecture* (2008)
8. M. Bowman, L.C. Briand and Y. Labiche, *Solving the class responsibility assignment problem in object-oriented analysis with multi-objective genetic algorithms* (2002)
9. O.A. Deryugina, Proceedings of MIPT, **7**, 146 (2015)
10. M. E. Volovich and O. A. Deryugina, Cloud sci., **2**, 138 (2015)
11. M. Sergievskiy, International Journal of Advanced Computer Science and Applications, **7**, (2016)

ITM Web of Conferences 6, 03004 (2016)
DOI: 10.1051/itmconf/20160603004

Terrain objects edge detection in noisy GPS images

Natalya N. Grinchenko[1, a], Aleksey I. Baranchikov[1] and Anton V. Tokarev[1]

[1]Ryazan state radio engineering university, Electronic computing machines department, 390005 Ryazan, Russia

Abstract. This paper presents the algorithm of terrain objects edge detection in GPS images. This objective is relevant for two reasons. Firstly, in case of distortions occurring in the process of data transmission through communication channel, and secondly, in many cases preliminary data processing requires edge detection. To solve the first issue we utilize quasi-2D filtration, and to solve the second we use an algorithm based on Canny edge detection algorithm.

1 Introduction

Nowadays the industry of Earth remote sensing (ERS) devices grows very rapidly. As a consequence, the amount of GPS information increased as well as the number of tasks connected with processing of such information. Apart from filtration, visual augmentation and restoration of missing areas, there are analytical tasks such as evaluation of different parameters (probabilistic characteristics, position and shape of objects etc.), object detection and identification etc. A lot of analytical tasks require preprocessing of images including edge detection.

Since this task is uncommon and multistep it causes certain problems. The most wide spread problem is the noise in images. In such case edge detection may give invalid results spoiled by vague edges or gaps. It often occurs during terrain (different terrain objects such as lakes, rivers, mountains, buildings etc.) observation.

As long as most of edge detection methods employ gradient methods, the distortions will negatively affect the objects detection and identification on GPS images. To solve the task effectively it is necessary to eliminate the described distortions, which may be completed by utilizing quasi-two-dimensional (Q2D) filtration methods. Since group and single distortions has a fairly predictable structure, they are clearly seen in spectral representations of the image.

2 Theoretical grounds

Any raster image is a matrix, the monolithic atomic unit of which is a pixel. Edge detection is mostly influenced by group noises, which can occur in two forms: the noise that affects the whole line or the noise that affects only a part of the line, which corresponds to the model of a noise that distorts a line in an image with a certain probability p (Figure 1). The following distortion process may be described as follows (1)[1]:

$$g(x,y)=\begin{cases} f(x,y), if\ R(x,y)=0, \\ 0, if\ R(x,y)=1. \end{cases} \quad (1)$$

Where $R(x,y)$ describes distortion spot depending on values p and p_l, where p – probability of noise in the line and p_l – random value equal to noise length.

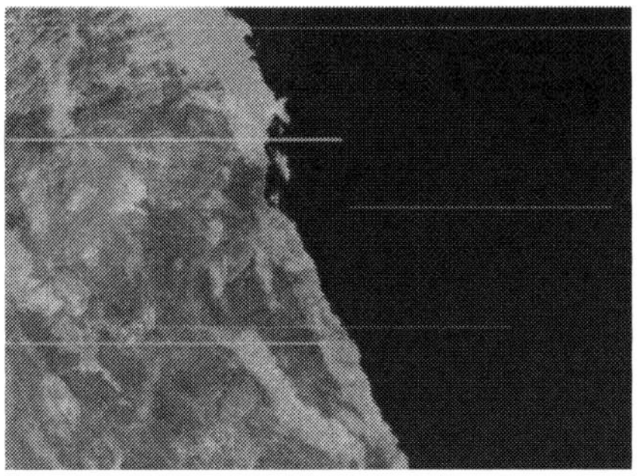

Figure 1. Types of Group noises.

Quasi-two-dimensional filtration method is as follows. Direct Walsh transform is performed according to the formula (2):

$$F = H_W g, \quad (2)$$

where H_W – Walsh-Adamar matrix; g – Image matrix.

Investigation of quasi-two-dimensional spectrum of group noises on a smooth background is likely to reveal sufficient runouts, connected with the presence of noise. On this basis we may conclude that the following run outs influence quasi-two-dimensional spectrum as well.

The elements of the spectrum may be divided into distorted and not distorted. The division is based on noise

[a] Corresponding author: grinchenko_nn@mail.ru

runouts in quasi-two-dimensional spectrum. The algorithm checks the relation of the central element to certain local environment (3):

$$\begin{cases} 0, if \left|F(u-1,y)-F(u,y)\right| \le s, \\ 0, if \left|F(u+1,y)-F(u,y)\right| \le s, \\ 1, \text{in any other case.} \end{cases} \quad (3)$$

where $M(u)$ – line of number of lines of possible location of a group noise, S – some threshold.

Threshold is selected for the whole spectrum but it can be adjusted for different images. Then you may use the following approach: interpolation of spectrum lines related to the noise with the nearest undistorted values of the spectrum. (4)[2]:

$$\hat{F}(u,y) = \begin{cases} F(u,y), u \notin M \\ \dfrac{F(u-1,y)+F(u+1,y), u \in M}{2} \end{cases}, \quad (4)$$

Reverse Walsh transform (5):

$$I = H_W \hat{F}, \quad (5)$$

where I – restored image.

The second type of noises is the impulsive noise or dotty noises («salt and pepper» Figure 2). Impulsive noises may be described in the following manner: if the value in point $f(i,j)=0$, it corresponds to black noise, if it is $f(i,j)=255$ – then it is white noise (6). Therefore

$$g(x,y) = \begin{cases} f(x,y) \text{ if } R(x,y)=0, \\ b, \text{if } R(x,y)=1, \end{cases} \quad (6)$$

where $R(x,y)$ describes noise spot, b – noise value in the spot, which can be only 0 or 255.

Figure 2. Dotty noises.

The most effective method for eliminating this noise is applying median filter (dimensionality of 3x3 [3, 4, 5]) to the noisy image (7).

$$f(x,y) = \underset{k=1,n}{med} \{g(x,y,k)\}, \quad (7)$$

where $\hat{f}(x,y)$ – processed image, $g(x,y,k)$ – filter mask with dimension of 3×3 pixels.

In general terms the quasi-two-dimensional algorithm consists of the following steps [6]:

1. Applying of non trigonometric spectrum restrain theorem to quasi-two-dimensional spectrum;
2. Applying of median theorem (8) to the obtained image:

$$\hat{f}(x,y) = \underset{k=1,n}{med} \{g(x,y,k)\}, \quad (8)$$

3. Subtraction of the obtained image from the image with impulse noises (9):

$$M = f - \hat{f}, \quad (9)$$

where f – image matrix, $\hat{f}$ – new image matrix, M – impulse noise value mask;

4. Using the values of the mask, apply the formula (10):

$$b = f + M, \quad (10)$$

where b – restored image matrix.

Since size of GPS survey objects is small, edge detection must be very precise and the most appropriate algorithm that may be used here is the one proposed by John Canny. This algorithm has the following advantages

1. Fine detection
2. Fine localization
3. One response for one edge

These features allow the use of this algorithm for detecting wide range of edges with high precision.

This is a multistep algorithm that includes the following steps.

2.1 Use Sobel operator to define edge points

Sobel operator is a differential operator, which calculates gradient value in each point as well as its vector direction [2, 3].

The calculation involves germ folds of the following form:

$$G_x = \begin{bmatrix} +1 & 0 & -1 \\ +2 & 0 & -2 \\ +1 & 0 & -1 \end{bmatrix}, G_y = \begin{bmatrix} +1 & +2 & +1 \\ 0 & 0 & 0 \\ -1 & -2 & -1 \end{bmatrix}. \quad (11)$$

With the help of the germs (11) initial image is folded for horizontal and vertical evaluation of approximate values of the derivatives (12).

$$b_{ij} = \sum_{i=1}^{3} \sum_{j=1}^{3} a_{ij} g_{ij}, \quad (12)$$

where b_{ij} – element of matrix B, which contains pixels of the final image; a_{ij} – element of matrix A, which contains pixels of the initial image; g_{ij} – element of matrix G.

Approximate gradient value in each point of the image is calculated as follows (13)

$$B = \sqrt{B_x^2 + B_y^2}; \quad C = arctg\left(\frac{B_y}{B_x}\right), \quad (13)$$

where B – matrix of gradient values, C – matrix of gradient direction.

This method is very sensitive to different noises (Figure 3a,b)

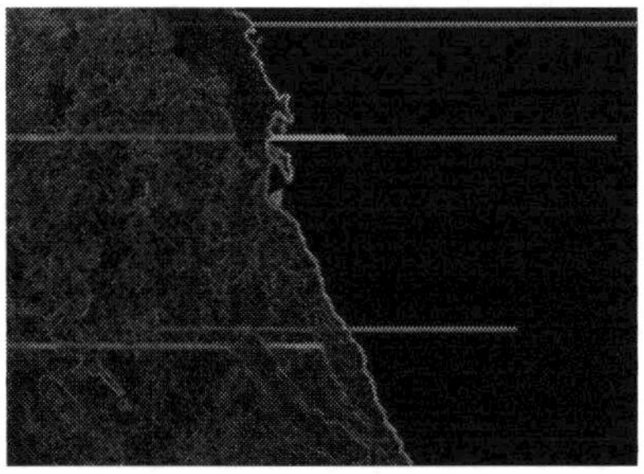

Figure 3. a) Sobel operator applied to image with group noises.

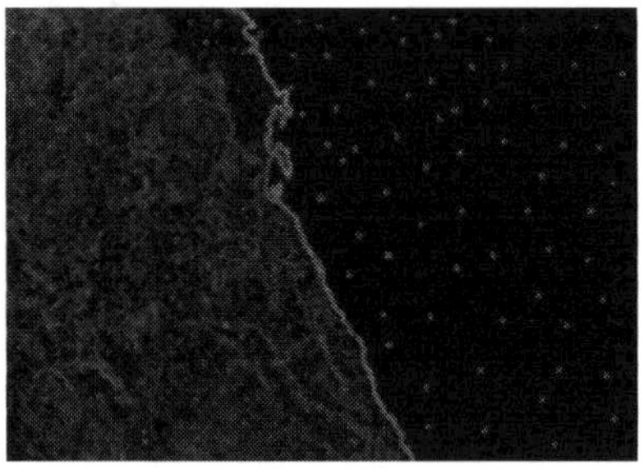

Figure 3.b) Sobel operator applied to image with dotty noises.

2.2 Operation proposed by the author

According to Canny algorithm the next step is an operation proposed by the author, which is reduction of no maximums. At this step each pixel is checked whether its gradient value is the local maximum in the gradient direction on the condition that the angle of the direction vector is rounded to the nearest multiple of 45 degrees.

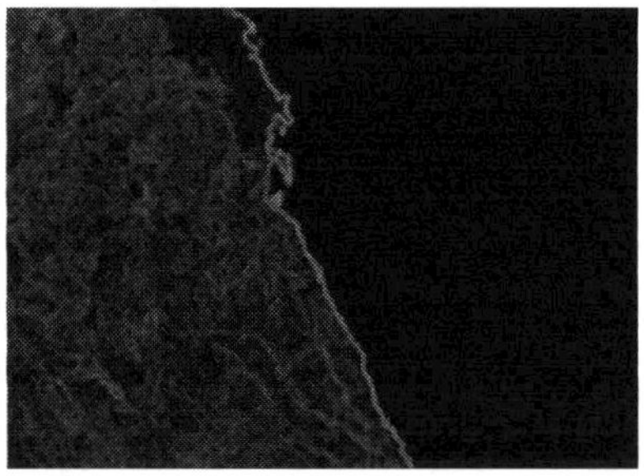

Figure 3. c) Sobel operator applied to the image after using quasi-two-dimensional filtration algorithm.

E.g. if the rounded angle of the gradient direction vector is equal to zero degrees (the edge is running from north to south), the pixel is considered to be the edge point, if its gradient value is higher than that of pixels which are to the north or to the south from it. The operation results in suppression of no maximum values, only local maximums marked as the borders and the edges become thinner and less blurry.

2.3 Threshold filtration

The next step is threshold filtration, which is carried out to define whether the edge is really situated in the chosen spot. The distinctive feature of filtration in Canny algorithm is that it uses two thresholds: if the pixel value is higher than the upper limit, it takes maximum value, if it is lower, then it is suppressed, points with values that are between the thresholds take the average value. This step is a little dubious due to the fact that if to reduce threshold the number of detected edges will increase, however, the result will be «noisier». From the other hand, high threshold may ignore weak edges, which may cause fragmented borders. As we eliminated all the noises in the beginning of the algorithm, the range of values that we consider as borders, may be wider (Figure 3c).

2.4 Highlighting groups of pixels

At the last step the task reduces to highlighting groups of pixels that gained average values at the previous step and relating them to the border or their suppression. Suppression takes place when pixel is not bound to the determined (strong) edge (Figure 4).

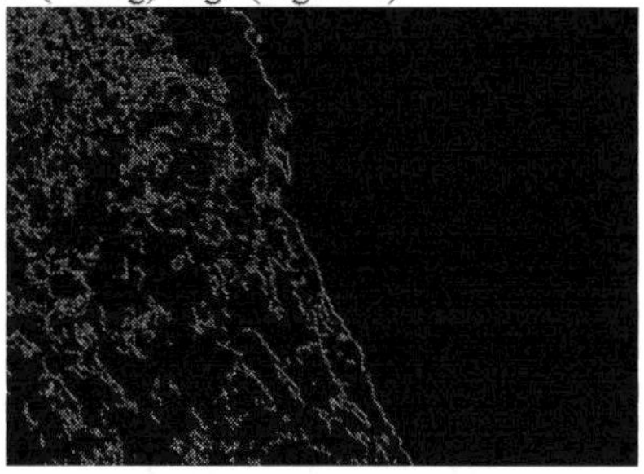

Figure 4. Final borders (edges) of terrain objects.

3 Conclusion

As the result, in images processed with the present algorithm, firstly, various distortions have been eliminated, and secondly, contours of terrain objects are sharp and thin.

References

1. N. Ahmed and K.R. Rao, *Orthogonal Transforms for Digital Signal Processing* (Springer, 1975)
2. R.C. Gonzalez and R.E. Woods, *Digital Image Processing* (Prentice Hall, 2002)
3. V.N. Ruchkin, B.V. Kostrov and E.V. Ruchkina *Communication Technologies 2015 4th Mediterranean Conference on Embedded Computing*, pp. 254-257 (2015)
4. A. Kolesenkov, B. Kostrov, E. Ruchkina and V. Ruchkin, *Proceedings 2014 3rd Mediterranean Conference on Embedded Computing, MECO 2014 - Including ECyPS 2014*, pp. 166-168 (2014)
5. E.V. Ruchkina, N.N. Grinchenko, V.N. Ruchkin, B.V. Kostrov and D.S. Stepanov *2015 4th*

Mediterranean Conference on Embedded Computing, 134-138 (2015)
6. A.N. Kolesnikov, B.V. Kostrov and V.N. Ruchkin, *Proceedings – 2013 2nd Mediterranean Conference on Embedded Computing, MECO–2013*, pp. 263–265 (2013)

ITM Web of Conferences 6, 03005 (2016)
DOI: 10.1051/itmconf/20160603005

Computerized tools in psychology: cross cultural and genetically informative studies of memory

V. Ismatullina[1], I. Zakharov[1], E. Nikulchev[2] and S. Malykh[1, a]

[1]Psychological Institute of Russian Academy of Education, Laboratory of developmental behaviour genetics, 125009 Moscow, Russia
[2]Moscow Technological Institute, 119334 Moscow, Russia

Abstract. In this article we presented the computerized tools for psychological studies of memory. The importance of implementing computerized automated tools for psychological studies is discussed. It has been shown that this tools can be used both for cross-cultural and genetically informative studies. The validity of these tools for cross-cultural and genetically informative studies of memory can be seen as the first step to use automated computerized tools for big data collection in psychology.

1. Introduction

In the modern era of managed care and socialized medicine, a pragmatic concern for practitioners is the extent to which computers can save them time and money. In the recent time period the use of online computerized in psychological research is growing fast. It is becoming standard practice to administer various forms of questionnaires via social networks and special web-sites (e.g., https://www.1ka.si). In addition, the development of touch-sensitive screens, touchpens, and voice-activated software allows examinees to make responses through a variety of input media. Advantages include increased efficiency, the achievement of highly standardized administrations, and automated response recording that would be difficult to accomplish by hand. For example, response times can be recorded with millisecond precision. There is also the possibility of adapting tests to suit the test-taker's ability level [1]. It has been shown, that performance scores is stable across different types of web-browsers and devices [2].

One example of computerized tool for psychological assessment is CANTAB [3]. Although the original aim of the CANTAB was to assess patterns of cognitive decline insubtypes of dementia in elderly participants, it has since been employed in clinical neuropsychological research across age groups. Performance has been characterized in a variety of psychiatric and neurological conditions, including attention deficit hyperactivity disorder [4], schizophrenia [5], affective disorders [6, 7], anxiety disorders [8], Alzheimer's dementia [9] and Parkinson's disease [10]. Today it is of immense practical importanceto obtain baseline data on healthy samples who are representative of different age and ability levels to define a standard against which the performanceof various patient groups can be assessed.

It was empirically demonstrated that task performance is comparable in children who are native versus nonnative English speakers when English is the language used to present each task [11]. In general, children found the computerized testing format to be interesting and motivating. It is worth noting that it is not only the overall testing format that is suitable for children. Children can be tested on the same tests and using exactly the same item sets that are employed in adult studies. Thus, this battery has been successfully used, without modification, to measure cognitive functions in individuals from ages 4 to over 90 years. In 4–12-year-old children, internal consistency coefficients are uniformly high, ranging from .73 for a measure of reaction time latency to .95 [11].

The most current version of the battery is a Windows-based program that operates on a PC platform and utilizes touch screen technology. The battery consists of 13 subtests that include measures of motor skill, visual attention, memory, and working memory. All task stimuli are nonverbal, consisting of geometric designs or simple shapes, and language proficiency is necessary only to understand the instructions prior to task initiation. The validity of the CANTAB for assessing brain–behavior relations in adults has been supported by numerous patients with brain lesions, degenerative disorders, and psychiatric illness [12, 13]. The impacts of psycho-pharmacological treatments on performance have also been examined [14, 15].

Functional magnetic resonance imaging (fMRI) and positron emission tomography (PET) have provided information regarding the neural substrates underlying adults_ performance on several tasks [16]. These findings indicate that the CANTAB is sensitive to the presence of brain dysfunction in adults and that discrimination among subtypes of brain disorder ispossible using profile

[a] Corresponding author: malykhsb@mail.ru

interpretation. It seems promising to use CANTAB tests together with brain activity recording, which are becoming widely available due to the progress in mass production of EEG headsets (e.g., https://emotiv.com/ epoc.php). In this article we want to present the use of computerized tools in cross cultural and genetically informative studies.

2 Material and methods

In our study, we used computerized tests of cognition, The Cambridge Neuropsychological Test Automated Battery [3]. CANTAB is relatively new to the field of quantitative genetic studies, using the accuracy and rigour of computerised psychological testing whilst also allowing for a wide range of ability avoiding ceiling and floor effects in the young [14] and old [17], respectively. As have been noted, the tests are culture and language free (and can even be administered without verbal instruction).

The testability of CANTAB in different samples has been showed in clinical and normal samples. At the same time there are only few studies dedicated to availability of using CANTAB tests in children population [11, 18]. CANTAB has been reported to have high applicability in the evaluation of children. In 4–12-year-old children, internal consistency coefficients are uniformly high, rangingfrom .73 for a measure of reaction time latency to .95 for performance on the self-ordered search task. We showed that reliability of SWM and PRM preformancescoresreliabilityis .71–.73.

We used two CANTAB subtests, Spatial Working Memory and Pattern recognition Memory in several experiments [19, 20]. We used memory subtests as memory is one of the most important cognitive functions which ensures unity an dintegrity of human behavior. Memory consists of a number of different entities relying on different brain systems. Memory can be categorized according to the nature of the material memorized. Investigation of unique features of visual recognition and spatial working memory is particularly interesting due to the fact that it contributes to a broader understanding of memory mechanisms ingeneral.

All tasks were administered through the use of a touch-screen computer.

2.1 Spatial Working memory test

Spatial Working Memory (SWM) task is self-ordered serial search task, where the participants were shown a group of boxes on the computer screen. They were told that a token was hidden beneath one of the boxes on the screen and they had to search through the boxes to find it. Participants did this by touching a box to discover whether or not a token was hidden beneath it. After participants found the token, they were shown the same set of boxes and instructed to find the next token. Participants were told that once a token had been found under a particular box, the box would never again hide a token. In a set of trials, each box eventually had a hidden token beneath it. Thus, to perform this task with the fewest number of errors, the participants needed to remember which of the boxes had previously hidden a token within a set of trials. The number of boxes on the screen, under which the participants needed to find the tokens determined the level of working memory load. Either four, six, or eight boxes were presented on the screen at one time. As the memory load increased from four to six to eight boxes, the participants needed to remember whether or not a token had been previously located under a larger number of boxes and over a larger number of trials. After a participant had found every token in a set of boxes, both the color and position of the boxes changed to begin the next set of trials; the dimensions of the boxes did not change throughout the task. Each memory load condition (i.e., number of boxes on the screen) was presented four times, with the four 4-box sets followed by the four 6-box sets and then the four 8-box sets. Thus, a total of 72 tokens needed to be located in 12 search sets. To insure that participants understood the task, testing began with a practice set in which targets were hidden sequentially beneath three search boxes.

2.2 Pattern recognition memory test

Pattern Recognition Memory (PRM) is a test of visual pattern recognition memory in a 2-choice forced discrimination paradigm. This test is sensitive to dysfunction in medial temporal areas of the brain and relatively insensitive to dysfunction in the frontal lobe. The subject is presented with series of 12 visual patterns, one at a time, in the center of the screen. The patterns are designed so that they cannot easily be given verbal labels. In the recognition phase, the subject is required to choose between a pattern they have already seen and a novel pattern. In this phase, the test patterns are presented in there verse presentation. The sub-test is repeated with a new set of 12 patterns to be remembered.

2.3 Statistical analysis

In our study we used two approaches: cross-cultural and genetically informative designs. To compare the groups in cross-cultural approach we analyzed standard descriptive statistics and performed a univariate ANOVA.

The contributions of genetic and environmental influences on individual differences in cognitive abilities were estimated using the structural equation modeling [21]. The data from MZ and DZ twins are used to estimate the contributions of the following components of phenotypic variance: additive (A) and non-additive (D) genetic factors, shared (C) and non-shared (E) environmental factors. The last component also includes the estimation of variance that comes from measurement error.

3 Results

3.1 Experiment 1. Cross-cultural study

3.1.1. SWM subtest. The study involved 289 adolescents, 172 of them were from Kyrgyzstan and 117 – from Russia (Mean age 12.9 years, SD=2,12 years).The participants were assessed using the SWM subtest. To compare the groups by country we performed a univariate ANOVA. There were no significant differences in means across countries (Between errors: F [1, 287]=0.022, p=0.881; Total errors: F [1, 287]=0.038, p=0.846; Strategy F [1, 287]=0.687, p=0.408; see also Table 1). It should be noted that means and standard deviations in Russian and Kyrgyz adolescents corresponded with the CANTAB norms.

3.1.2. PRM subtest. The study involved 343 adolescents, 223 of them were from Kyrgyzstan and 120 – from Russia (Meanage 12.9 years, SD=2,19years).

To compare the groups by country we performed a univariate ANOVA. There were no significant differences in means across countries, but there were difference in the number of correct answers. Though it was significant, the effect size of 1 correct answer is negligible (Meanlatency: F[1,343]=0.778, p=0.378; Correctanwsers: F[1,343]=8.195, p=.023; see also Table 2).

It should be noted that means and standard deviations in Russian and Kyrgyz adolescents corresponded with the CANTAB norms.

Table 1. Descriptive statistics for SWM test.

		Mean	SD	SE	95% CI
Betweenerrors	Kyrgyz	38.86	19.496	1.487	[35.93, 41.79]
	Russian	38.52	18.025	1.666	[35.22, 41.82]
Strategy	Kyrgyz	35.09	5.057	0.386	[34.33, 35.85]
	Russian	35.54	3.659	0.338	[34.87, 36.21]
Totalerrors	Kyrgyz	39.50	19.799	1.510	[36.52, 42.48]
	Russian	39.05	18.288	1.691	[35.70, 42.40]

Table 2. Descriptive statistics for PRM test.

		Mean	SD	SE	95% CI
Mean latency	Kyrgyz	1970.39	480,56	33.35	[35.93, 41.79]
	Russian	1920.57	470.43	45.57	[35.22, 41.82]
Correct anwsers	Kyrgyz	20.63	2.57	0.168	[34.33, 35.85]
	Russian	21.45	2.42	0.230	[34.87, 36.21]

3.2 Experiment 2. Genetically informative study

Previously, different authors reported the results of research in specific cognitive abilities such as processing speed, working memory, spatial ability and verbal ability in which have shown heritabilities that range from 30% to 60% in both young and elderly subjects. Such studies have employed the cognitive tests such as the 'pencil and paper' tests used in the Hawaii Family Study of Cognition [22] and 'Working Memory Span' tasks [23]. However, these testing procedures of testing doesn't allow for studying the pure cognitive component of the task [24]. In a study of executive functions, Friedman [25] showed that 31-71% of individual differences can be explained by genetic factors, while the environmental impact range from 50 to 71%.

3.2.1. SWM subtest. Our genetically informative sample for SWM subtest consisted of 688 adolescences (339 twin pairs, MZ=118, DZ=143) aged from 10 to 16 years (mean age 12.99, SD 2.18).

Cross-twin correlations of "Between errors" WM measure were 0.592 for MZ and 0.352 for DZ. The individual differences in "Between errors" measure were explained by additive genetic (A= 60%) and non-shared environmental (E= 40%) effects. For "Total errors" parameter the cross-twin correlations were 0.594 for MZ and 0.350for DZ. Most suitable model was also genetic (A = 60%, E = 40%). "Mean time to last response 8 boxes" measure was explained by shared environmental (C= 41%), and non-shared environmental (59%) effects. Cross-twin correlations for "Strategy" measure were 0.406 for MZ and 0.151 for DZ. For this parameter most suitable model was additive genetic model where A = 39% and E = 61%.

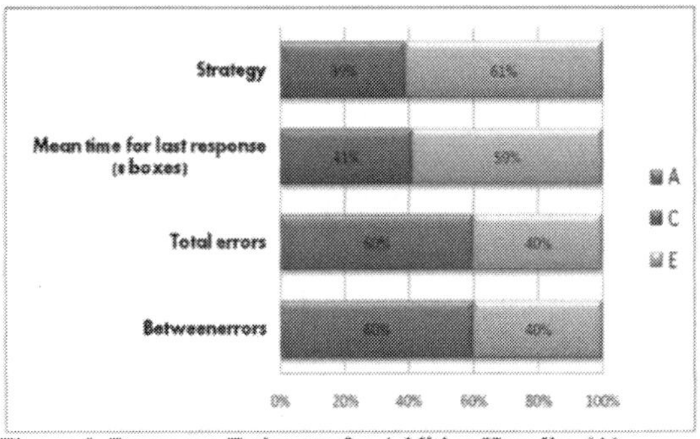

Figure 1. Parameter Estimates for Additive Heredity (A), Common Environment (C), and Unique Environmental Influences (E) by Equation Modeling of SWM test

MZ co-twin correlations were higher than DZ co-twin correlations for most variables. All variables were tested for assumption of ACE estimation. After testing "Within errors", "Double errors", "Mean time to first response (8 boxes)" parameters were excluded from model fitting test.

3.2.2. PRM subtest. The PRM sample included 339 twins pairs (118 MZ, 221 DZ), aged from 10 to 17 years (mean age 13, SD 2.19).

Cross-twin correlations of "Mean correct latency" PRM measure were 0.39 for MZ and 0.14 for DZ. The individual differences in "Mean correct latency" measure were explained by additive genetic (A= 37%) and non-shared environmental (E= 63%) effects. For "Number correct" parameter the cross-twin correlations were 0.33 for MZ and 0.29 for DZ. Most suitable model was full model where A = 13%, C = 22%, and E = 64%.

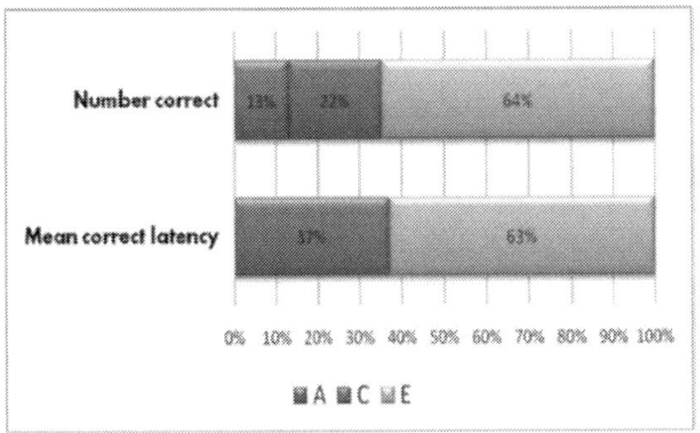

Figure 2. Parameter Estimates for Additive Heredity (A), Common Environment (C), and Unique Environmental Influences (E) by Equation Modeling of PRM test

Thus, different measures of pattern recognition memory were associated with additive genetic and common environment factors with substantial impact of non-shared environment.

4 Conclusions

It is important for psychological studies today to keep up with current trends such as using big data for research. Computerized tools provide incredible source of information given wide prevalence of social media and web-site in everyday people life. It gives unique chance to enlarge study samples that can be invaluable for such areas as cross cultural or genetically informative studies [27, 28]. We showed that CANTAB is sutiable for that purpose. CANTAB, like other computerized tests, has limitations. It may be important for practitioners, in formulating treatment to facilitate the collection and storage of vast amounts of normative developmental and clinical data, that can lead to new hypotheses and knowledge regarding cross cultural, genetic, and environmental sources of individual differences.

References

1. B.L. Roper, Y.S. Ben-Porath and J.N. Butcher, Journal of Personality Assessment, **65**, 358 (1995)
2. A. Chetverikov and P. Upravitelev. Behavior Research Methods (2015)
3. E. Strauss, E.M.S Sheman and O. Spreen, *A Compendium of Neuropsychological Tests: Administration, Norms, and Commentary (3rd. Ed)* (Oxford University Press, 2006)
4. T.W. Robbins, M.A. Mehta and B.J. Sahakian. Science, **290**, 2275 (2000)
5. R. Elliott, P.J. McKenna, T.W. Robbins and B.J. Sahakian, Psychological Medicine, **25**, 619 (1995)
6. B.C. Beats, B.J. Sahakian and R. Levy. Psychological Medicine, **26**, 591 (1996)
7. R. Elliott, S.C. Baker, R.D. Rogers, D.A. O'leary, E.S. Paykel, C.D. Frith, R.J. Dolan, and B.J. Sahakian. Psychological Medicine, **27**, 931 (1997)
8. D.M. Veale, B.J. Sahakian, A.M. Owen and I.M. Marks, Psychological Medicine, **26**, 1261 (1996)
9. K.W. Lange, B. J. Sahakian, N.P. Quinn, C.D. Marsden and T. W. Robbins. Journal of Neurology, Neurosurgery & Psychiatry, 58, 598 (1995)
10. A.M. Owen, J.L Iddon, J.R. Hodges, B.A. Summers and T.W. Robbins, Neuropsychologia, 35, 519 (1997)
11. M. Luciana and C.A. Nelson, Developmental Neuropsychology, 22, 595 (2002)
12. K.S. Fowler, M.M. Saling, E.L. Conway, J.M. Semple and W.J. Louis, Journal of the International Neuropsychological Society, 3, 139 (1997)
13. S. Rahman, T.W. Robbins and B.J. Sahakian, Dementia and Geriatric Cognitive Disorders, 10, 15 (1999)
14. J.T. Coull, H.C. Middleton, T.W. Robbins and B.J. Sahakian, Psychopharmacology, 120, 322 (1995)
15. R. Elliott, B.J. Sahakian, K. Matthews, A. Bannerjea, J. Rimmer and T. W. Robbins. Psychopharmacology, 131, 196 (1997)
16. A.C.H. Lee, A.M. Owen, R.D. Rogers, B.J. Sahakian and T.W. Robbins, Utility of CANTAB in functional neuroimaging, pp. 366-378 (2000)
17. B.J. Sahakian, R.G. Morris, J.L. Evenden, A. Heald, R. Levy, M. Philpot and T.W. Robbins, Brain, **111**, 695 (1988)
18. C.R. De Luca, S.J. Wood, V. Anderson, J. Buchanan, T. M. Proffitt, K. Mahony and C. Pantelis, Journal of Clinical and Experimental Neuropsychology, **25**, 242 (2003)
19. V. Ismatullina, I. Voronin, A. Shelemetieva and S. Malykh, Procedia – Social and Behavioral Science, **146**, 353 (2014)
20. Y. Davydova, V. Ismatullina, I. Voronin, O. Ovcharova, E. Sabirova and S. Malykh, Procedia – Social and Behavioral Sciences, **86**, 419 (2013)
21. M. Neale and L. Cardon. *Methodology for Genetic Studies of Twins and Families* (Springer, 1992)
22. J.C. DeFries, R.C. Johnson, A.R. Kuse, G.E. McClearn, J. Polovina, S.G. Vandenberg and J.R. Wilson, Behavior Genetics, **9**, 23 (1979)
23. M.K. Healey and A. Miyake, Quarterly Journal of Experimental Psychology, **62**, 733 (2006)
24. P. Schatz and J. Browndyke, The Journal of head trauma rehabilitation, **17**, 395 (2002)
25. N.P. Friedman, A. Miyake, S.E. Young, J.C. DeFries, R.P. Corley and J.K. Hewitt, Journal of Experimental Psychology: General, **137**, 201 (2008)
26. I. Zakharov, V. Ismatullina and S Malykh, Theoretical and Experimental Psychology, **7**, 79 (2014)
27. I. Zakharov, V. Ismatullina and I. Voronin, Theoretical and Experimental Psychology, **8**, in press.

ITM Web of Conferences 6, 03006 (2016)
DOI: 10.1051/itmconf/20160603006

System analysis of sagittal plane human motion wearing an exoskeleton using marker technology

Sergey Jatsun[1, a], Sergei Savin[1], Boris Lushnikov[1] and Andrey Yatsun[1]

[1]*Southwest State University, Department of mechanics, mechatronics and robotics, 305040 Kursk, Russia*

Abstract. This paper discusses various methods of obtaining time functions for joint angle that describe a exoskeleton's motion during sit-to-stand motion. This article demonstrates that functions obtained by solving the inverse kinematics problem can be effectively used as inputs to the control system of the robot. Comparison with experimentally data obtained using marker technology is done.

1 Introduction

Nowadays systems composed of two main elements- man and machine have become more common in robotics. These systems include devices called exoskeletons which are used to extend human abilities and enhance performance. The interaction of these two components determines the quality of the system as a whole.

A new generation of exoskeletons that allows a person to move even in the case of damage of the lower extremities recently came into service. In addition it becomes possible to significantly expand human capabilities when a person performs tasks that impose high demands on endurance and physical strength.

Obviously the creation of such devices is possible with a well-developed theory of the functioning of "man-machine" systems with particular emphasis being given to control. This also demands consideration of the man-machine interaction. Common problems in the theory of walking mechanisms have been developed in [1-10] and other publications. The focus of those publications is controlled walking which includes a wide range of problems such as gait generation and motion planning [1–3, 5, 10], stability [2, 4] and obstacle negotiation [8, 9]. At the same time we should note that for a normal person walking is preceded by the process of standing up. The problem of performing controllable motion when standing up is not as well studied as walking. There is a number of medical and technical papers discussing different aspects of sit-to-stand motion [11–17]. In papers [11–13] the use of robot suits that help paraplegic patients [11–12] and elderly people [13] to stand is discussed. Papers [14–15] analyze the use of fuzzy logic applications in exoskeletons performing this kind of motion with emphasis on the use of wearable sensors. Paper [17] discusses the use of an assistant robot that helps a person to stand up. In paper [18] experimental data obtained from studying sit-to-stand motion of a person was shown and different methods of approximating it by smooth functions were compared.

[a] Corresponding author: teormeh@inbox.ru

After analysing the amount of presented work we can conclude that there hasn't been enough research in the area of experimental study of the motion of a person wearing an exoskeleton during the process of standing up as well as the analysis of methods of verification, processing and application of such data.

In this work an experimental study of a motion of a human wearing exoskeleton is carried out. We will use the data obtained from experiment discussed in the paper [18]. The measurements are done with sensors and using visual markers and camera footage to obtain certain kinematic parameters. The data is used to produce trajectories of exoskeleton parts that will drive the machine from sitting to standing position. This approach of obtaining such trajectories is an alternative to the one proposed in [19] where the trajectories were generated by solving the inverse kinematics problem. The advantage of using experimental data to generate the trajectories is the possibility of taking into account more individual features of the moving patterns of a person wearing an exoskeleton, thus making the machine more adaptive for the user.

2 Statement of the problem

The person's position is determined by generalized coordinates. In this paper we consider the case when a system of three generalized coordinates defines the orientation of the shin, hip and trunk. These parts of the human body execute plane-parallel motions whilst the foot remains stationary. Hence it turns out that the person's movement can be considered as that of a four-link mechanism with one fixed link (fig. 1).

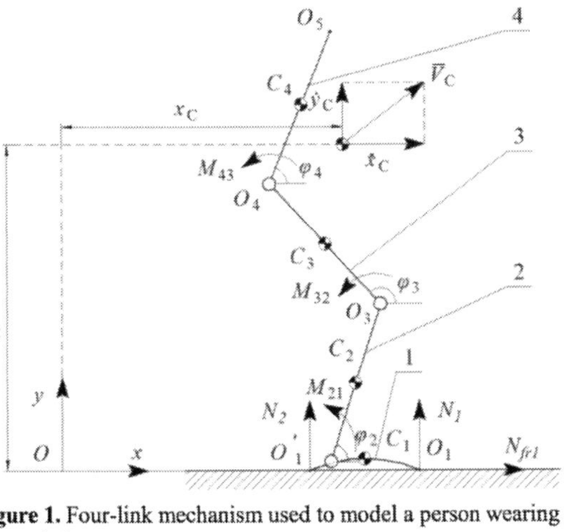

Figure 1. Four-link mechanism used to model a person wearing an exoskeleton.

The shin's orientation is determined by angle φ_2, the hip's orientation – by angle φ_3, and the trunk's orientation – by angle φ_4. The links have length l_i and mass m_i, $i=\overline{1,4}$. $M_{i,i-1}$ are torques acting on the *i-th* link.

The forward kinematics of the mechanism are described by the following expressions:

$$\vec{r}_{Ci}^{\,(0)} = \begin{bmatrix} x_{O1} + \sum_{j=1}^{i-1} l_j \cos(\varphi_j) + 0.5 l_i \cos(\varphi_i) \\ y_{O1} + \sum_{j=1}^{i-1} l_j \sin(\varphi_j) + 0.5 l_i \sin(\varphi_i) \end{bmatrix}, \quad (1)$$

$$\vec{r}_{Oi+1}^{\,(0)} = \begin{bmatrix} x_{O1} + \sum_{j=1}^{i} l_j \cos(\varphi_j) \\ y_{O1} + \sum_{j=1}^{i} l_j \sin(\varphi_j) \end{bmatrix}, \quad (2)$$

where $\vec{r}_{Ci}^{\,(0)}$ and $\vec{r}_{Oi}^{\,(0)}$ are radius vectors, describing position of points C_i and O_i respectively; x_{O1}, y_{O1} - coordinates that describe the position of point O_1.

Assuming $x_{O1} = y_{O1} = 0$ the position of the center of mass (CM) of the mechanism is described by the vector $\vec{r}_C^{\,(0)}$ (see [18]):

$$\vec{r}_C^{\,(0)} = \begin{bmatrix} x_C \\ y_C \end{bmatrix} = \begin{bmatrix} \sum_{i=1}^{4} K_i \cos(\varphi_i) \\ \sum_{i=1}^{4} K_i \sin(\varphi_i) \end{bmatrix}, K_i = \left(\sum_{j=i}^{4} m_j - 0.5 m_i\right)\left(\sum_{j=1}^{4} m_j\right)^{-1} l_i. \quad (3)$$

We will consider the case when the person's CM moves along a line described by a parametric equation during the process of standing up. Then we can solve the inverse kinematics problem and obtain expressions for φ_2 and φ_3 that drive the CM along that trajectory:

$$\varphi_2 = -\cos^{-1}\left(\frac{\|b\|^2 + K_1^2 - K_2^2}{2K_1\|b\|}\right) + \cos^{-1}\left(\frac{b_1}{\|b\|}\right),$$
$$\varphi_3 = \cos^{-1}\left(\frac{\|b\|^2 + K_2^2 - K_1^2}{2K_2\|b\|}\right) + \cos^{-1}\left(\frac{b_1}{\|b\|}\right), \quad (4)$$

where $b = \begin{bmatrix} x_C^*(t) - K_1\cos(\varphi_1) - K_4\cos(\varphi_4) \\ y_C^*(t) - K_1\sin(\varphi_1) - K_4\sin(\varphi_4) \end{bmatrix}$, $t \in [t_1 \quad t_2]$.

and $x_C^*(t), y_C^*(t)$ are functions that give parametric representation of the CM's trajectory. φ_4 can be chosen arbitrarily provided that for any value of φ_4 it should be possible to form a triangle with sides K_2, K_3 and $\|b\|$. We will choose φ_4 to be a polynomial function

$$\varphi_4 = \sum_{p=1}^{4} a_p^{(\varphi 4)} t^p, t \in [t_1 \quad t_2].$$

We should note that before starting the verticalization process the mechanism should relocate its center of mass such that the mechanism would be statically stable. This can be done by lowering the 4-th link. We will call this part of motion the "preliminary phase". A similar kind of motion is performed by a person when standing up from a chair. The motion of the 4-th link during preliminary phase is described by a polynomial function

$$\varphi_4 = \sum_{p=1}^{4} b_p^{(\varphi 4)} t^p, \ t \in [t_0 \quad t_1).$$

The obtained expressions are shown in fig. 2. The time interval 0<t<1 s corresponds to the preliminary phase.

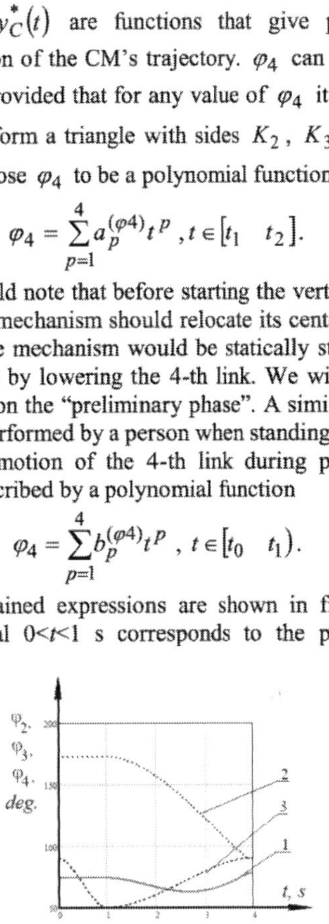

Figure 2. Graphs of 1 - φ_2, 2 - φ_3, 3 - φ_4.

We should note that in practice if all computations are done on the robot's on-board computer the use of expressions (4) may not be optimal. Using a spline approximations for functions φ_2 and φ_3 might speed up computations by alleviating the need for computing inverse cosines.

The dynamics of the mechanism can be described by three equations of motion:

$$\ddot{\varphi}_2(J_{C2} + l_2^2(\frac{m_2}{4} + m_3 + m_4)) + \ddot{\varphi}_3(m_3 + 2m_4)\frac{l_2 l_3}{2}\cos(\varphi_3 - \varphi_2)$$
$$+ \ddot{\varphi}_4 m_4 \frac{l_2 l_4}{2}\cos(\varphi_4 - \varphi_2) + \dot{\varphi}_3^2(m_3 + 2m_4)\frac{l_2 l_3}{2}\sin(\varphi_2 - \varphi_3) +$$
$$+ \dot{\varphi}_4^2 m_4 \frac{l_2 l_4}{2}\sin(\varphi_2 - \varphi_4) =$$
$$= -g\frac{l_2}{2}(m_2 + 2m_3 + 2m_4)\cos(\varphi_2) - \mu_2\dot{\varphi}_2 + M_{21} - M_{23}.$$

$$\ddot{\varphi}_3\left(J_{C3} + m_3\frac{l_3^2}{4} + m_4 l_3^2\right) + \ddot{\varphi}_4 m_4 \frac{l_3 l_4}{2}\cos(\varphi_4 - \varphi_3) +$$
$$+ \ddot{\varphi}_2(m_3 + 2m_4)\frac{l_2 l_3}{2}\cos(\varphi_2 - \varphi_3) + \dot{\varphi}_2^2(m_3 + 2m_4)\frac{l_2 l_3}{2}\sin(\varphi_3 - \varphi_2) +$$
$$+ \dot{\varphi}_4^2 m_4 \frac{l_3 l_4}{2}\sin(\varphi_3 - \varphi_4) =$$
$$= -g\frac{l_3}{2}(m_3 + 2m_4)\cos(\varphi_3) - \mu_3(\dot{\varphi}_3 - \dot{\varphi}_2) + M_{32} - M_{34}.$$

$$\ddot{\varphi}_4\left(J_{C4} + m_4\frac{l_4^2}{4}\right) + \ddot{\varphi}_3 m_4 \frac{l_3 l_4}{2}\cos(\varphi_3 - \varphi_4) +$$
$$+ \ddot{\varphi}_2 m_4 \frac{l_2 l_4}{2}\cos(\varphi_2 - \varphi_4) + \dot{\varphi}_2^2 m_4 \frac{l_2 l_4}{2}\sin(\varphi_4 - \varphi_2) +$$
$$+ \dot{\varphi}_3^2 m_4 \frac{l_3 l_4}{2}\sin(\varphi_4 - \varphi_3) = -\frac{1}{2}g l_4 m_4\cos(\varphi_4) - \mu_4(\dot{\varphi}_4 - \dot{\varphi}_3) + M_{43}.$$

From these equations we can derive expressions for torques $M_{i,i-1}$ as functions of generalized coordinates and their derivatives. The graphs of $M_{i,i-1}$ are shown in fig. 3.

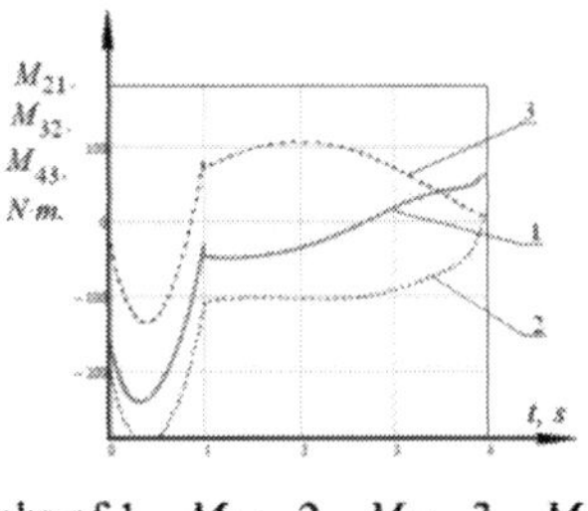

Figure 3. Graphs of 1 - M_{21}, 2 - M_{32}, 3 - M_{43}.

We observe that during the preliminary phase the torque graphs have a parabolic shape and after the end of this phase they rapidly change their form, producing small peaks at $t = 1$ s. This peak appears because of the instantaneous change in the second derivatives of φ_2, φ_3, φ_4.

In practice it is not always possible to use the torques obtained by inverse dynamics to control a mechanical system. Small disturbances that were not taken into account when building the model can lead to loss of stability of the mechanism. To amend this feedback control is used (see fig. 4).

Here we consider a control system with a MIMO (multi input multi output) controller. Details on the implementation of this control strategy for an exoskeleton can be found in paper [18]. The graphs of φ_2, φ_3 and φ_4 obtained for the case with feedback control are shown in fig. 5.

The graphs shown in fig. 5 are very similar to the ones shown in fig. 2. There is a slight difference during the preliminary phase. Graphs of torques $M_{i,i-1}$ generated by the control system (see fig. 6) show a more visible difference from the graphs shown in fig. 3.

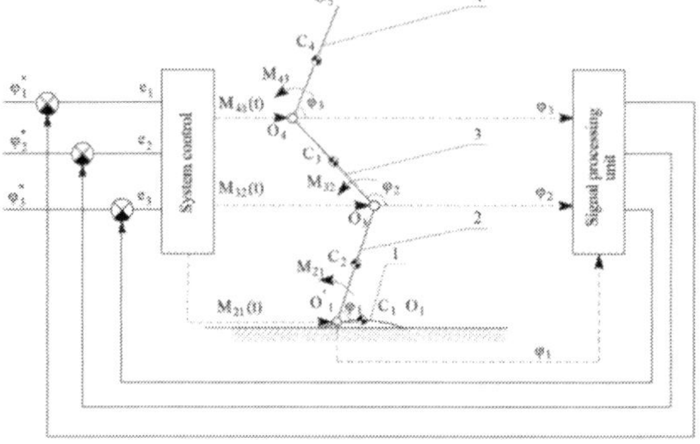

Figure 4. Mechanism with feedback control system.

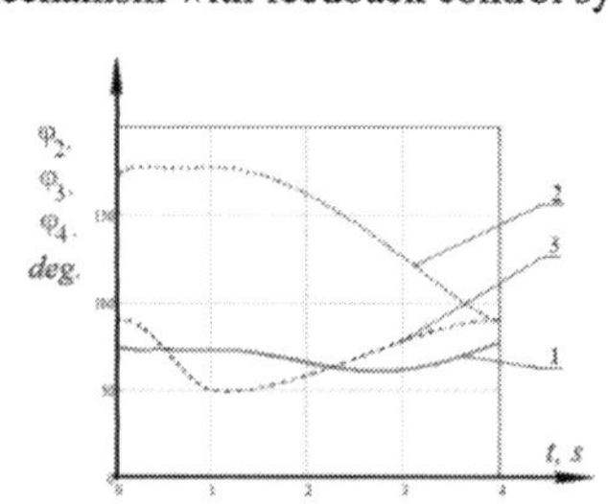

Figure 5. Graphs of 1 - φ_2, 2 - φ_3, 3 - φ_4 obtained for the case with feedback control.

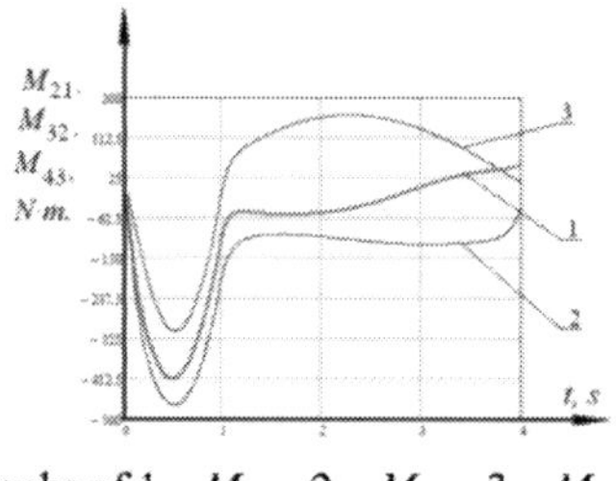

Figure 6. Graphs of 1 - M_{21}, 2 - M_{32}, 3 - M_{43} obtained for the case with feedback control.

We note that the peaks observed earlier are smoothed out, while the shape of the graphs is mostly preserved. This indicates that feedback control is well suited for implementation of this type of motion.

3 Experimental study

In the last section we showed that the graphs of joint angles obtained by solving inverse kinematics problem and angles that come from solving equations of motion for the mechanism are similar, which suggest that it is possible to use feedback control to implement this type of motion of a four link mechanism. At the same time we should take into account the fact that the motion of the exoskeleton is performed both by the mechanism and the operator. If the motion is unnatural for the operator they will feel discomfort which may become an important issue if the person wears the exoskeleton daily.

To study the difference between the human's sit-to-stand motion and the motion discussed in the previous section we will use experimental data derived from experiments done in the laboratory of the department of Mechanics, Mechatronics and Robotics, Southwest State University. The sensor suit can be equipped with visual markers that allow use of cameras and video processing to obtain kinematic parameters of the motion. Fig. 7 shows the human in the rising process, wearing measuring system built in the laboratory. Some details of the experiments can be found in paper [19].

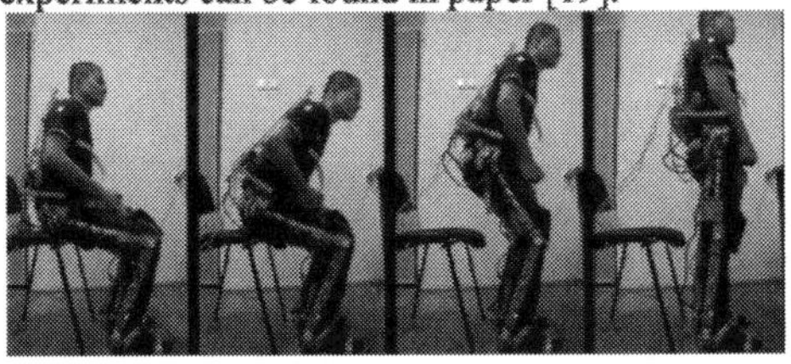

Figure 7. A person in the process of standing up.

The experimental setup shown in figure 6 consists of a seven-link mechanism that can be fixed on a human body such that the links are attached to the body parts by straps. When motion takes place in sagittal plane with the legs moving synchronously the three pairs of links move identically, which is why it is possible to use the four link mechanism as a model for this case. Each link has an accelerometer fixed on it in such a way that allows the use of the accelerometer for measuring angular displacements. Every joint is equipped with an encoder. The links strapped to the person's feet are equipped with pressure sensors.

The corresponding numerical dependences are shown in fig. 8.

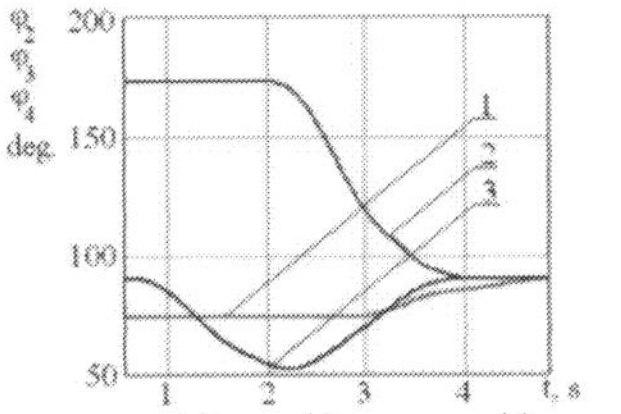

1, 2 and 3 – graphs $\varphi_2(t)$, $\varphi_3(t)$ and $\varphi_4(t)$, respectively

Figure 8. Experimental data after smoothing process.

The graphs shown in fig. 8 were obtained after averaging by a sliding window.

After comparing experimental data with expressions obtained by solving inverse kinematics problem we should not that the person in the experiment stands up faster, there are differences in the range of joint angles and at the end of the motion he stands up right with all angles being equal 90 degrees. The use of inverse kinematics to drive the exoskeleton into such a configuration presents great difficulty, because that is the mechanism's singular position. The difference in speed can be accounted for by changing the functions, $x_C^*(t), y_C^*(t)$ and parameter t_I.

It is possible to use experimental functions of joint angles as the control system's inputs. It is advantageous to approximate these functions by smooth functions.

In paper [19] various ways to approximate such experimentally obtained graphs by smooth functions are presented. It was shown that approximation by trigonometric polynomials has disadvantages in the constant parts of the graphs. Approximation by spline functions was shown to give more advantages.

To construct an approximation of the experimentally obtained graphs $\varphi_2(t)$, $\varphi_3(t)$ and $\varphi_4(t)$ we divide functions $\varphi_2(t)$ and $\varphi_3(t)$ into three portions and $\varphi_3(t)$ into four sections, as was done in [19]. Let this partitioning occur at the points corresponding to the time instants: $t_{21} = 3.48$ sec, $t_{22} = 4.93$ sec for the graph $\varphi_2(t)$, and $t_{31} = 2.69$ sec, $t_{32} = 4.4$ sec for the graph, $\varphi_3(t)$, and $t_{41} = 1.38$ sec, $t_{42} = 2.56$ sec, $t_{43} = 4.03$ sec for the graph, $\varphi_4(t)$. The first section and the last section of each spline are specified by a zero order polynomial and the rest is defined by a seventh order polynomials.

To calculate the polynomial coefficients, we can write the following conditions:

$$\begin{cases} S_2(t_{21}) = \varphi_2(t_{21}) \\ S_2(t_{22}) = \varphi_2(t_{22}) \\ \dot{S}_2(t_{21}) = 0 \\ \ddot{S}_2(t_{21}) = 0 \\ \dddot{S}_2(t_{21}) = 0 \\ \dot{S}_2(t_{22}) = 0 \\ \ddot{S}_2(t_{22}) = 0 \\ \dddot{S}_2(t_{22}) = 0 \end{cases} \quad \begin{cases} S_3(t_{31}) = \varphi_3(t_{31}) \\ S_3(t_{32}) = \varphi_3(t_{32}) \\ \dot{S}_3(t_{31}) = 0 \\ \ddot{S}_3(t_{31}) = 0 \\ \dddot{S}_3(t_{31}) = 0 \\ \dot{S}_3(t_{32}) = 0 \\ \ddot{S}_3(t_{32}) = 0 \\ \dddot{S}_3(t_{32}) = 0 \end{cases} \quad \begin{cases} S_4(t_{41}) = \varphi_4(t_{41}) \\ S_4(t_{42}) = \varphi_4(t_{42}) \\ S_4(t_{43}) = \varphi_4(t_{43}) \\ \dot{S}_4(t_{41}) = 0 \\ \ddot{S}_4(t_{41}) = 0 \\ \dddot{S}_4(t_{41}) = 0 \\ \dot{S}_4(t_{42}) = 0 \\ \ddot{S}_4(t_{42}) = 0 \\ \dddot{S}_4(t_{42}) = 0 \\ \dot{S}_4(t_{43}) = 0 \\ \ddot{S}_4(t_{43}) = 0 \\ \dddot{S}_4(t_{43}) = 0 \end{cases} \quad (5)$$

where $S_2(t), S_3(t), S_4(t)$ are the spline functions used to approximate the functions, $\varphi_2(t)$, $\varphi_3(t)$ and $\varphi_4(t)$, respectively.

Splines that fit conditions (5) are shown in fig. 9, a). Their first and second derivatives are shown in fig. 9, b) and c).

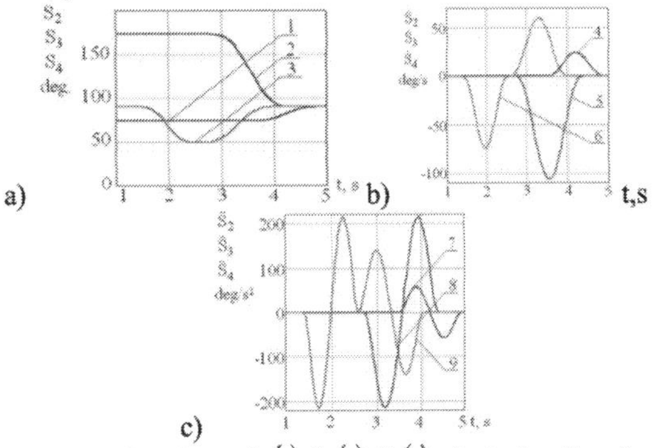

1, 2, 3 – functions $S_2(t), S_3(t), S_4(t)$, 4, 5, 6 – functions $\dot{S}_2(t), \dot{S}_3(t), \dot{S}_4(t)$, 7,8,9 – functions $\ddot{S}_2(t), \ddot{S}_3(t), \ddot{S}_4(t)$

Figure 9. Graphs: a) spline functions, b) first order time-derivatives of spline functions, c) second order time-derivatives of spline functions (see [19]).

It is possible to achieve the absence of function discontinuities in the graphs of the time functions of generalized velocities and accelerations (fig. 9 (b) and (c)) because of the seven order spline functions.

4 Conclusion

This paper discusses the approach to obtain and study trajectories the sit-to-stand motion of an exoskeleton. A comparison between the trajectories obtained by solving inverse kinematics problem and the ones from solving equation of motion was carried out. It was shown that the obtained time functions of generalized coordinates can be used as an input to the feedback control system to produce the desired motion. Experimental data collected from experiments carried out at the department of Mechanics, Mechatronics and Robotics at Southwest State University was used to assess how much that motion disagrees with natural human movements during standing up process. The results of the comparison were discussed. It was noted that it is also possible to use the experimental data as input to the control system. To do that approximation by spline functions was done.

Acknowledgments

Work is performed with RSF, Project № 14-39-00008

References

1. S. Kajita, F. Kanehiro, K. Kaneko, K. Yokoi and H. Hirukawa, *2001 IEEE/RSJ International Conference on Intelligent Robots and Systems, 2001. Proceedings,* **1**, 239-246 (2001)
2. S. Kajita, F. Kanehiro, K. Kaneko, K. Fujiwara, K. Harada, K. Yokoi and H. Hirukawa, *IEEE International Conference on Robotics and Automation, 2003. ICRA'03,* **2**, pp. 1620-1626 (2003).
3. K. Harada, S. Kajita, F. Kanehiro, K. Fujiwara, K. Kaneko, K. Yokoi and H. Hirukawa, IEEE/ASME Transactions on Mechatronics, **12**, 53 (2007)
4. S. Kajita, M. Morisawa, K. Miura, S. Nakaoka, K. Harada, K. Kaneko and K. Yokoi, *2010 IEEE/RSJ International Conference on Intelligent Robots and Systems (IROS)*, pp. 4489-4496 (2010)
5. Q. Huang, K. Yokoi, S. Kajita, K. Kaneko, H. Arai, N. Koyachi and K. Tanie, IEEE Transactions on Robotics and Automation, **17**, 280 (2001)
6. R. Sellaouti, O. Stasse, S. Kajita, K. Yokoi and A. Kheddar, *2006 IEEE/RSJ International Conference on Intelligent Robots and Systems*, pp. 4909-4914 (2006).
7. H. Arisumi, S. Miossec, J.R. Chardonnet and K. Yokoi, *IEEE/RSJ International Conference on Intelligent Robots and Systems, IROS 2008*, pp. 668-675 (2008)
8. E. Yoshida, C. Esteves, T. Sakaguchi, J.P. Laumond, and K. Yokoi, *2006 IEEE/RSJ International Conference on Intelligent Robots and Systems*, pp. 827-832 (2006)
9. B. Verrelst, O. Stasse, K. Yokoi and B. Vanderborght, *2006 6th IEEE-RAS International Conference on Humanoid Robots*, pp. 117-123. (2006)
10. O. Brock and O. Khatib, The International Journal of Robotics Research, **21**, 1031 (2002)
11. A. Tsukahara, Y. Hasegawa and Y. Sankai, *IEEE International Conference on Rehabilitation Robotics, ICORR 2009*, pp. 211-217 (2009)
12. A. Tsukahara, R. Kawanishi, Y. Hasegawa and Y. Sankai, Advanced robotics, **24**, 1615 (2010)
13. H.G. Jun, Y.Y. Chang, B.J. Dan, B.R. Jo, B.H. Min, H. Yang and J. Kim, *2011 IEEE International Conference on Rehabilitation Robotics (ICORR),* pp. 1-5 (2011)
14. S.M. Taslim Reza, N. Ahmad, I.A. Choudhury, & R.A.R. Ghazilla, Sensors, **14**, 4342 (2014)
15. O. Salah, A.A. Ramadan, S. Sessa, A.A. Ismail, M. Fujie and A. Takanishi, International Journal of Automation and Computing, **10**, 405 (2013)
16. A.M. Mughal and K. Iqbal, *2010 IEEE International Conference on Systems Man and Cybernetics (SMC)*, pp. 568-573 (2010).
17. A.M. López, J. Vaillant, F. Keith, P. Fraisse and A. Kheddar, *2014 14th IEEE-RAS International Conference on Humanoid Robots (Humanoids)*, pp. 817-822 (2014).
18. S. Jatsun, S. Savin, A. Yatsun and A. Malchikov, *Advances in Robot Design and Intelligent Control*, pp. 165-172 (Springer, 2016)
19. S. Jatsun, S. Savin and P. Bezmen, *New Developments in Pure and Applied Mathematics*, pp. 83-87 (2015)

ITM Web of Conferences 6, 03007 (2016)
DOI: 10.1051/itmconf/20160603007

The research of image segmentation algorithms based on Vilenkin-Crestensen functions

Boris V. Kostrov[1, a], Sergey I. Babaev[1], Anastasia G. Svirina[1]

[1]Ryazan state radioengineering university, Electronic computing machines department, 390005 Ryazan, Russia

Abstract The problem of Vilenkin-Crestenson functions (VCF) application to process aerospace images is considered. Theoretical grounds of VCF basis and its construction in the field of m-based numeric systems with operation of inversion by Walsh are discribed. Examples of basic functions system building on the basis of VCF with different bases and their application to image segmentation are shown. Avdvantages of using image segmentation algorithm based on VCF basis are discribed. Band pass spectrum restriction possibilities to highlight borders and edge the regions of similar density are given. Different forms of VCF spectrum restriction and its combinations with thier impact to image segmentation results are shown. Technical vision system application of sugested algorithm are shown. VCF basis abbility to highlight objects to be used in correlation-extreme navigation systems are shown. The experimental results of using VCF in comparasing with traditional Fourie basis are given.

1 Introduction

This paper is connected with general trends to develop aviation technology of the fifth generation as well as with the improvement of computer processing information systems from technical vision systems (TVS) of flight apparatus (FA) that allows to take a fresh look at the mathematical apparatus, which has been so far only of fundamental theoretical interest. Vilenkin-Crestenson functions known since the second half of the 20th century are considered to be such mathematical apparatus.

The increased role of vision systems used together with navigation and FA flight parameters and a priori information presented in the form of digital district maps (DDM) together with increased performance of onboard computing means distinguishes the current stage of aviation science and technology development, which is characterized by growing implementation of various management system types [1–3] in complex objects the activity of which is related to the analysis of a great number of parameters of constantly changing environment. This characterization fully corresponds to modern aircraft design.

The task of building autonomous navigation systems and correlation-extreme navigation systems (CESN) and navigation by means of geophysical fields are of the same type.

2 Theoretical grounds

Efficient use of correlation methods with a combination of images is connected with a number of difficulties relating to the large volume of computational operations [4, 5] and low productivity of onboard systems. In the basic approach to the construction of CESN the phase of preconditioning images processing is used in order to remove redundancy information and to select the elements being the most suitable for correlation algorithms.

This stage is commonly understood as the task of image segmentation [6], by allocating on it uniform brightness regions. The traditional scheme for determining the boundaries based on the methods of spatial differentiation involves the following steps:

- to contrast the image;
- to form a binary image.

A significant disadvantage of such multistage schemes of image processing is the large number of computational operations consequently leading to low performance.

The use of discrete exponential bases to construct extremal correlation algorithms allows to reduce information redundancy of correlated images using the filtering of respective spectral components. Using the mechanism of correlation and filtering in Vilenkin-Crestenson function space based on using the theorems of correlation and convolution it is necessary to introduce the elements of image matrix in the form of N real-valued periodic sequences of data. In this case, properties of correlation and convolution are the same as the properties of cyclic correlation and convolution for discrete Fourier transform [7] (DFT).

[a] Corresponding author: kostrov.b.v@evm.rsreu.ru

2.1 Vilenkin-Crestnson functions

Generally, VCF function is a complex function which can be defined as:

$$VKF(p,x) = w^{\sum_{i=1}^{n} p_i x_i}, \quad (1)$$

where $w = e^{2\pi j/m}$, p_i and x_i are the digits of integers p and x, represented in m-based numeric system.

In the simplest case, when $m=2$ and $w=e^{\pi j}=-1$ VCF is represented by Walsh function system. In another case, if $n=1$, the domain of functions definition is represented as $N=m^n=m$ so that VCF transforms to discrete exponential functions - $def(p,x) = e^{\frac{2\pi j}{N}px}$.

VCF is the function of two equal variables p and x, so any conclusion concerning the one variable can be equally attributed to the other. Consequently, the VCF matrix is symmetric.

VCF is a periodic function with the period of N:

$$VKF(p, x \pm N) = VKF(p,x) \quad (2)$$

Vilenkin-Crestenson system of functions is multiplicative:

$$VKF(p,x)\,VKF(q,x) = VKF(p+q,x) \quad (3)$$

Average value of any VCF with $p \neq 0$ is 0:

$$\sum_{x=0}^{N-1} VKF(p,x) = \left(e^{\frac{2\pi j}{N}pN} - 1\right) \Big/ \left(e^{\frac{2\pi j}{N}p} - 1\right) \quad (4)$$

VCF system is orthogonal:

$$\sum_{x=0}^{N-1} VKF(p,x) VKF(q,x) = \begin{cases} 0, p \neq q \\ N, p = q \end{cases} \quad (5)$$

As VCF are N-periodic functions, then the matrix can be rewritten with a minimum phase generated after subtracting from px integer factor of 2π

The VCF system could be determined both at even and odd interval of N.

VCF could be visualized at the plane as the rotating of unit length vector, whose projection on the abscissa and ordinate give the real and imaginary parts of the functions. The difference lies in the fact that in case of usual functions this vector rotates continuously, while in VCF it rotates abruptly.

2.2 Matrix representation of VCF

We will use only the aggregates of VCF being complete orthogonal systems, i.e. containing N orthogonal functions defined in N interval. Any such system of VCF could be represented as square orthogonal matrix of $N \times N$ size. CCF is a periodic function with m-based rational period, so they are determined on $N = m^n$ interval where m and n are integer numbers.

Alternation of functions in VCF system or arrangement of lines in VCF matrix may be different, which gives the opportunity to build different systems of VCF. The example of such systems is the Kronecker system of VCF. The matrix of this system, which we will denote as **VKF**(m,n) is n^{th} Kronecker factor of discreet exponential function $\mathbf{D_m}$

Let us consider building the system of base functions on VCF basis where the base of $m=4$. For easier understanding of basic functions system formation let $n=2$. The initial matrix of discrete exponential functions has the form:

$$\mathbf{D_m} = \begin{pmatrix} w_0 & w_0 & w_0 & w_0 \\ w_0 & w_1 & w_2 & w_3 \\ w_0 & w_2 & w_4 & w_6 \\ w_0 & w_3 & w_6 & w_9 \end{pmatrix}, \quad (6)$$

where $w = e^{j\frac{2\pi}{m}} = e^{j\frac{2\pi}{4}}$.

The constructive matrix is n[th] Kronecker factor of discrete exponential matrix with $m \times m$ size.

$$\mathbf{VKF}(m,n) = D_{\mathrm{m}}^{(n)}, \quad (7)$$

where (n) means Kronecker factor of $\mathbf{D}$ matrix.

According to (7) the required basis for $m = 4$ and $n = 2$ will be represented as the matrix:

$$\mathbf{VKF}(m,n) = \left(\begin{array}{cccc|c|cccc} w_0 & w_0 & w_0 & w_0 & & w_0 & w_0 & w_0 & w_0 \\ w_0 & w_1 & w_2 & w_3 & \cdots & w_0 & w_1 & w_2 & w_3 \\ w_0 & w_2 & w_4 & w_6 & & w_0 & w_2 & w_4 & w_6 \\ w_0 & w_3 & w_6 & w_9 & & w_0 & w_3 & w_6 & w_9 \\ \hline & \cdots & & & \cdots & & \cdots & & \\ \hline w_0 & w_0 & w_0 & w_0 & & w_0 & w_0 & w_0 & w_0 \\ w_0 & w_1 & w_2 & w_3 & \cdots & w_0 & w_1 & w_2 & w_3 \\ w_0 & w_2 & w_4 & w_6 & & w_0 & w_2 & w_4 & w_6 \\ w_0 & w_3 & w_6 & w_9 & & w_0 & w_3 & w_6 & w_9 \end{array}\right)$$

The resulting matrix is symmetric, i.e. its properties are the same for variables p and x. This property allows to use this transformation in forward and reverse directions without performing the transpose operation of matrices:

$$C = \mathbf{VKF}(m,n) B \mathbf{VKF}(m,n) \quad (8)$$

and

$$B = \mathbf{VKF}(m,n) C \mathbf{VKF}(m,n), \quad (9)$$

where C – spectral coefficients matrix, B – image matrix.

2.3 Using spectrum restriction in VCF base for image segmentation

Spectrum in VCF basis differs from the familiar Fourier spectrum because the component corresponding to the highest frequency falls into the lower-right corner when using the ordering of the spectrum by frequency. VCF spectrum has no symmetry and all of its components have a small amount of information about the image.

Thus, in harmonic analysis in general case we have to face the necessity either to analyse complex components, or consider both the amplitude and phase spectrum to obtain a complete picture. The advantage of VCF spectrum is that most of the information about the image carries the amplitude spectrum.

Let's describe the impact of signal spectrum limitation. Spectrum of processed image can be defined by the formula

$$C(u,v) = \hat{H}(u,v) \cdot B(u,v), \quad (10)$$

where $\hat{H}(u,v)$ – two-dimensional discrete function of frequency attenuation; multiplication is performed elementwise.

Attenuation function of frequency in the simplest case for two dimensional ideal high pass filter has the form:

$$\hat{H}_f(u,v)=\begin{cases}1, \text{если } D_f(u,v)\geq D_f,\\ 0, \text{если } D_f(u,v)<D_f,\end{cases} \quad (11)$$

where D_f – edge frequency, $D_f(u, v)$ – distance from point (u, v) to the beginning of coordinate system.

In VCF spectrum various functions of attenuation corresponding to different variants of two-dimensional filter attenuation of lower frequencies can be offered. Figure 1 shows the diagram of three such variants.

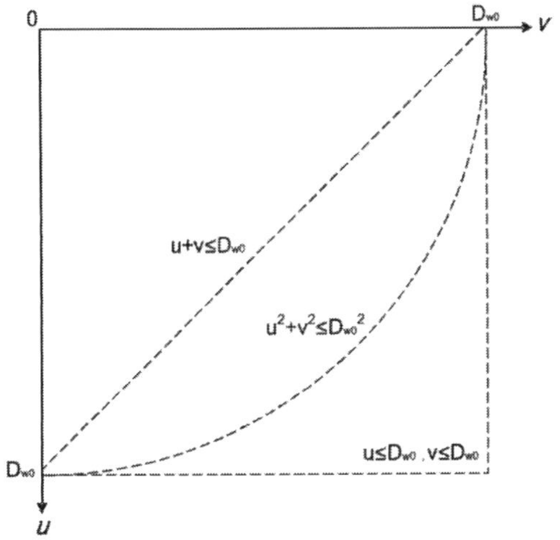

Figure 1. Two-dimensional area where three different borders of three filters are marked

Attenuation function for triangular region restriction option has the form:

$$\hat{H}_w(u,v)=\begin{cases}1, \text{если } u+v\geq D_w,\\ 0, \text{если } u+v<D_w.\end{cases} \quad (12)$$

Attenuation function for round region restriction option has the form:

$$\hat{H}_w(u,v)=\begin{cases}1, \text{если } u^2+v^2\geq D_w^2,\\ 0, \text{если } u^2+v^2<D_w^2.\end{cases} \quad (13)$$

Attenuation function for square region restriction option has the form:

$$\hat{H}_w(u,v)=\begin{cases}1, \text{если } u\leq D_w \text{ и } v\leq D_w,\\ 0, \text{если } u>D_w \text{ или } v>D_w.\end{cases} \quad (14)$$

3 Experiment results

According to this example you can build a VCF system with any fiyld of definition N. Taking into account (2) the basis for m = 4 and n = 4, N = 256 was built, its fragment is given in table 1. This fragment shows that if m = 4 the VCF functions elements are complex.

For research the package of applied programs MATLAB was used, using it in research and image processing was described in [8–10].

Table 1. Formed basis matrix fragment

1+0i	1+0i	1+0i	1+0i	1+0i	1+0i
1+0i	0+1i	–1+0i	0+1i	1+0i	0-1i
1+0i	–1+0i	1 +0i	–1+0i	1+0i	-1+0i
1+0i	0+1i	–1+0i	0–1i	1 +0i	0+1i
1+0i	1+0i	1+0i	1+0i	0–1i	0-1i
1+0i	0–1i	–1+0i	0+1i	0-1i	-1+0i

Test image fragment and its spectrum in VCF basis are presented at Figure 2.

Different types of spectrum fields limits (square, round, triangular) application, according to obtained experimental data did not lead to a significant difference between the results of their application. For further research of spectrum restriction effects was selected round area, as more comparable to the traditional method based on the Fourier basis.

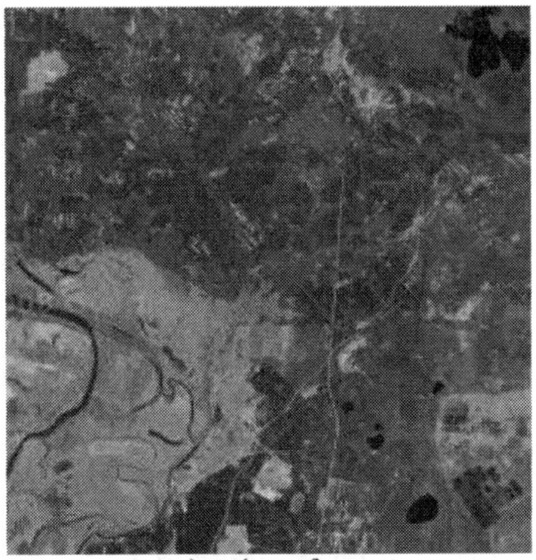

a) test image fragment

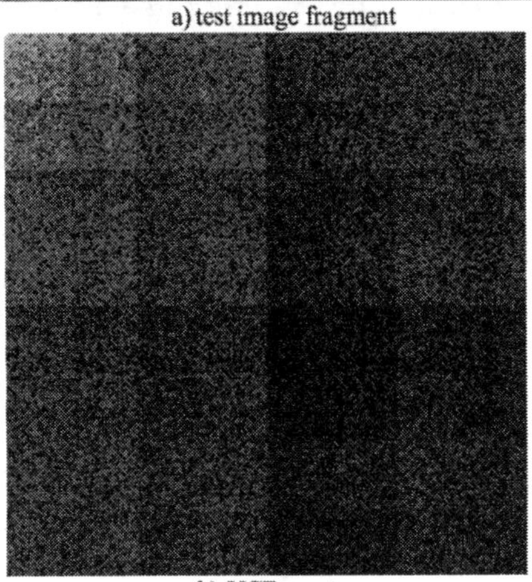

b) VCF spectrum

Figure 2. Test image fragment and its VCF spectrum in constructed basis.

During experimental studies, we analyzed the possible options of spectrum limit. Only high- or only low-frequency spectrum components restrictions did not give the desired results, however, the combination of simultaneous constraints high-frequency and low-frequency components gave results that together with the correction of the resulting image gave a result that can be used to highlight borders of informative regions in image sensors vision systems.

The results of the application so-called band-pass filters that limit the spectrum simultaneously with the upper and lower frequencies are shown at figure 3.

Restored image highlights areas characterized by comparable values of brightness at the respective samples. The line features are aggravated. This property can be used to select informative elements during the navigation systems data preliminary preparation..

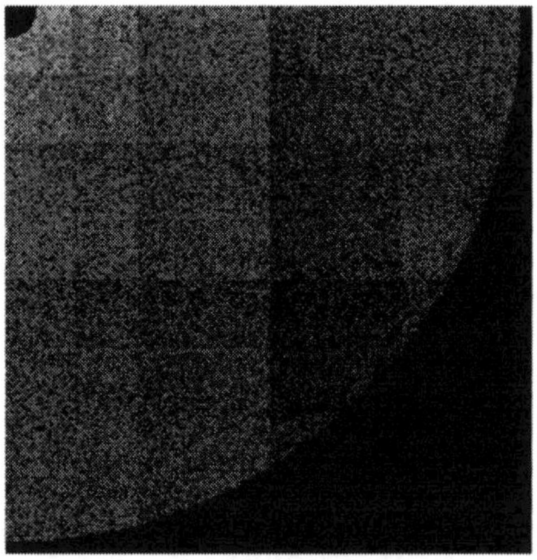

a) restricted spectrum

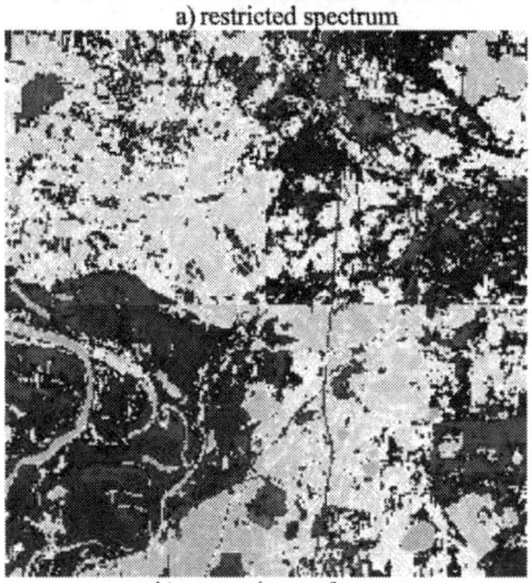

b) restore image fragment

Figure 3. Band-pass filtering results

Limit frequencies boundaries of described bandpass filter may vary based on the need to highlight or detract from certain image properties.

Changing boundary frequencies areas research showed the ability of band-pass filters to clearly identify comparable areas of small extent. The sensitivity of filter to such objects is determined by the frequency of the lower cutoff filter. The average brightness within areas characterized by an upper frequency cutoff of the filter.

The results of the changing cutoff frequencies are shown at Figure 4.

Restricted spectrum filters ability to highlight small areas can be applied in image processing where pixel brightness characterizes the density of the investigated object that can be applied in many related areas: radiography, medicine and so on.

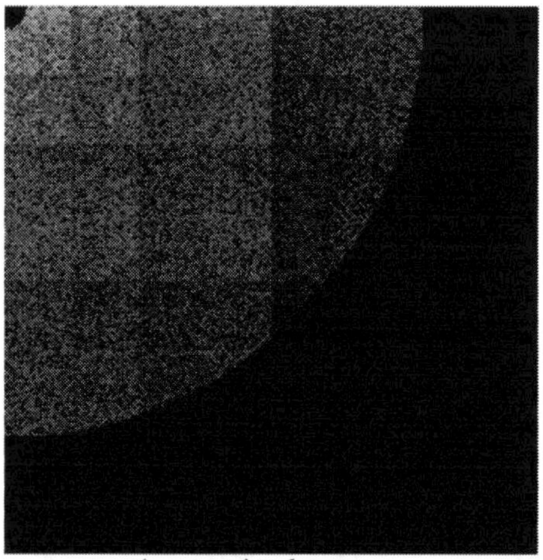

a) restricted spectrum

b) вorestore image

Figure 4. Band-pass filtering results

4 Conclusion

To compare the results of applying restrictive filters we used already studied Fourier basis and execute in it similar transformation of the spectra. The obtained restored image are comparable to the compliance using one of images difference measurement metrics. Similar images will be considered images, if difference between them is less than some threshold. Currently, the most popular and common metrics used to evaluate quality of restored images is the root mean square error (RMSE). MSE can be calculated by the formula:

$$\sigma = \sqrt{\frac{1}{MN} \sum_{x=0}^{M-1} \sum_{y=0}^{N-1} \left(\hat{f}(x,y) - f(x,y)\right)^2} \,. \quad (15)$$

Comparative characteristics for VCF basis to the Fourier basis are shown in table 2. The purpose of this experiment is as follows: in the limitation spectrum of the image four times around the same time the resolution must deteriorate. When you drop limited of spectral components, the image size is reduced four times. In the same spatial area of the image as elements of this image will be the pixel with the average brightness that can be taken as the standard of correctness of the algorithm.

Table 2. Comparative characteristics

Base	VCF	Fourie
Quantity of differentiae pixels	123	117
Mean squre root error (MSE)	0,1589	0,1154
Executing time, s	0,0151	0,0586

Analysis of data in table 2 shows that the proposed method can perform the same functions as the Fourier basis, with comparable quality of results.

References

1. A.N. Kolesenkov, B.V. Kostrov and V.N. Ruchkin, *2nd Mediterranean Conference on Embedded Computing, MECO 2013, Emergencies monitoring and preventing Proceedings*, pp. 263-265 (2013)
2. A. Kolesenkov, B. Kostrov, E. Ruchkina and V. Ruchkin, *3rd Mediterranean Conference on Embedded Computing, MECO 2014, Anthropogenic situation express monitoring on the base of the fuzzy neural networks Proceedings*, pp. 166-168 (2014)
3. A.N. Kolesenkov, B.V. Kostrov, V.N. Ruchkin and E.V. Ruchkina, *4th Mediterranean Conference on Embedded Computing, Algorithms of Fire seat Detection, Modeling Their Dynamics and Observation of Forest Fires via Communication Technologies*, pp.254 -257 (2015)
4. S.E. Umbaugh, *Computer Imaging: Digital Image Analysis and Processing* (CRC Press, 2005)
5. M. Seul, L. O'Gorman and M. J. Sammon, *Practical Algorithms for Image Analysis* (Cambridge, 2000)
6. M. Petrou, P. Bosdogianni, *Image Processing: The Fundamentals* (John Wiley & Sons, 1999)
7. S.W. Smith, *The Scientist and Engineer's Guide to Digital Signal Processing* (California Technical Publishing, 1999)
8. W.L. Martinez, A.R. Martinez, *Exploratory Data Analysis with MATLAB* (CRC Press, 2005)
9. F. Gustafsonand, N. Bergman, *MATLAB for Engineers Explained* (Springer, 2003)
10. C.F. Van Loan, *Introduction to Scientific Computing: A Matrix-Vector Approach Using MATLAB* (Prentice Hall, 1999)

ITM Web of Conferences 6, 03008 (2016)
DOI: 10.1051/itmconf/20160603008

Applied problems of the identification and regression analysis in stochastic structures with multimodal properties

Vladimir Kulikov[1, a], Alexander Kulikov[1], vb.kulikov@yandex.ru

[1]Nizhny Novgorod State Technical University n. a. R. E. Alekseev, Nizhny Novgorod, Russia

Abstract. We have been elaborating an approach founded on the identification of multimodal laws of the complex structure distribution in medicine, biology, chemistry of ultrapure materials and membrane technology as well as in technical applications. The method is based on the formulation and solution of inverse problems in mathematical physics for the respective probability density functions. The verification of the used algorithmic tools is carried out on model limited-scope samples. For stochastic structures and systems under study the method is supplemented with an original option of a regression analysis taking into account the identified stochastic laws displaying numerical parameters into the binary space. The proposed approach has been tested on clinical material in practical medicine.

1 Introduction

Applied problems for the identification of distribution laws with multimodal specificity may be based on the solution of inverse problems in mathematical physics. Nevertheless, there are some approaches based on the classical methods of constructing histograms, the Parzen-Rosenblatt algorithms, the application of the goodness-of-fit criteria for testing of hypotheses regarding stochastic phenomena under study. In publications [1, 2] the issues are discussed, which relate to the selection of the (kernel) weight function in constructing the probability density estimate by the Parzen-Rosenblatt type and the conditions for using sign-variable higher-order kernels to improve the identification algorithm quality. D.B.H. Klein [1] introduced the term of "the admissible weight function" and established the necessary ratios to minimize an integral squared error within the ***L2*** approach and in the assumption of sufficient smoothness of the ***p (x)*** function. In metric C $[-\infty, \infty]$ the admissibility condition may be omitted [2].

The kernel function selection is herewith always limited by a priori suggestion of a researcher on the smoothness of the estimated density and the sample scope.

To this block of problems quite naturally the regression analysis method and the least-squares method are linked up. However, without a proper analysis of the stability of solutions obtained their development, for example, with the approximation of stochastic data by linear varieties with the dimensionality less than the dimension of initial data spaces (method of principal components) is not quite correct.

In publications of a number of the USA scientists, to study the considerable data arrays on the level of gene expression in the mRNA (messenger ribonucleic acid) they initially applied the principal components analysis (PCA), which generated linear representations of uncorrelated components [3].

Later works have already shown in the context of the gene expression the significance of the ICA (Independent Components Analysis), which is especially effective with the assumption of dependence within the data generation process – Liebermeister [4].

The approach using the solution of inverse problems [5] enables to suggest in addition a method combining the said principles for the identification of the distribution densities and regression algorithms. This combination forms a method for the interpretation of experimental data and includes a new version of regression.

The method is universal and its testing has been carried out with the factual material in clinical immunology. It is expected that the results of works such as the solution principles of inverse stochastic problems, correct algorithms, programs will become a tooling in the field of biotechnology and modern "personalized" medicine. As it has been previously shown [5], a number of indicators in immunology have such peculiarities as complex distribution laws. To great disturbances in the immune system (in response to infection or therapy) shall correspond in this case the similar features of processes in non-equilibrium dissipative structures leaving the point of dynamic equilibrium.

The structure changes from the normal state to the chaotic one with loosing its conservative properties, its parameters outreach normal ranges. With further dynamics external fluctuations become significant in bifurcation points.

[a] Corresponding author: vb.kulikov@yandex.ru

In mathematical immunology the most known are the studies of the viral infections dynamics.

The review www.cytokines.uspb.ru of S.R. Kuznetsov, V.I. Shishin (the St. Petersburg State University) includes the latest achievements of mathematical immunology.

The review "describes examples of the effective use of major mathematical methods in order to study the immune system dynamics, to estimate values inaccessible for the direct measurement, to carry out computer experiments".

It is noted that "in the recent decade a number of new measurement techniques has come into existence, which enable to make high-quality analyzes *in vivo*, it is worth noting among them the multiphoton microscopy and the resonance transfer of fluorescence energy; the X-ray investigation, MRI and ultrasonic diagnostics have been also extended to a micro-level" [6, 7].

The results of monitoring for such processes (experimental data) require correct interpretation models and stable processing algorithms.

2 Statement of identification and verification problems

The method used by the author for the reconstruction of distribution densities with many modes [5] is supplemented by stochastic verification: the analysis of "simulated" distributions with known properties.

For this purpose based on a number of fundamental work results there were carried out tests of samples generated under programs developed by the corporate authors under the direction of Professor B.Y. Lemeshko (NSTU, Novosibirsk) - following different distribution laws as well as their identification as per the suggested approach. The sample volume L had herewith a range of 100-600 units.

The random variable samples were studied, which related to theoretically quite continuous distributions: gamma-, Cauchy, exponential, normal, Weibull distribution.

Samples of discrete readings of "reference" distribution densities were studied but in fact there were excluded from the consideration the mechanisms for the generation of singular distributions typical to theoretically fractal realizations (Cantor "dust" etc.).

For example, such factual data may be obtained by using the EGEG method (EGEG – Elektrogastroenterography). They possess the persistence characteristic of singular (fractal-like) processes. It is noted in the author's publications that the use of regularizing methods for the identification of distribution laws combined with prediction algorithms enables also to expand significantly the scope of the analysis for fractal-like structures of any natural, technological, biological, social and other nature.

The research results show that the conclusion persists on the available peculiarities of composite (Cauchy, exponential) distributions, which result in the need for an increasing number of smooth functions to represent the approximate solution: about 20 harmonics for Cauchy, 10–23 for exponential distributions. In the latter case the shape of the distribution curve is structurally improved by increasing the sample scope from 100 to 300 units.

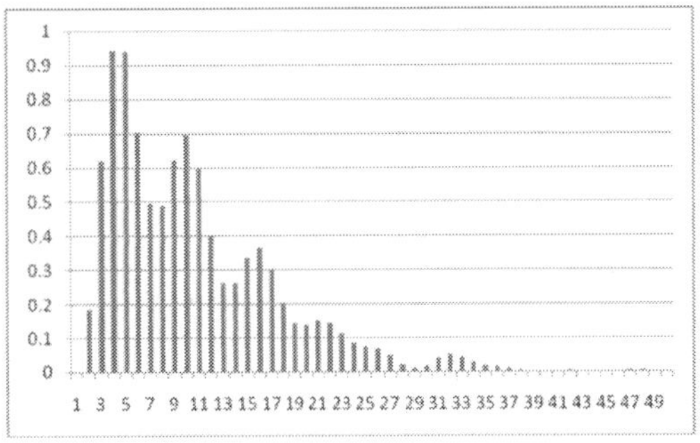

Figure 1. The Reconstructed Exponential Distribution (L=300 readings)

A similar conclusion may be also made in normal law at increasing the sample scope. Though, even for $L = 100$ the goodness-of-fit criteria give a close fit of the sample to the Gaussian distribution.

The proposed method fundamentally distinguishes the main difference for samples generated as per the normal type (scopes were studied with $L = 100, 200, 300, 600$), that is the number of expansion terms N is low and is within the range of $N = 2$-4. The solution expansion coefficients in the system of trigonometric functions for the sample of 200 units have, for example, the following value: $\alpha = 0.01393$; $\beta = - 0.83330$; $\gamma = - 0.50181$.

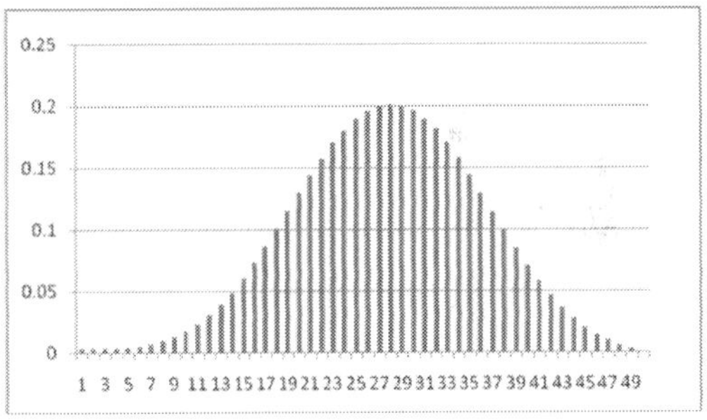

Figure 2. The Reconstructed Normal Distribution (L=300 readings)

The authors suppose that this is a fundamental feature for this type of distributions. The identified property of random variables with the Gaussian probability density distribution may be used as an additional argument in the identification of the distribution law in applied mathematical statistics. The "bell" form of the Gaussian distribution and the three sigma rule are complemented by new identification criterion.

3 Regression approach

To complement identification algorithms for multimodal stochastic structures, the following regression approach is suggested, which takes into account the identified distribution laws.

The fact is that a researcher prior to constructing any mathematical model has a priori information on the interval of hypothetical or practically accepted norms for desired variable x_i (usually assumed with a significant margin). Such norm may be a permissible instrumental error, limits of the physiological norm for clinical evidence, the stability zone in adjustment, the degree of the technological component quality (the said concept is not to be confused with the norm of elements for normalized spaces of the functional analysis). This a priori information on the parameter norm is taken as the basis for the proposed method. Let us consider its essence on the example of immunological clinical tests within the framework of the suggested regression model.

We assume normal ranges for each indicator according to recognized intervals. We convert an initial data table to a binary-form table, i.e., we compress the initial information in a special way. In this case, in each binary matrix cell the figure of one is recorded, if the resultant value of the initial cell is within the normal range, and zero is recorded, if otherwise. Zero values for binary matrix elements are resulting from those readings, which are above or below the norm. The actual testing of the method was carried out with a binary matrix for several dozens of patients in 12 parameters of blood, lymph, hormones. There were obtained unique vectors displaying the status of patients with respect to the "parameter norm" characteristics.

The coded data differ from the original laboratory data in the most comprehensive provision of information about an object just by two gradations. As shown below, it gives the considerable obviousness and simplicity for the analysis in the "patient-index" plane, forms in a naturally way algorithms and methods for the immunological data processing. Such binary matrices are used in the graph theory.

The regression coefficients shall be determined from the matrix equation $\boldsymbol{Az} = \boldsymbol{u}$ (the system coefficients - are binary digits) with regularization algorithm. The identified parameters belong to the set $\mathbf{R}^1$ and assign the mathematical model of a process or structure.

Further, if the norm-limits of the index are very wide, they may be "compressed" by using the form of the previously identified distribution density for each immunological parameter. In this case, information is used on the availability or lack of higher modes, their offset to one or another direction of the parameter norm, calculated point estimates in the form of the mathematical expectation and variance. Such compression may be performed based on the Jaynes' maximum entropy principle or otherwise. Then, the algorithm for determining the regression coefficients is repeated.

Let us compare the proposed interpretation method to the classical regression model in the standard Euclidean space of the initial data. In the both cases, the linear regression recovery occurs on a sample of short length ($L = 50 \ldots 100$).

3.1 Classical Regression Model Based on the Initial Data Matrix

1. The linearization of the model of a phenomenon under study based on a volitional decision.

2. The method for the recovery of sample regression coefficients by the linear regularization methods in case of ill-conditioning system.

3. The ranking of the solution components in a natural way – by small values of the eigenvalues corresponding to these components; the assessment of the each individual factor actual contribution to the output value is generally hindered.

4. There is no possibility for the direct functional relationship of this regression model with hypothetical or practically accepted norms for each variable x_i (permissible error range, the limits of physiological norm for clinical evidence, the stability zone in adjustment, etc.).

5. The introduction of the quantitative characteristics for the solution components, the variable regression and factors is hindered from the position of a universal and formalized approach if the information theory.

6. There is only one degree of freedom in the study of the behavior characteristics of the subject under study – an increase in the sample length.

3.2 Regression Model Based on the Binary Coding of Input Data Matrix - Capabilities and Peculiarities of the Approach

1. The linearization of the model of the phenomenon under study in a natural way is the display of input data into binary space $\mathbf{D[0.1]}$ according to the sign of belonging to the field of norm x_i.

2. The mode for the recovery of sample regression coefficients is by the linear regularization methods under ill conditio sine qua non (ill conditioning).

3. The regression recovery by binary matrices occurs with the certain decorrelation of sample data (both on lines and columns of the matrix operator), thus, increasing the degree of the problem correctness.

4. The availability of the natural bond of this regression model with hypothetical or practically accepted norms x_i.

5. The second degree of freedom is added in the study of the behaviour characteristics of the subject of research- the change in the length of the field of the norm for each variable model (usually the contraction) on the input principle of the error regularization - the principle of Pareto (80%–20%), Jaynes or any other.

6. The said approach implements a new operator on $\mathbf{D}$ (binary matrix), the relevant regression model and it checks the properties of the object or phenomenon under study for its stability with respect to the norm of the subject parameter.

7. Such functions derivative from the "matrix of norms" are introduced in a natural way as the monitoring frequency of the number of norms on the input parameter vector, the model arguments in the sample series, their cumulative characteristics as well as the "measure" of the output value amount in binary units of the norm.

8. The ranking of the solution components apparently occurs in the following combination: a) a natural

component of the rank – by small values of the eigenvalues corresponding to these components – as per the method of solving the problem based on conditionality, b) the assessment of the partial contribution of each factor to the output value pursuant to the homogeneity of the binary description of vectors of input parameters and the output value.

9. The introduction of the quantitative characteristics of the variable regression and factors becomes possible from the viewpoint of the information theory – each model factor for estimates of probability for occurrence of ones and zeros is considered as the source of messages with respective entropy *H*.

The proposed method is in general enhances greatly possibilities for the correct, formalized and systematic study of phenomena in interpretation problems in engineering, economics, medicine and other fields.

Acknowledgement

The work was performed with the financial support by the RF Ministry of Education and Science (Agreement №14.577.21.0098 on Granting Aid Grant of 08.26.2014, Unique Project IdentifieRFMEFI57714X0098

References

1. D.B.H. Cline, Ann. Statist, **16**, 1421 (1988)
2. H.-G. Muller, Ann. Statist, **12**, 766 (1984)
3. O. Alter, P.O. Brown and D. Botstein, Proceedings of the National Academy of Sciences, **100**, 3351 (2003)
4. W. Liebermeister, Bioinformatics, **18**, 51(2002)
5. V. Kulikov, Applied Mathematical Sciences, **9**, 6827 (2015)
6. A.R. Kherlopian, T. Song, Q. Duan, M.A. Neimark, M.J. Po, J.K. Gohagan and A.F. Laine, BMC Syst. Biol., **12**, 74 (2008)
7. T.M. Przytycka, M. Singh and D.K. Slonim, Brief Bioinform., **11**, 15 (2010)

ITM Web of Conferences 6, 03009 (2016)
DOI: 10.1051/itmconf/20160603009

Methodology of profiling network operations in software for distributed information systems

Oleg Lukyanchikov[1, a], Vyacheslav Filatov[2], Dmitry Biryukov[1] and Evgeniy Pluzhnik[1]

[1] Moscow Technological Institute, Leninskiy pr., 38A, Moscow, Russian Federation, 119334
[2] Moscow Technological University, Vernadskogo pr., 78, Moscow, Russian Federation, 119454

Abstract. Network operations take up large amounts of resources in distributed systems and in this case, existing profilers can correctly construct the execution tree of the program code and correctly identify the runtime, so you need other methods that will allow finding bottlenecks in the. The article discusses various approaches on the time efficiency assessment software, and based on a new method for profiling distributed systems, also an example of its use on a system built with agent technology-relational mapping. As a demonstration of the proposed method there's presented an example of the system, built using the technology of agent-relational mapping that performs network operations in distributed transactions. Thus showing that for the ease of using this technology we have to pay with lots of operations to monitor network transactions.

1 Introduction

One of the important qualities of information systems and applications is the temporal efficiency of the implementation. Particularly acute it affects the efficiency indicators of QoS in cloud systems.

Already in the process of developing software the developer has an idea about a possible "narrow" places, as in the limitation of time is taken more convenient implementation, but not more effective. For effectiveness evaluation in the development lifecycle there is only one stage in the course of which it is possible to detect and, if necessary, correct the most resource-intensive places software. Using life cycle according to [1], this stage is the test program, including the conduct of pre-state, interagency, acceptance and other testing and correction of program and program documentation according to test results. At this stage, functional testing, security testing is the performance testing includes load testing, stress testing, stability testing or reliability and volume testing. Profiling relates to load testing.

Profiling is the process of observing and recording metrics about the behavior of regions of code or an entire application. The profiling software may be implemented by the programmer in the process of developing software, implementing in code, fixing the execution time of basic operations, but more convenient after the development using CASE-tools called profilers. Today there are many profiling tools that are built into the composition of development tools and distributed separately (TAU Performance System, MPI Parallel Environment, GProf, Intel VTune Performance Analyzer), which allow us to construct the execution tree for the source code, control operations and even the control of multiple threads. Based on the analysis of bottlenecks using profilers, the developer is taking measures to improve the efficiency of implementation, namely: threading operations between threads, and reduces unnecessary passages cycles, selects specialized data storage structures (lists, queues, hash tables, etc.).

Network operations take up large amounts of resources in distributed systems and in this case, the profilers can correctly construct the execution tree of the program code and the right to determine the time, as it is affected by many factors such as:

- the operation is performed on remote compute nodes, whose characteristics are not always known and at the time of the operation accidentally downloaded, so it is not possible to accurately determine the runtime operations;
- network load isn't taken into account;
- number of users constantly changes.

Therefore, profiling methods are not applicable to distributed systems and other methods are needed that will allow to find the system bottleneck.

2 Methodology of profiling distributed systems

There are three approaches to evaluating execution time of a task on a computing resource[2].

1. Analysis of source code, based on an analytical model of internal system algorithms and key

[a] Corresponding author : bidmal@mail.ru

characteristics of the input data, an example of which is considered in [3].

2. Code profiling, during which run the calculations on plank data sets, and determine the system performance for the studied type of code, such as profilers.

3. Statistical methods of forecasting in which is stored results of past runs of the solving, and then used to predict the time of new work, examples of which are described in [4], and a system database for this purpose is described in [5].

Each approach has its limitations and large errors in the evaluation, so they should complement each other and be used together, especially for evaluating the run-time network operations.

For source code analysis and profiling is cost oriented graph that describes the routes code, where program blocks are nodes connected by edges, if the control can pass from one block to another. This graph is built by analyzing program code and using the Profiler, examples of this are described in [6]. When considering distributed systems, the priority for analysis are network operations, so to simplify the graph minor local operations can be neglected. Also in terms of the popularity of UML is more convenient and more correct instead of count to describe the route code of the activity diagram notations in UML, mainly due to the possibility to indicate parallel processes.

The developer of distributed systems knows about the basic processes occurring in the system, which can describe the sequence of actions when a network share, and build a graph or chart of activity. However, the developer uses third-party technologies and libraries for it can submit a "black box" [5]. Also in the analysis of code a developer has to consider many system operations, or to count them is not substantial, neglecting them, therefore, to analyze code not always immediate right. Hence the required experiments and analyze statistically the collected data, confirming the correctness of earlier estimates of operations.

Based on the foregoing, it is proposed the following method for profiling distributed systems:

1. Building a directed graph or chart activity notation in UML to describe the routes code.

2. The mathematical formula for calculating average time of the operations.

3. The tests for evaluating run-time operations, under varying number of computing nodes.

4. The correct mathematical formula of the test results.

5. If the test results failed to clearly confirm the correctness of the formula the addition of artificial delays and step 2, otherwise 6.

6. Definition of bottlenecks in the system, thus impacting the system performance.

3 Profiling distributed systems based on agent-relational mapping technologies

For an example of the proposed method, consider profiling a distributed system, built on the basis of agent-relational mapping technology (ARO), the principles of which are described in [7–9]. This technology is a hybrid technology of object-relational mapping (ORM) and remoting technologies (technologies of remote objects, remote procedure call, and are focused on message processing). As a result, the technology has ARO ORM interface and allows you to perform relational commands (select, update, insert, delete) to the database and other remote locations. This technology, due to its versatility, allows you to build almost any system architecture.

For research distributed system will be built consisting of a single database and a variable number of applications distributed between multiple computing nodes, as shown in Fig. 1. System specifications:

– Compute node 1 CPU Pentium Dual-Core E5200 2.5 GHz, 4Gb RAM, Windows 7 operating system on which the application is the initiator of operations, and note the time of operations and PostgreSQL database on 5 thousand records.

– Many computing nodes as virtual machines, raised on a separate server running VMwareEXSi, for each allocated 1 CPU, 1Gb RAM, Windows XP.

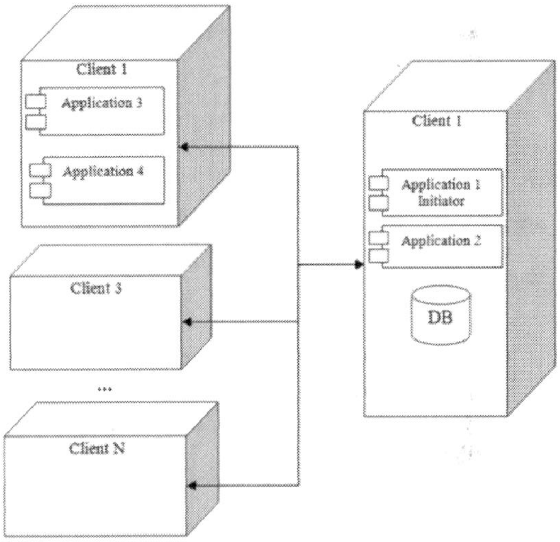

Figure 1. Experimental stand.

Researches on the effectiveness of this architecture are aimed to assess delays in data synchronization during the execution of update operations. This is the following sequence of actions:

– instruction is being generated;

– message with an instruction is sent to all clients and DBs;

– all remote objects on different compute nodes and the application performs the operation asynchronously and if successful, sent back to the initiator a message indicating successful execution, parallel operations are executed on all distributed databases;

– the initiator while finally collecting messages from all clients successfully captures the change and sends all other clients and the DB message with the command commit changes.

Based on the above process the activity diagram notation in UML will be built, as shown in Fig. 2.

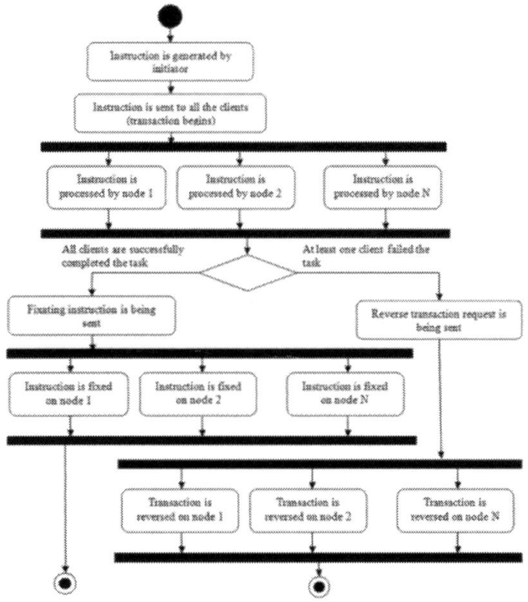

Figure 2. The activity diagram of the update operation for agent-relational mapping technology with UML notation

The average mathematical performance evaluation of a distributed system with distributed databases using the ARO will have the following form:

$$\overline{T}=\overline{t}_g+2\sum_{i=1}^{N+M}\left(\overline{t}_{z_i}\right)+\max\left(\max_{i=1,N}\left(k\overline{T}_{o_i}+\overline{t}_{a_i}\right),\max_{i=1,M}\left(\overline{T}_{db_i}+\overline{t}_{a_i}\right)\right)+\overline{t}_c,$$

where $\overline{T}$ – average estimated time for a single operation; $\overline{t}_z$ – average time before request for operation is sent; $\overline{t}$ – average time of generating SQL request; $\overline{T}_o$ – average time of processing the operation by the object; $\overline{t}$ – average time for reply with operation results; $\overline{T}_{db}$ – average time of processing request on DBMS; $\overline{t}_c$ – average time of operation fixation; N – number of remote nodes; k – number of remote objects on a node; M – number of DBs.

This estimation does not include the loading units, location storing a record in a data structure, the probability of unsuccessful operations and other factors, so all times are the average value. To confirm the mathematical evaluation of the execution time of the update operation (1), conducted a series of experiments, the average results of which are shown in Fig. 3.

As can be seen from the graphs the mathematical evaluation of (1) is true. The deviation of graph values without delay from the values of schedule delay of the operation is different about the forced time delay, thus confirming that this operation will be executed in parallel on all the compute nodes.

A completely different kind of schedule has a delay of data transmission, it has a linear increase as in arithmetical progression, thus showing that the operation data is "narrow" place in the system.

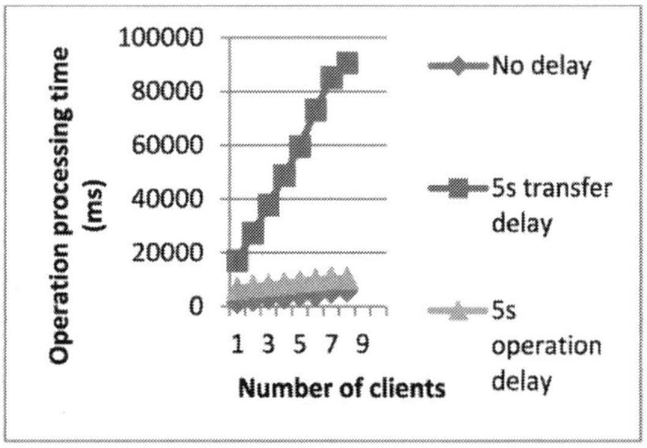

Figure 3. The results of the experiments to assess changes in run-time modification operations from changing the number of clients.

4 Conclusion

The article discusses various approaches on the time efficiency assessment software, and based on this a new method for profiling distributed systems. An example of application using this method is given on a distributed system containing one DB and many clients, built on the basis of technology ARO. The proposed method will more accurately assess the existing architecture of distributed systems, to identify among them the most efficient one and to generate recommendations for the design of new systems.

References

1. ISO/IEC 12207 (2008)
2. M.A. Iverson, F. Ozguner and L.C. Potter, *Proc. Eighth Heterogeneous Computing Workshop (HCW'99)*, pp. 99–111 (1999).
3. D.J. Kerbyson, H.J. Wasserman and A. Hoisie, *International Workshop on Innovative Architecture for Future Generation High Performance Processors and Systems*, pp. 27–37 (2002)
4. M.V. Devarakonda and R.K. Iyer, IEEE Trans. on Software Engineering, **15**, 1579 (1989)
5. E. Pluzhnik; E. Nikulchev and S. Payain, *2014 IEEE World Congress on Services (SERVICES)*, pp. 458-461 (2014)
6. S. Hao, D. Li, W. G. Halfond, and R. Govindan, *2013 35th International Conference on Software Engineering (ICSE)*, pp. 92-101 (2013).
7. E. Nikulchev, E. Pluzhnik, D. Biryukov O. Lukyanchikov and Simon Payain, International Journal of Advanced Computer Science and Applications, **6**, 22 (2015)
8. E. Nikulchev, O. Lukyanchikov, E. Pluzhnik and D. Biryukov, International Journal of Advanced Computer Science and Applications, **7**, 30 (2016)
9. M. Aubakirov and E. Nikulchev, International Journal of Advanced Computer Science and Applications, **7** (2016)

ITM Web of Conferences 6, 03010 (2016)
DOI: 10.1051/itmconf/20160603010

Project management offices in Russian engineering companies

Natalya Novikova[1,a], Nikolay Barchan[1], Elena Vikhodtseva[2], Maria Guseva[2] and Sergei Nikitin[2]

[1]*Moscow Technological Institute, 119334 Moscow, Russia*
[2]*State University of Management, 109542 Moscow, Russia*

Abstract. Project management offices (or PMOs) are becoming a very well known concept and widely used organizational unit which is organized to support and develop project management systems and methodologies in companies in various sectors of economy. PMOs are being organized in more and more Russian engineering companies. However, PMOs have different forms and functions in different organizational context. It is very useful for theory and practice to analyze the real practice and define which characteristics and forms of PMOs are more accepted. The research presented in the article shows that PMOs are very popular among Russian engineering companies and the trends in their development are in line with the trends in other countries and industries.

1 Introduction

Over the last decade, engineering companies in Russia and worldwide have been facing new challenges related to increased competition, accelerated pace of innovations, shortened lifecycles of products, general economic volatility. As a response to these new challenges engineering companies are adopting new managerial frameworks and developing new organizational forms in order to implement more flexible and responsive project management approaches. One of the relatively new project-based organizational forms implemented in some engineering companies is the project management office or PMO. The theoretical aspects of PMOs have been extensively covered in the professional literature [1; 2]. But the empirical research on functions, forms and efficiency of PMOs in engineering companies is not sufficient in the current literature stream.

2 Forms and functions of PMO

Recent studies revealed extreme variety in forms and functions of PMOs [3]. Furthermore, some researchers discovered the high level of instability of PMOs which means that in the same organization PMO can change significantly its form, functions, level of subordination, number and scope of projects under control during short period of time [4]. Hobbs, Aubry and Thuillier (2008) explain these specificities of PMOs in the way that PMOs should be considered as constant organizational innovation that are still in the process of experimentation and search for the best practices [5].

Several attempts to produce the typology of PMOs have been made by several researchers. For instance, Kerzner (2003) identified such types as 'Client PMO', 'Functinal PMO' and 'Corporate PMO' [6]. Crawford (2011) distinguished between 'Control project office', 'Business unit project office', 'Strategic project office'. [1]. Englund, Graham and Dinsmore (2003) proposed the typology of PMOs which included 'Project support office', 'Project management centre of excellence' and 'Program management office' [2]. Kendall and Rollins (2003) identified four different models of PMO: 'Project repository model', 'Coach model', 'Enterprise model' and 'Delivery now model' [7]. There are other typologies of PMOs, but according to the convincing analysis of Dai and Wells (2004) all existing typologies are very vague, do not correspond to each other and do not provide clear basis for classification [8]. They suggest that instead of identification of different types it is more practically usefull and scientifically rigorous to use four dimensions along which PMOs differ. These dimensions are the place of PMO in the organizational structure of a company (level of management), the scope of control (how many projects are under control of PMO), the number of full-time employees in PMO, the number and the nature of functions performed by PMO.

The problem of PMO functions needs more attention because this dimension is the most powerful source of variety of PMOs in companies. Again, as in the case with the types of PMO, different authors propose different lists of PMO functions [4; 8-11]. After the discussion of different lists of PMO functions with the sample of respondents the list elaborated by Dai and Wells (2004) [8] was selected as the most comprehensible and convenient for the purposes of this research. Another advantage of the list suggested by Dai and Wells is that it was used in several empirical researches of PMO forms and functions. This list includes the following PMO functions:

[a] Corresponding author: s_titov@mti.edu.ru

- Development, deployment and support of project management standards and methods;
- Trainings and education in project management area;
- Management of documents and archives, knowledge management;
- Administrative and technical support and help for project managers;
- Consulting and methodological support of project managers;
- Recruiting and talent development in project management area;
- Monitoring and audit of projects;
- Program and portfolio management;
- Financial supervision and budgeting.

3 Research methodology

This research was organized as a survey with the participation of the practicing engineers from Russian engineering companies.

Russian National Association of Engineers was approached and asked for the permission to send the invitation to members of the association to participate in the survey about PMOs in their companies. From 175 members positive responses were received and to these people questionnaires were sent. Correctly and unambiguously filled forms were received from 115 engineers.

The respondents had on average 12 years of work experience and about 5 years of the professional participation in project management activities in their companies. 72% of respondents worked for engineering companies and the rest worked in engineering departments of companies without engineering specialization.

The respondents were asked about their knowledge about PMOs and the existence of PMOs in their companies. Those respondents who reported that PMO were organized in their companies were asked several questions about the forms and functions of their PMOs.

4 Research findings

The answers of the respondents showed that from 115 participants only 17 respondents did not hear about PMOs and did not have any knowledge of them. Another 21 respondents said that they heard of PMOs, but had very vague knowledge of them and never saw them functioning in real practice. Yet another 33 people reported that they had good knowledge of PMOs, their functions and forms, but their companies did not have PMOs. Finally, 44 engineers (from different companies) said that their companies organized PMOs and still have them as functioning organizational entity.

From 44 PMOs in engineering companies 17 (38,6%) were established at the top level of management with a manager of PMO reported directly to CEO. 24 PMOs (54,5%) were organized at the middle managerial level with the subordination to one of the directors of departments. The rest of PMOs (3, or 6,9%) were introduced at the low level of the organizational structure and considered as more technical rather than managerial.

Table 1. Distribution of respondents according to their knowledge of PMO and practical establishment of PMOs in their companies.

Attitude towards PMO	**Number of respondents**	**Number of respondents (in %)**
Lack of knowledge about PMO	17	14,8%
Limited/ vague knowledge about PMO	21	18,3%
Good knowledge about PMO without implementation	33	28,7%
Practical knowledge about PMO with implementation in companies	44	38,3%
Total	115	100%

According to the last group of respondents, the majority of PMOs in Russian engineering companies were organized in the 2010s (see Figure 1).

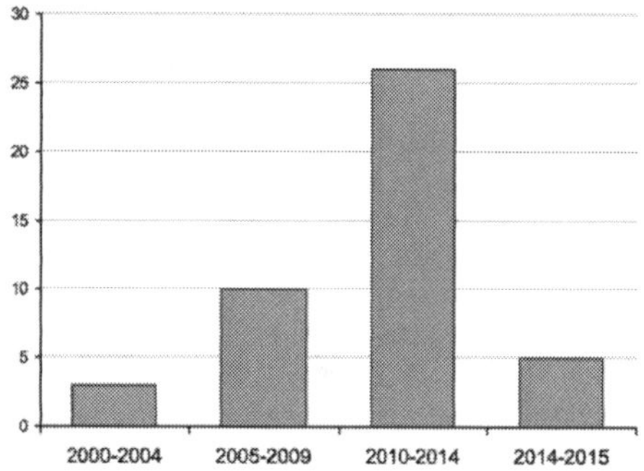

Figure 1. The number of PMOs established in Russian engineering companies

None of the PMOs controlled from 90 to 100% of the company's projects. 12 PMOs supervised from 75 to 89% companies' projects. 19 PMOs had from 50 to 74% of projects under their control. 8 PMOs controlled from 25 to 49% of projects and other 3 PMOs did not have projects under their supervision.

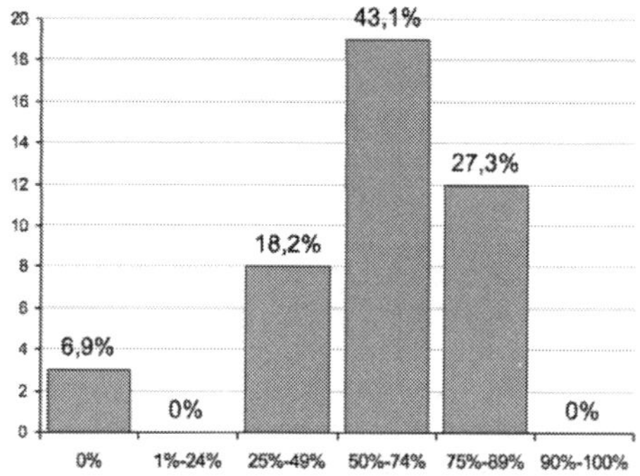

Figure 2. Scope of control of PMOs (in % of company's projects under control)

From all 44 PMOs 14 had the number of staff less than 5 employees, 18 PMOs had from 6 to 10 people of permanent staff and 12 PMOs had the staff with 11 or more employees.

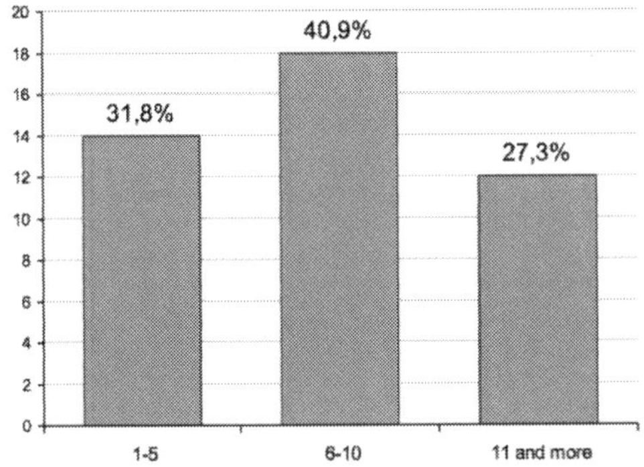

Figure 3. The full-time staff of PMOs established in Russian engineering companies

The respondents which reported the existence of PMO in their companies were asked about the functions that PMOs perform. The list of PMO functions defined above in the article was used in the survey questionnaire. The respondents were able to choose any number of PMO functions from the list. The distribution of the positive answers of respondents across PMO functions is presented in Table 2.

5 Discussion on research results

One of the most interesting findings of the research is the discovery of the fact that PMO in the community of Russian engineering community is a well known concept. The overwhelming majority of the respondents (85,2%) has limited or good knowledge of PMO, its organizational mission and functions. The proportion of engineering companies which already established PMO is rather high. Dai and Wells (2004) [8] analyzed how often PMO is established and used in different companies across various sectors of economy and found that at the highest level PMOs are used in software, communication and hardware companies. But even in these companies the portion of companies with PMO is about 10-15% which is much lower than discovered level in Russian engineering companies. In the research of Dai and Wells (2004) the percentage of engineering companies with PMOs was only 5%. Though that can be explained by the fact that the research of Dai and Wells was made in 2004, and the popularity of PMO has been increasing since that year.

In terms of the forms of PMO the trends in Russian engineering companies is more or less similar to the global trends. The majority of PMOs are established at the middle managerial level (54,2%) with the rather wide scope of control (70,4% of PMOs have more than 50% companies' projects under supervision). The bulk of PMOs has the full-time staff 10 people and less. According to the research by Hobbs and Aubry (2008) which cover more than 200 PMOs in different countries and sectors of economy, the companies tend to organize PMOs at the middle level of authority, with middle-to-high scope of control and with the full-time staff from 5 to 15 employees [12].

Table 2. Performance of PMO functions in Russian engineering companies.

PMO function	Number of respondents which reported about performance of the PMO function in their companies	Number of respondents which reported about performance of the PMO function in their companies (in %)
Development, deployment and support of project management standards and methods	110	95,7%
Trainings and education in project management area	85	73,9%
Management of documents and archives, knowledge management	54	47,0%
Administrative and technical support and help for project managers	52	45,2%
Consulting and methodological support of project managers	44	38,3%
Recruiting and talent development in project management area	23	20,0%
Monitoring and audit of projects	19	16,5%
Program and portfolio management	4	3,5%
Financial supervision and budgeting	2	1,7%
Total	115	100,0%

It is interesting to compare the PMO functions in Russian engineering companies with the functions of other analyzed PMOs. Dai and Wells (2004) investigated the popularity of different functions in about 100 PMOs in different companies. Due to the fact that in this research we used the same list of PMO function it is possible to compare the results. The comparison of the results of two studies is presented in Figure 4.

From Figure 4 we see that such functions as 'Development, deployment and support of PM standards and methods', 'Trainings and education in PM area', 'Recruiting and talent development in PM area', 'Program and portfolio management' and 'Financial supervision and budgeting' are performed in Russian engineering companies almost as frequently as in other companies analyzed by Dai and Wells (2004) [8].

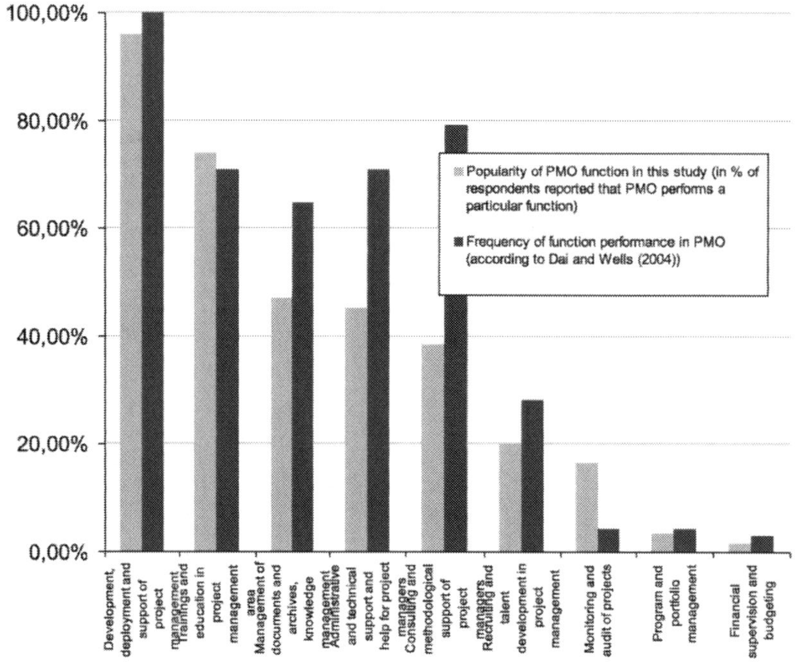

Figure 4. The full-time staff of PMOs established in Russian engineering companies

Functions 'Management of documents, archives and knowledge management', 'Administrative and technical support for PMs', 'Consulting and methodological support of PMs' are performed in Russian engineering companies notable less frequently than in the sample research by Dai and Wells. 'Monitoring and audit of projects' is a more popular function among Russian engineering companies than in other companies. However, admitting all the identified differences, the general patterns of the frequencies of PMO functions are very similar in both studies.

6 Conclusion

It is worth emphasizing that the popularity of PMO among Russian engineering companies is very high by world standards. PMO can be considered as a widely excepted organizational unit which officially established in engineering companies in order to support and develop corporate project management systems and methodologies.

The discovered variety of forms and functions of PMOs in Russian engineering companies are similar to those that were analyzed by other researchers in other companies in the world.

References

1. J.K. Crawford, *The Strategic Project Office* (Marcel Dekker, 2002)
2. R.L. Englund, R.J. Graham and P.C. Dinsmore, *Creating the Project Office: A Manager's Guide to Leading Organizational Change* (Jossey-Bass, 2003)
3. G.M. Hill, Inform Syst Manage, **21**, 45 (2004)
4. B. Hobbs and M. Aubry, PMJ, **38**, 74 (2007)
5. B. Hobbs, M. Aubry and D. Thuillier, Int J Proj Manage, **26**, 547 (2008)
6. H. Kerzner, PMJ, **34**, 13 (2003)
7. G.I. Kendall, and S.C. Rollins, *Advanced Project Portfolio Management and the PMO: Multiplying ROI at Warp Speed* (J.Ross Publishing, 2003)
8. X.C. Dai and W.G. Wells, Int J Proj Manage, **22**, 523 (2004)
9. H. Kerzner, *Project Management Best Practices: Achieving Global Excellence* (Wiley, 2006)
10. S. Pellegrinelli and L. Garagna, Int J Proj Manage, **27**, 649 (2009)
11. K.C. Desouza and J.R. Evaristo, Int J Inform Manage, **26**, 414 (2006)
12. B. Hobbs and M. Aubry, PMJ, **39**, 69 (2008)

ITM Web of Conferences 6, 03011 (2016)
DOI: 10.1051/itmconf/20160603011

Using social network analysis techniques to study the efficiency of interproject communication

Dmitry Plokhov[1, 2], Ilya V. Osipov[1,a] and Gregory Bubnov[1, 2]

[1]Moscow Technological Institute, 119334 Moscow, Russia
[2]Moscow Institute of Physics and Technology, 141700 Dolgoprudny Moscow reg., Russia

Abstract: Traditional performance monitoring techniques in project management are based on classical measures – costs, schedule and scope of work. But focusing our view on these indices and their derivatives we can overlook one of the most important elements of project management – project participants. Degrees of their coordination, cohesion and collaboration directly influence on the extent to which project goals could be achieved. Communications and relations between participants play a vital role of special glue holding project parts together. Besides, communication environment integrate within itself information about all aspects of a project – successes, failures and conflicts. Character of interpersonal relations and structure of communications between participants are proposed as indicators of successfulness or failures. In present report project participants are considered as a social network. Using social network analysis (SNA) techniques provides opportunities to examine links between structural characteristics of interproject communication networks and project performance.

1 Introduction

A project can be viewed as a temporal organization formed within an enterprise for achieving unique goals [1]. In addition to create a unique product, service or result, particular characters of projects are dynamic environment in which a project is managed and high level of uncertainty. Of course, processes optimization and agile management techniques are of high importance for the project success. However, as were rightly pointed out in the article of T. Cooke-Davies [2], project results are delivered by people, not by processes and systems. Interacting each other and the environment, project participants should constantly adopt their work to new conditions and challenges tactics to eventually achieve the major strategic goal – to meet customer needs. Communications and relation between people determine the quality of the processes, and therefore the quality of project management in general [3].

The most common approach for evaluating project management performance is based on comparison of actual project measures with approved constraints on costs, time and specification of work. This approach, that can be rightly called classical, makes possible to get bird-eye view on the situation through a set of formal metrics. Although an analysis by classical metrics and their derivatives is clear and well-formalized, it seems extremely difficult to use such metrics to evaluate impact of major social factors – communications and social relations that that move the project team from efficient to effective [4].

A communication environment acts not only as a data transfer system or a messenger, but it also integrates not only for messaging, but it also integrates all information in broad terms about the project. Project initiation proceeds in parallel with forming of a social ties network, the members of which are the project participants. The communication structure is inevitably interwoven with informal relations that also have great impact on the work environment and complement relations based on functional and hierarchical links [5]. Problems or failures during the work, as well as their overcoming and successes affect participants and how they interact with each other. Thus, on the one hand, participants' places in the network are determined by their formal (functional and hierarchical) positions, on the other hand, by such imprescriptible factors as social prestige, readiness to cooperate, sympathy or antipathy towards others.

The social nature of project management is also reflected in a link between emerging mismatches or contradictions and conflicts between participants. There are two opposing points of view on the role of conflict. Traditional views supporters consider conflicts as a threat to a project and its environment. So conflicts should be avoided. Given the modern behavioral framework in management, conflicts are inevitable parts of the human organization, and with proper approach they can bring benefits and give right clues to resolve contradictions [6]. The study [7] conducted was focused on identifying the main causes of conflict in projects and covered almost all aspects of project management. The general consensus of

[a] Corresponding author: ilya@osipov.ru

proponents of traditional and behavioral viewpoints is that conflicts can be symptoms of problems in project management and, not being solved, potentially lead to damages [8]. In the current research, we aim to investigate a communication structures and their character in projects that were in a conflict state. During the study of three projects, information about communication between the main participants were collected and considered. An analysis of a links between communications structures and the project's success rate is fulfilled.

2 Social network analysis techniques for studying interproject communication

Techniques of social network analysis (SNA) are used extensively for studying of relations within organizations and between them. The main part of such research is based on analysis of corporate communications and information from the participants obtained through surveys and interviews. In relation to the project management, researches interests are targeted on features of interaction within virtual teams and the evaluation of their performance [9, 10], the issues of building effective communication between organization / project members [11], optimal conditions for spreading of practices and knowledge [12].

Communication issues were the central topics of the significant number of researches in the context of studying project management practices in construction and engineering industries. In [13–16] the authors considered the possibility of applying the social networks concept and analysis techniques to improve the efficiency of construction projects. The analysis of the links between the structure of teams' communications and innovative projects effectiveness was undertaken by S. A. Titov [18].

The growth of interest in SNA methods results from their flexibility that allows possibility to explore the communities and organizations of all sizes, to identify and visualize the formal and informal networks, to evaluate the quantitative parameters of communication structures and conduct a comparative analysis on their basis. In addition, several powerful software products, including free, were developed for supporting researchers to use SNA methods. These user-friendly products allow building and analyzing networks of various sizes. All this makes the use of social network analysis methods is very promising for the studies of organization and project communication networks.

2.1 Research methods

Earlier it was noted that communication structures and their character are the essential success factors on projects. From the full variety of project communication issues this study considered links between the structural balance of the project network and the project success rate by the end of the conflict. According to the theory of F. Heider [19], there is structural balance in a social network when in do not contain relations – "positive attitudes (friendship, cooperation) between A and B and between B and C, but negative attitudes (hostility, rivalry) between B and C". It is supposed that balanced networks are more comfortable for participants and more stable than unbalanced. Thus, the conflict should split a network into balanced sub-groups (conflict parties) consisting of like-minded people who share similar points of view.

The studied project networks were built information by using data about communications between the participants by formal and informal ways, directly related to the certain project. Also intensity (evaluated in the form of a numeric attribute) and character (attitude) of communications are taken into account.

The authors distinguished three levels of communication intensity: low, medium and high, which were associated with the values 0, 1 and 2 respectively. Consideration was given to mutual directed communication, i.e. the intensity of the evaluated communications between the certain participants pair was the same from the point of view of each of them.

Character (attitude) of communication communications associated with the "+" sign, if the communications were friendly, i.e. participants had mutual sympathy or common ground, or "–"sign in case of antipathy or difference in views. In each of the projects previously mentioned regarding the subject matter of the conflict. The positions conditionally designated as "Agree", "Disagree" or "Neutral".

The basis for the study was the information about the following three projects:

- *The project A.* 14 participants. The main object: development of the online educational games [19]. The conflict subject: disagreements about the final versions of the game concept and scenarios. Summary of the conflict: disagreements were finally overcome by harmonizing the wishes of all parties, but time was substantially out of schedule. Overall assessment of project results given by the participants is positive.
- *The project B.* 9 participants. The main object: development of an enterprise information system. The conflict subject: different views on technical solutions and disagreements about quality assessment of project results. Summary of the conflict: the parties were not able to reach a consensus which led fail to meet the project deadlines, and, subsequently, the project was cancelled.
- *The project C.* 7 participants. The main object: developing of educational online service [20]. The conflict subject: reforming of the project organization structure, attracting new members. Summary of the conflict: the deadlines were broken; some of the participants were out of the project. A key problem raised by participants was an impossibility of compromise on the conflict issue.

Summary data about communications (intensity and character) are presented in tables 1-3. These tables indicate the participants' position on the matter of the conflicts (A – "Agree"; D – "Disagree"; N – "Neutral").

It should be noted that the projects have been implemented in different organizations and by different teams, even though planned times of project duration had roughly the same.

Table 1. The matrix of communications in the project A.

Participant	A1	A2	A3	A4	A5	A6	A7	A8	A9	A10	A11	A12	A13	A14
A1		2	-1									1		1
A2			1	1								2	1	1
A3				2	1	2		-1				1		
A4						1		1		1		2		
A5							1	2	1					
A6							2	2	1	1	1	1	2	
A7								2	1	2	1			
A8									2	1	2			
A9											1			
A10											1			
A11														
A12													2	2
A13														2
A14														
Position	D	N	D	D	A	N	A	A	N	A	N	N	N	N

Table 2. The matrix of communications in the project B.

Participant	B1	B2	B3	B4	B5	B6	B7	B8	B9
B1		1	1					1	
B2			1	2	2	1	1	2	-1
B3				1				1	
B4					2	2	2	-2	-2
B5						2		-1	-2
B6								-1	-1
B7								2	2
B8									2
B9									
Position	A	A	A	D	D	N	N	A	A

Table 3. The matrix of communications in the project C.

Participant	C1	C2	C3	C4	C5	C6	C7
C1		2	2	-2	1	-1	2
C2			1			1	
C3				-1	1	1	
C4					2	-1	
C5							
C6							
C7							
Position	A	A	A	D	D	N	N

2.2 Analysis of result

The data about the structure of project communications were investigated using the freeware Pajek [23], presented by its authors to open access.

Visualization models of networks' structure are illustrated by graphs whose vertices correspond to the project participants and edges reflects meaningful communication between them. Since initially it was assumed that existed communications were mutual directed, undirected graphs was used for building the models. The models of communication networks for the investigated projects are shown in the figures 1, 3, 5. The communications with positive character are shown by solid line and with positive character – by dashed. The participants' positions in the conflicts are illustrated by color of its vertices: white color is corresponding "Agree", black – "Disagree", gray – "Neutral".

The rule of finding a balanced solution for a particular network can be formulated as follows: the balanced solution should contain that partition of the network into subgroups (clusters) in which all positive ties are within clusters and negative are located between them. It should be given that the formulated rule describes an ideal situation, in which positive and negative ties between network members are placed respectively strictly inside the clusters or outside. It do not occurs always in real life, so researchers using the error weight factor α can control the program threshold for penalizing of erroneous negative ties within subgroups (valid values range from 0 to 1). The error weight factor for erroneous positive ties between subgroups counts automatically as $(1-\alpha)$. For the present study it is used α=0,5. This factor can be explained from a socio-psychological point of view. Before selecting a value of α researcher should assess participants' tolerance to those with whom they have a negative attitude. If, in the opinion of the researcher, project members exist in an atmosphere of strong rejection of the opposite point of view, α should be defined close to 1. On the contrary, in the case where someone's disagreement does not prevent to consider him part of the team, α can be lowered closer to 0.

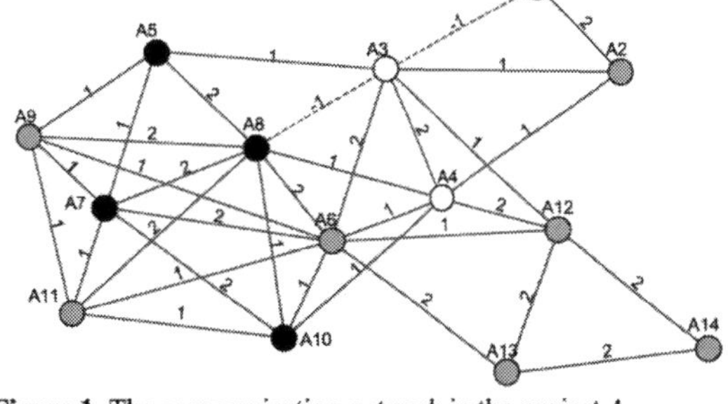

Figure 1. The communication network in the project A.

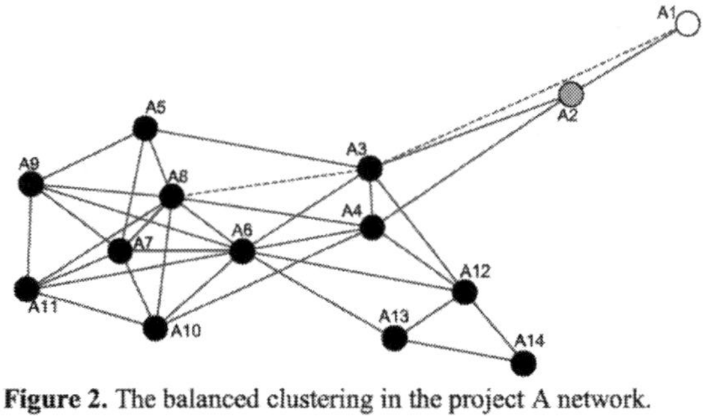

Figure 2. The balanced clustering in the project A network.

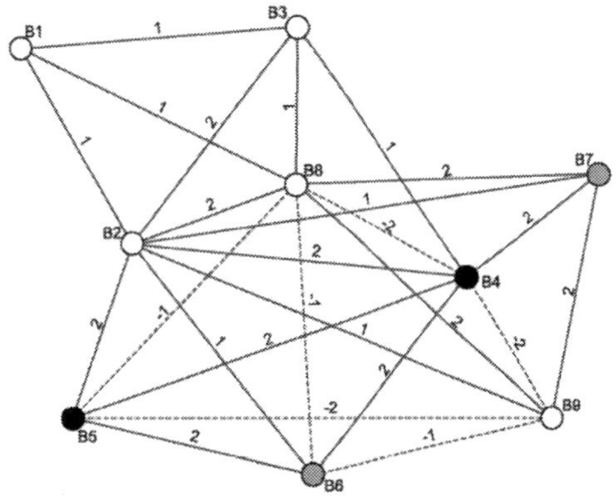

Figure 3. The communication network in the project B.

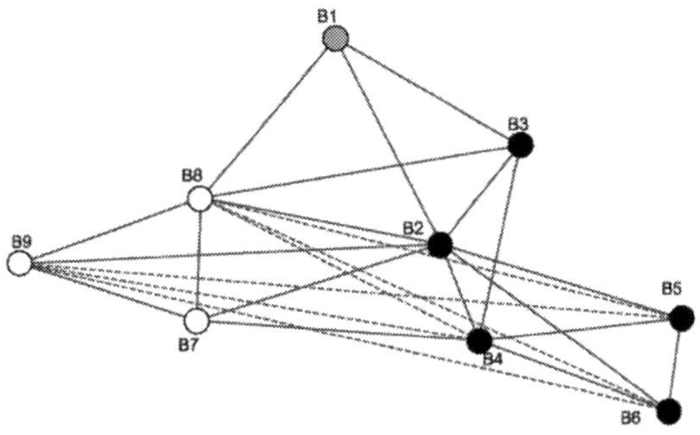

Figure 4. The balanced clustering in the project B network.

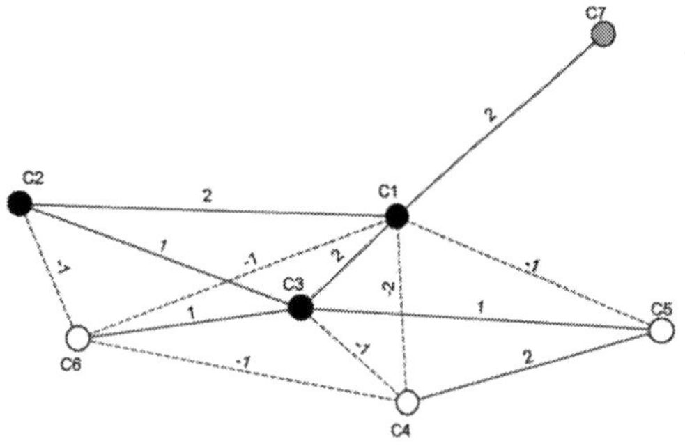

Figure 5. The communication network in the project C.

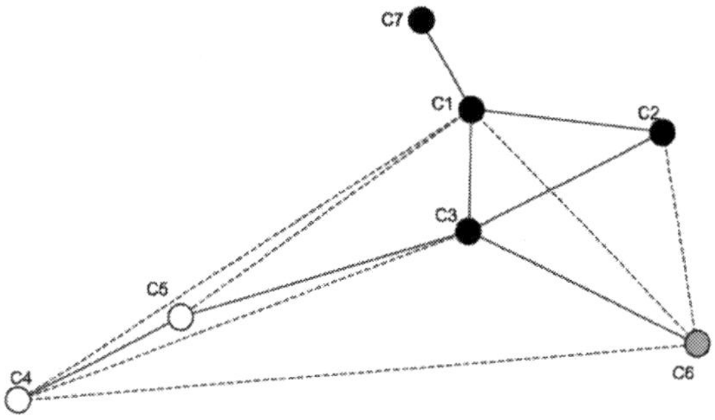

Figure 6. The balanced clustering in the project C network.

Found balanced solutions are presented in the Figures 2, 4, 6. In this case used color coding are corresponding its membership of a new subgroup and not to the initial participant's position in the conflict. For example, in the project A the participant A3 initially demonstrated position «Agree» (its vertex in the figure 1 is white), but in the balanced network he joined the main subgroups (the black vertices in the figure 2). In the figure 3 the participant B1 was also marked with «Agree» position, but this project B member is the only participant in the grey-colored subgroup separated from the rest.

Comparing the found solutions with factual information about the projects it can be come to the following conclusions. In the project A there were 7 members in the open contradiction that is half of the total number of participants. The rest showed neutrality. It should be noted that the project A network contain only two negative ties in the communication structure. The balance analysis revealed that the 12 members belonged to the common subgroup. This fact shows about high emotional and psychological stability and cohesion of the project team, which is not influenced by differences of opinion, and therefore, about the high efficiency of communications management. Apparently, it was a significant factor contributing to overcoming conflict stage.

Comparing with project A, there is a big share of negative relations in the communication structure of the project B. It can be assumed that in the situation with project B the conflict this project proceeded in a more critical stage adversely affecting the people relations. It is noteworthy that participants with the "Agree" position more than their opponents (5 vs. 2). But the figure 4 with balanced network is showing the presence of 2 subgroups, almost the same number of participants. The nature of the relations between the parties became a potential cause of a more radical separation, and therefore it reduced the level of mutual cooperation. So the negative attitude in the communications of participants B6 with B8 and B9 contributes to transition B6 from the neutral position to the opposition to them. For the participants B2 and B3 who shared the "Agree" position the results are more interesting because next these persons joined to subgroup with one's opponents B4 and B5. Such situation when a network member has better relations with opponents than with supporters is reinforcing the dissociation. Divergent views, the lack of sympathy in relationships with peers have a negative impact on decision making. The participants of the project B pointed to the lack of coherence in the goals understanding. The analysis of the balanced network showed that the participants, among whom there was the nominal consent could turn out to be opponents.

The project C network divided clearly into 3 subgroups, between which negative attitudes are dominated. It can be noted that the participants C4 and C6 have only one positive link with the other that is blocking effective cooperation. Observing the pattern of the balanced network in the project C, the withdrawal of the several team members from the project seems to be in a predictable step. Communications and relationships between the participants are not contributing to the conflict resolution, and therefore, in this case it is hardly to expect achieving the project goals.

In the project A the communication network was stable when a conflict occurred. Its members had opposing points of view but could maintain positive attitudes with their opponents. Consequently, the team remained cohesive and kept the common goals and vision. In contrast, separate subgroups, in opposition to each other were clearly distinguished. Prevailing negative relationships between subgroups hindered information exchange and reduced the overall productivity of the teams. The lack of situation analysis in which the projects B and C were and insufficient efforts in relation to communication management became possible causes of disunity and the project failures.

3 Conclusions

Interproject communications are the integration environment for the participants, transforming them from individual actors into a united team. Using modern approaches in the organization theory, project teams can be classified as specific social networks. Formal and informal communications taken together constitute the project communication environment. Relations characters and their structure depend on project management effectiveness, and, therefore, can serve as indicators of project success.

Using the social network concept as a basis, the authors present the study communication characters and structure in the several projects that were in a conflict state. SNA techniques were chosen in order to examine structural balance of the project network. The analysis results gave opportunities to advance explanations regarding outcomes for each project taking into account social ties and member partitioning in the conflicts.

The use of SNA methods seems promising as a tool for analyzing of communication management effectiveness in addition to traditional methods for assessing quality of project management. This would pay more attention on human and social factors because project participants are essential element which deliver project results.

References

1. J.R. Turner and R. Müller, Int J Project Manage, **21**, 1 (2003)
2. T. Cooke-Davies, Int J Proj Manage, **20**, 185 (2002)
3. M.B. Pinto and J.K. Pinto, JPIM, 7, 200 (1990)
4. P.S. Chinowsky, J. Diekmann and J. O'Brien, JCEM, **136**, 452 (2009)
5. P. Dietrich, IJPM, **37**, 49 (2006)
6. H. Kerzner, *Advanced project management: Best practices on implementation* (2004)
7. H.J. Thamhaim and D. L. Wilemon, SLOAN MANAGE REV., **16**, 31 (1975)
8. W.A. Reed, *Doctoral dissertation* (2006)
9. D. Hinds and R. M. Lee, *Hawaii International Conference on System Sciences, Proceedings of the 41st Annual, IEEE*, pp. 323-323 (2008)
10. P. He, B. Li and Y. Huang, *Second International Conference on CGC*, pp. 418-423 (2012)
11. R. Alsamadani, M. Hallowell and A. N. Javernick-Will, CEM, **31**, 568 (2013)
12. T. Mueller-Prothmann and I. Finke, J. UCS, **10**, 691 (2004)
13. S.D. Pryke, Construct Manag Econ, **23**, 927 (2005)
14. A. El-Sheikh and S.D. Pryke, Construct Manag Econ, **28**, 1205 (2010)
15. P. Chinowsky, J. Diekmann and V. Galotti, JCEM, **134**, 804 (2008)
16. P. Chinowsky and J.E. Taylor, EPOJ, **2**, 15 (2012)
17. H.R. Kerzner, *Project management: a systems approach to planning, scheduling, and controlling* (2013)
18. S. A. Titov, Cloud of science, **1**, 665 (2014)
19. I.V. Osipov, A.A. Volinsky and V.V. Grishin, International Journal of advanced computer science and applications, **6**, 11 (2015)
20. I.V. Osipov, E. Nikulchev, A.A. Volinsky and A.Y. Prasikova, International Journal of advanced computer science and applications, **6**, 71 (2015)
21. S. Wasserman and K. Faust, *Social Network Analysis: Methods and Applications* (1994)
22. W. De Nooy, A. Mrvar and V. Batagelj, *Exploratory social network analysis with Pajek*, **27** (2011)

ITM Web of Conferences 6, 03012 (2016)
DOI: 10.1051/itmconf/20160603012

The new approach to the problem-driven object programming

Alexander Prutzkow[1,a] and Dmitriy Tsybulko[2]

[1]Ryazan State Radioengineering University, Department of computational and applied mathematics, 390005 Ryazan, Russia
[2]Ryazan State Radioengineering University, Department of computational and applied mathematics, 390005 Ryazan, Russia

Abstract. Using more and more computing devices requires a new programming approach. The programming approach should be simple for an ordinary device user and problem-driven. So we propose a new programming concept for easy code writing by any non-programmer. We named it the Problem-Driven Object Programming or PDOP. According to the concept, program is a control flow by program objects. Every object is a action for a problem solvation and has the same structure. The object structure is defined by formal grammar rules. During code writing, the user programs a control flow and sets type and parameters of the object. The PDOP is also a simplified programming language with user-friendly graphical representation.

1 Introduction

Writing a programming code requires adequate programming approaches. Currently, there are a few different approaches available to programmers: structural, object-oriented, logical, functional, etc. Born in the 1970s of the 20th century, the object-oriented programming approach has become more common. Back then, leading programming experts had to face a task how to achieve a greater conciliation of data and programs. A solution to the set task called for a change of von Neumann's presupposition according to which "data and programs are indistinguishable in machine's memory" [1]. The basis of the outlined conception rests on three founding principles: inheritance, encapsulation and polymorphism. The approach built on these principles was named object-oriented programming (OOP).

OOP is a universal approach to describing task solution as unified consistent data structures. OOP was offered as a way to reduce duplicating codes. To use this approach a programmer has to have certain knowledge and skills.

Firstly, it is important to understand such basic concepts as classes, inheritance, dynamic binding, modules, abstract data types and the like. Studying the principles of how data encapsulation functions takes a great deal of time, whereas designing classes seems to be the most challenging. This task is more complicated than their usage. Secondly, to be able to settle the problem a specialist ought to possess quite a lot of experience. An OOP-based program design is rather complicated and is solely the responsibility of a programmer. Thirdly, a right set-up of the structure allows for an easy check-out and exploitation of the program. A fully satisfactory object model makes target software more scalable and flexible. The quality of the designed model depends on the competence of a specialist who creates the product.

2 Problem-driven object programming concept

A great number of consumer microprocessing devices and related operational systems and software to run them generated a need to write a simplified programming language that could allow any user to learn programming tools and solve focused tasks.

Normally, the solution to focused tasks motivates users to resort to 5-10 different commands. Using basic operations from sophisticated programming languages, one can group atomic statements into blocks that enable a user to write problem solution. A user needs a language with a limited number of commands to solve a problem. This will help a user to settle problems for a specific subject area quite effectively. This approach to problem solving was called Problem-Driven Object Programming or abbreviated PDOP [2].

For the PDOP, any operation is described by an object that consists of two main parts – hidden and open [3]. The hidden part performs actions, checks conditions for control transfer to another object and is inaccessible to the user.

The open part includes the following sections:

- a field section (parameters used by the object to perform actions);
- an initialization section that contains commands acted out by the object on getting control;
- a condition section that contains commands for transferring global data and controlling functions to other objects according to datum conditions.

The user can set different characteristics for these sections, necessary for problem solving.

The objects exchange global data through a special storage area that can be structured as a stack, a queue or a memory space with direct access (array variable). The

[a] Corresponding author: mail@prutzkow.com

memory access is done through the initialization section or condition section.

Logically, programs in PDOP is a bifurcated structure and can be identified as an aggregate of objects sending each other global data and control.

We can describe PDOP with the help of formal grammar rules:

```
object = indentificator «=» type «{» { parameter
{parameter} } { transfer_condition {transfer_condition} }
«}».

parameter = indentificator « : » (symbol | digit { symbol |
digit } ) «;».

transfer_condition = if (parameter | «_nocondition») «call»
identificator «;».

type = identificator.
identificator = letter{symbol}.
symbol = letter | digit | «_».
letter = 'A'...'Z' | 'a' ...'z'.
digit = "0" | "1" | "2" | "3" | "4" | "5" | "6" | "7" | "8" |"9".
```

The record «{element {element}}» means one or more elements of the rule «{element}».

A full description of the formal grammar of the PDOP language is provided in the article [4].

To illustrate our reasoning, we propose the following description of types of objects that are used in the knowledge test script: Q – show a question on the screen and get an answer (figure 1), T – show an explanation on the screen (figure 2), R – show a knowledge test result on the screen (figure 3).

```
Q1 = Question
{
   // data section
   Question: "Text for question 1"
   Option1: "Option 1"
   Option2: "Option 2"
   Option3: "Option 3"
   Option4: "Option 4"
   Correct: Option1
   // condition section
         if yes
         call Q2;
         if no
         call T1;
}
```

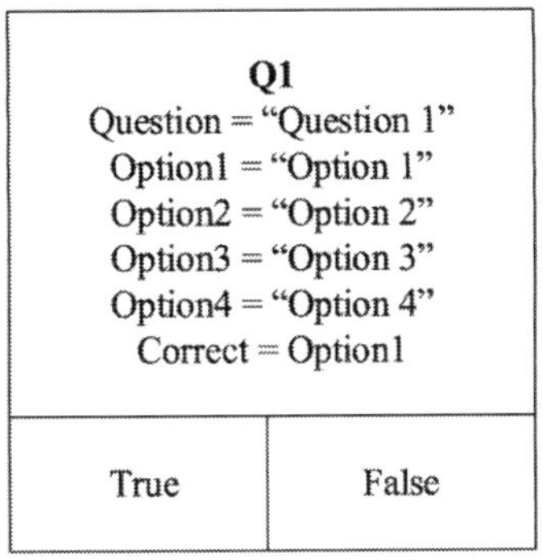

Figure 1. Question Object Type

```
T1 = Tip
{
  Text: "Text of explanation";
  ifnocondition
     call Q2;
}
```

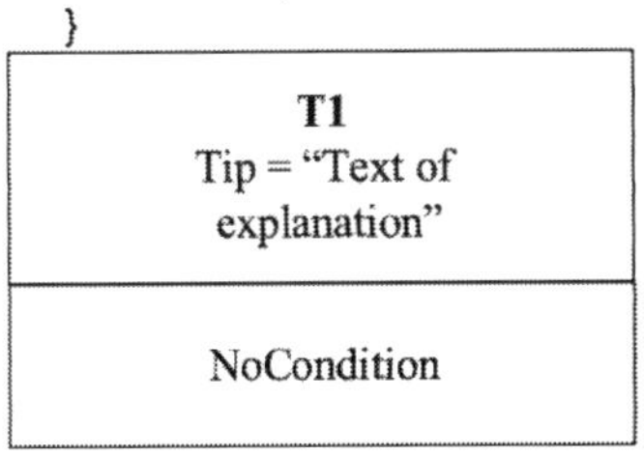

Figure 2. Tip Object Type

```
R1 = Result
{
    ifnocondition
       end;
}
```

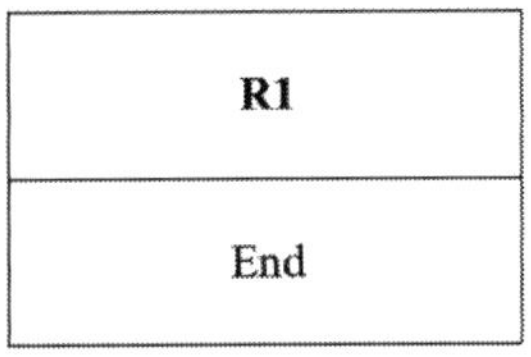

Figure 3. Result Object Type

The objects' description means the following. Object Q1 takes the question and variants of answers onto the screen. If the answer is correct, control is transferred to object Q2, otherwise the control function is given to object T1 for showing explanations. After object T1 shows explanations, control is also transferred to object Q3 (figure 4). After all questions and answers have been shown on the screen, control is then transferred to object R1 – show the final result.

Objects of the PDOP program can be represented not only in the form of a text, but as graphics as well (for example, figure 4). It consequently allows programming problem solution through a visual editor.

3 Self-Similarity

To make the code less abundant, PDOP uses the approach which was named "self-similarity". A user can form any sequence of objects as one complex object.

Description of scripts for automated teaching is a possible subject area in which we can use PDOP [2]. A few simple operations ought to exist: "show text material", "show image", "show video", etc. They are all similar and can be used to make the object "do a training lesson". For a knowledge test, it is needed to activate the objects "ask question", "show help", "show correct answer", "show result". These can well be used to write a more sophisticate script "build a test".

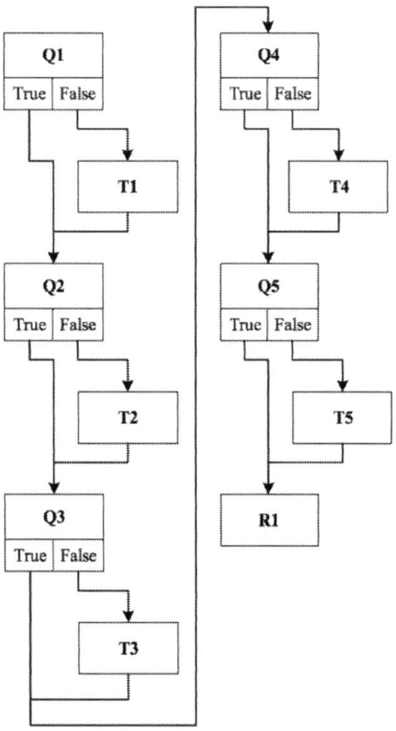

Figure 4. Graphical representation of the PDOP program objects

Using self-similarity makes it possible to avoid code duplication and re-use existing elements in the structure of more sophisticated objects, the fact that takes less time to write a program.

4 Conclusion

A specialist does not need to take into account an object's implementation arrangements. He or she should only know the function it performs and its section structure. For example, as it is shown in the article [5], we can describe the elements of structural programming with the help of PDOP. Their combination can generate objects that perform operations identical to such operations as a condition, a cycle with a precondition, a cycle with a post-condition, a cycle with a parameter. It allows writing scripts similar to methods in the OOP languages or the functions of structural programming. Application of such objects affords an opportunity to use PDOP for different ends and in different subject areas that require complicated operational algorithms.

Regardless of unlimited functionality of the OOP mechanism, it is not always easy or handy to work with this paradigm, which is especially challenging to an untrained user who lacks target programming skills. Using the described PDOP framework encourages the user to concentrate on commands effective for problem solution rather than to delve into conceptual details and the programming language.

Nowadays, PDOP is used to implement linguistic algorithms (algorithms for word-form generation and recognition [6] on the basis of a word-form building model [7]) and other algorithms.

References

1. V.A. Kamaev and V.V. Kosterin, *Tekhnologii Programmirovaniya* (2006) [Rus]
2. A.V. Prutzkow and D.M. Tsybulko, Vestnik of RSREU (Herald of RSREU), **45** (2013)
3. D.M. Tsybulko, Cloud of Science, **1**, 129 (2014) [Rus]
4. D.M. Tsybulko, *Student. nauch. soob-vo: issledovaniya i innovatsii – 2015*, pp. 117 (2015) [Rus]
5. A.V. Prutzkow, D.M. Tsybulko, Vestnik of RSREU (Herald of RSREU), **47** (2014)
6. A.V. Prutzkow, *2014 International conference on computer technologies in physical and engineering applications (ICCTPEA)*, p. 157 (2014)
7. A.V. Prutzkow, Cloud of Science, **1**, 88 (2014) [Rus]

ITM Web of Conferences **6**, 03013 (2016)
DOI: 10.1051/itmconf/20160603013

The fast vocabulary-based algorithm for natural language word form analysis

Alexey Rozanov[1,a]

[1]*Ryazan State Radioengineering University, Department of computational and applied mathematics, Ryazan*

In the field of Natural Language Processing, identifying word forms and, more precisely, identifying part-of-speech and grammatical information for each of the words in the input text usually comprises the very first level of text processing (or immediately follows splitting the text into words, should such task be non-trivial), therefore development of approaches to speed up the word form analysis pose significant interest. In this work, by using the work [1] as a basis, we present an approach to analysis of word forms for natural languages with postfix inflection, following the work done in [3]. We propose a way of representing the postfix inflection rules associated with a natural language and an algorithm for word form analysis based on it. In conclusion, we provide the benchmark data indicating the increase in speed compared to known analysis methods.

1 Introduction

In his works, A. Prutzkow proposed a universal model for representing the word form generation rules [1] and an algorithm for word form analysis of a natural language [2].

All rules in the aforementioned model are described as chains of elementary transformations of strings, each one possessing the properties of **unambiguity** (the same word is always transformed with the same result) and **reversibility** (for each transformation P, there is exactly one transformation P^{-1} such that $P^{-1}(P(s)) = s$ for any string s the transformation P is applicable to).

Albeit the model and the algorithm utilizing it, both proposed in [1], do have the advantages of being language-independent and bi-directional (i.e. allowing both generation and analysis), the speed of word form analysis is significantly lower compared to known analogues.

In this article we only consider word form analysis for languages with postfix inflection, i.e., languages in which word form generation rules only replace postfixes in the word, leaving the stem unchanged. As shown in [3], the model described above is redundant for such languages and can be reduced to a much simpler model, which allows using a more efficient algorithm for word form analysis.

Then we propose an approach to structuration of vocabulary for word form analysis software. It allows representing complex word paradigms efficiently. We consider the advantages of proposed vocabulary structuration and conclude the article with the performance test data.

2 Organizing the rule set

It is shown in [3] that, given the language inflection is strictly postfix, every word form generation rule can be represented by using a single postfix substitution operation, which is easily seen to be unambiguous (deterministic) and reversible.

Therefore, one might represent the whole set of such rules as distinct connections C_i between two prefix trees L (left) and R (right), correspondingly representing the set of postfixes the initial forms possess and the set of their replacements. Figure 1 displays the resulting data structure.

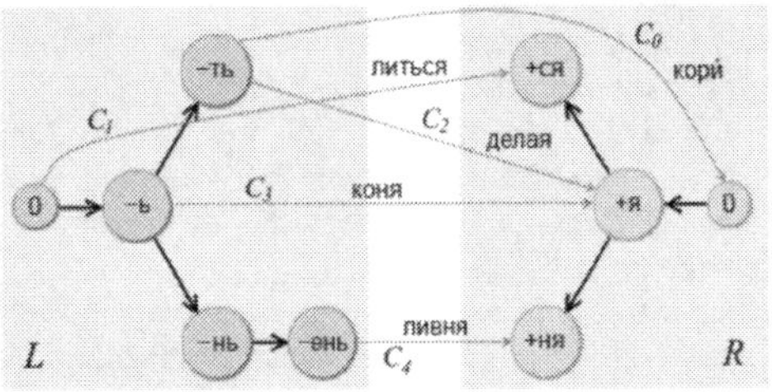

Figure 1. Connections between prefix trees defining rules for word form generation.

The data structure shown in Figure 1 illustrates how the rules for word form generation are stored in memory. In this example, a few rules for the Russian language are shown: C_0 represents the generation of imperative (“*кори́*”) for the Russian verb “*кори́ть*” (Eng. *to blame*), as well as many other Russian verbs, C_1 is used to obtain the reflexive form (“*литься*”) of the verb “*лить*” (Eng. *to pour*), C_2 provides the rule for obtaining the gerund form of the verb “*делать*” (Eng. *to do*), C_3 shows how to

[a] e-mail : thehdotx@gmail.com

generate genitive (or accusative, as said two forms of this word do not differ) for the noun "конь" (Eng. *male horse*), C_4 generates the genitive (but not accusative) for the noun "ливень" (Eng. *downpour*).

In the above figure, each node of the left tree *L* represents a certain valid Russian postfix (i.e. at least one word has it in the initial form). This postfix is what should be removed in order to obtain a word form that differs from the initial one. The "zero" node corresponds to the null postfix meaning that no remove is needed.

Similarly, each node of the right tree *R* represents a certain valid (at least for a single word in its non-initial form) Russian postfix. The said postfix is what should replace the removed postfix of the initial form of the word. The "zero" node represents the null postfix, meaning that no new postfix is needed.

Then, given the above mentioned data structure represents the complete inflection rule set, the algorithm for word form analysis, contains the following steps:

(a) obtaining the chain *Z* of right tree nodes that matches the characters of the input word taken in the reverse order, thus eliminating most of the rules as impossible for the given input word;

(b) taking the next possible way of splitting the input word into a [*stem+postfix*] pair by iterating thtough $\{Z_i\}$;

(c) scanning through all rules associated with node Z_i to filter out the rules whose inversions, being applied to the input word, do not produce the initial form they were initially associated with;

(d) the set of the rules obtained gives the information on all possible interpretations of the input word, as well as the initial word forms for each of the interpretations found at step (c), so the word is considered unknown if the resulting set is empty.

Thus, it can be seen (and is shown in [3]) that

- the set of the rules to iterate through when analyzing a word is reduced to a small (compared to the entire Russian rule set) set of the rules represented by the connections C_k linked to the nodes of a single chain of the tree *R* (and not the whole tree);
- the application of any given rule to a word is as trivial as the postfix replacement is in the programming language the programmer decided to implement the algorithm in;
- the memory overhead is negligible (around 2Mb for the trees built from the test vocabulary containing over 8000 words in initial form) in comparison to the vocabulary size (said vocabulary, when deserialized, took about 20Mb of RAM), therefore the analysis method is suitable for running on devices possessing small amounts of RAM;
- the analysis can be executed in parallel very well, as it requires no writing to shared memory, therefore the speed of analysis increases proportionally to the number of parallel execution threads.

3 Representing grammatical information

When planning the vocabulary structure of the word form analysis system, we usually face the problem of organizing the initial word forms into groups sharing similar (or equal) word form generation rule sets. In languages with complex inflection rules, the structure of a word paradigm may depend on a number of circumstances including the values of certain categories (e.g. perfective or imperfective aspect of a verb, comparability of an adjective) associated with the word in question. Therefore, we need to divide the whole set of vocabulary words so that the amount of duplicate rules in similar word groups would be as small as possible.

In [4], the author proposes a hierarchical representation of the vocabulary and demonstrates that it is sufficient to describe the full paradigm structure for Russian words. The proposed model is largely language-independent, as well as it does not depend on the word generation rule kinds existing in the language. The proposed model can be described using the following sequence of definitions:

1. The whole set of **grammatical categories** of the language is stored in a special global registry, i.e.

$$GValues = \{GValue_1, GValue_2, \dots, GValue_N\}$$

$$GTypes = \{(GType_1, GValues_1), \dots, (GType_2, GValues_2)\}$$

Examples of particular grammatical categories descriptions for the Russian language are

(Case, {Nominative, Genitive, ..., Prepositional})

(Number, {Singular, Plural})

(Animacy, {Inanimate,Animate})

2. When describing words and sets of words, it is imperative that the word or word group being described can have only one or zero GValues per GType. In the latter case we say that the grammatical category in question is not applicable (e.g. verb-related categories for nouns), or is undefined. The description (be it partial or complete) is called a **grammatical value map** (GValueMap). Examples for the Russian language are

(1) "*делами*":

{{*Case:Instrumental*}, {*Number:Plural*}, {*Animacy:Inanimate*}, {*Gender:Neuter*}}

(the initial word form "*дело*" is the Russian for "*deed*")

(2) *animate feminine nouns*:

{{*Animacy:Animate*},{*Gender:Feminine*}}

Grammatical value maps are used in the proposed model both for representing the analysis results and describing word groups.

3. Thus, the word form generation rules are represented as the (*Operation, GValueMap*) pairs where *Operation* is the exact low-level string manipulation procedure for obtaining the word form from the initial (vocabulary) form, and *GValueMap* is the grammatical information. For example, the word "*делами*" is generated by rule

R = (–о+ами):{{*Case:Instrumental*},{*Number:Plural*}}.

Note how no animacy is included in GValueMap, as it is already set for the word family containing the word.

4. GTypes often depend on each other: for example, in Russian, gender is undefined in plural forms; possible participles depend on aspect and transitivity. Due to that, listing all variable GTypes is not enough to efficiently describe a paradigm; therefore, the concept of **Inflection Maps** is introduced.

The idea behind inflection maps is to present the paradigm structure by splitting it into subsets formed by groups of independent GTypes. Each inflection map is composed of a GValueMap listing all invariant GValues, a set of variable GTypes, and a set of restrictions forced upon particular variable GTypes.

To illustrate how the inflection maps can be used to describe the structure of the paradigm for a group of words, we consider the paradigm of Russian adjective "ясный" (Eng. *clear*) as an example (Table 1).

Table 1. Full Russian adjective paradigm structure.

Number, Gender, Animacy / Comparison degree, short/long forms, Cases			Singular			Plural, Animate/ Inanimate
			Masculine Animate/ Inanimate	Feminine	Neuter	
Positive	Long form	Nom.	ясный	ясная	ясное	ясные
		Gen.	ясного	ясной	ясного	ясных
		Dat.	ясному	ясной	ясному	ясным
		Acc.	ясного/ ясный	ясную	ясное	ясных/ ясные
		Inst.	ясным	ясной/ ясною	ясным	ясными
		Prep.	ясном	ясной	ясном	ясных
	Short form		ясен	ясна	ясно	ясны
Comparative			яснее			

It is easily seen that GTypes shown in the table above are not independent, and for these six GTypes (*Number*, *Gender*, *Animacy*, *Comparison degree*, *Adjective form* (short or long), and *Grammatical Case*), there are just 30 distinct combinations of GValues that are grammatically correct (out of 288 theoretically possible, yielded as the product of GValue counters for each of the GTypes listed, i.e. 2×3×2×2×2×6). Therefore, we present the paradigm structure using 8 inflection maps:

$InflectionMap_1$: $(\{\{Number{:}Plural\},\{Form{:}Short\}\},\varnothing,\varnothing)$
(short plural form is unique)

$InflectionMap_2$: $(\{\{Number{:}Singular\},\{Form{:}Short\}\},\{Gender\},\varnothing)$
(short singular)

$InflectionMap_3$: $(\{\{ComparisonDegree{:}Comparative\}\},\varnothing,\varnothing)$
(comparative is unique too)

$InflectionMap_4$: $(\{\{Number{:}Plural\}\},\{Case\},\{Case{\neq}Accusative\})$
(long form, plural)

$InflectionMap_5$:
$(\{\{Number{:}Singular\}\},\{Case,Gender\},\{Case{\neq}Accusative\})$
(long form, singular)

$InflectionMap_6$:
$(\{\{Number{:}Plural\},\{Case{:}Accusative\}\},\{Animacy\},\varnothing)$
(Inflection maps 6..8 describe all accusative forms)

$InflectionMap_7$:
$(\{\{Number{:}Singular\},\{Case{:}Accusative\}\},\{Gender\},$
$\{Gender{\neq}Masculine\})$

$InflectionMap_8$:
$(\{\{Number{:}Singular\},\{Case{:}Accusative\},\{Gender{:}Masculine\}\},$
$\{Animacy\},\varnothing)$

5. Next, the whole set of words in initial forms is divided into subsets sharing the same sets of word form generation rules. Each of such subsets is associated with a special shared GValueMap describing the invariant grammatical information such as gender and animacy for nouns.

At this point, we should have no trouble building the word form analyser, as the analysis is the process of determining the initial word form and the grammatical values map for the input word. Once an applicable rule is found, the latter goal is achieved by merging the GValueMap associated with the found rule with the GValueMap associated with the word subset the found rule belongs to, and the former goal is achieved by applying the reverse of the rule to the input word.

However, further structuration of the vocabulary is necessary because otherwise the process of filling it with new words requires much more redundant actions. The advantages of the proposed additional hierarchical vocabulary structuration include

(a) automatic generation of paradigm templates for new words based on their classification (for Russian verbs, given its aspect and transitivity, the complete paradigm template differs);

(b) guessing of particular rules for such templates can be done more precisely by taking into account how close to the new word was the existing rule in the hierarchy.

6. In the proposed model, the hierarchy of word types contains three levels (**Supertypes** – **Kinds** – **Families**) described below.

(a) **Supertypes** are the largest sets of words sharing the same invariant grammatical information structure. Also, at the supertype level, the set of all possible infection maps is described. For example, Russian nouns are presented as the supertype containing 2 invariant GTypes (Animacy and Gender) and a single inflection map (∅, {*Case*, *Number*}, ∅), which means that in Russian most nouns have 12 distinct forms, with some exceptions discussed below.

(b) **Kinds** are the subsets comprising supertypes, which are characterized by a GValueMap (shared by each of the words in the subset), a set of applicable inflection maps (some of the maps declared in the supertype might be inapplicable to some of the words comprising said Supertype), a set of words grouped in **families** (which are discussed below), and a set of **restrictions** (often empty) forced upon particular inflection maps. For example, in the supertype describing Russian nouns, there are 8 kinds, namely *Inanimate Masculine*, *Inanimate Feminine*, *Animate Masculine*, *Animate Feminine*, *Neuter*, *Plural Nouns*, *Singular Nouns*, *Indeclinable nouns*. The kind for *Plural Nouns*, for example, has a non-empty GValueMap {{*Number:Plural*}}, which reduces the amount of possible word forms to 6, (i.e. one per grammatical case).

(c) Families are the smallest subsets of words containing words that share the same word form generation rule set. For example, one of the biggest families of Russian nouns is the family of inanimate masculine nouns containing the word "*телефон*" (Eng. *phone*). The complete rule set associated with this family consists of the following 12 rules:

$R_1 = 0{:}\{\{Case{:}Nominative\},\{Number{:}Singular\}\}$
$R_2 = (+\text{а}){:}\{\{Case{:}Genitive\},\{Number{:}Singular\}\}$
$R_3 = (+\text{у}){:}\{\{Case{:}Dative\},\{Number{:}Singular\}\}$
$R_4 = 0{:}\{\{Case{:}Accusative\},\{Number{:}Singular\}\}$
$R_5 = (+\text{ом}){:}\{\{Case{:}Instrumental\},\{Number{:}Singular\}\}$
$R_6 = (+\text{е}){:}\{\{Case{:}Prepositional\},\{Number{:}Singular\}\}$
$R_7 = (+\text{ы}){:}\{\{Case{:}Nominative\},\{Number{:}Plural\}\}$
$R_8 = (+\text{ов}){:}\{\{Case{:}Genitive\},\{Number{:}Plural\}\}$
$R_9 = (+\text{ам}){:}\{\{Case{:}Dative\},\{Number{:}Plural\}\}$
$R_{10} = (+\text{ы}){:}\{\{Case{:}Accusative\},\{Number{:}Plural\}\}$
$R_{11} = (+\text{ами}){:}\{\{Case{:}Instrumental\},\{Number{:}Plural\}\}$
$R_{12} = (+\text{ах}){:}\{\{Case{:}Prepositional\},\{Number{:}Plural\}\}$

Note how rules R_1 and R_4 have zero transformation because Russian inanimate non-feminine nouns have the same singular form in nominative and accusative cases, and nominative singular is considered the initial form for all Russian nouns that have it.

4 Performance comparison

In order to test the analysis speed, the author prepared a vocabulary containing some of the most frequently used Russian words (figure 2 shows the vocabulary statistics).

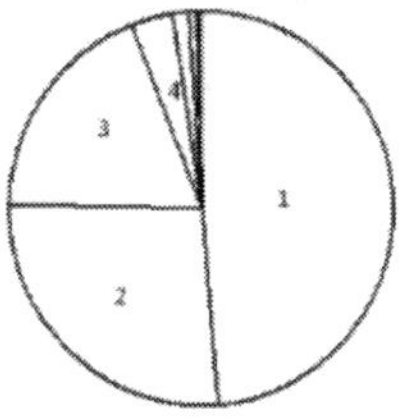

Figure 2. Test Russian vocabulary statistics.

Although the vocabulary only slightly exceeds 8000 initial word forms, the full bank of all recognizable word forms buildable from said initial forms would contain over 240000 words. As a result, more than 70% of the test input was recognized properly, thus allowing estimating the analysis speed and comparing it to that of the Mystem analyzer [5].

The performance tests were carried out on an Intel Core i7-4800MQ (2.7GHz), 16Gb RAM, running Windows 7. The algorithms were implemented in C# 6.0 (using .NET 4.5 framework).

In the test scenario involving a big corpora of words containing no duplicates (to exclude the effects of caching), the implementation of the proposed algorithm written by the author turned out to be slower than Mystem (the speed ratio varied from 1 to 0.5 depending on the amount of unknown words in the input text).

On the other hand, in the scenario involving a regular text (containing lots of repeating words), the implementation of the proposed algorithm has shown better speed (ratio varying from 1.5 to 2) and, thanks to caching, analyzing text B twice as big as text A never took twice as long as analyzing text A.

The roughly averaged sample absolute values are presented in table 2.

Table 2. Word analysis speed comparison.

	Proposed algorithm implementation	Mystem	Speed Ratio
No repeating words, 250000 words	55000 words/second	80000 words/second	0.69
Regular Russian text, 250000 words	180000 words/second	120000 words/second	1.5

5 Conclusion

In this article, we have demonstrated an approach to natural language word forms analysis using a general algorithm independent of particular language inflection rules, as long as all rules can be reduced to postfix replacement.

Given the fact that the performance tests were carried out using a high-level programming language, we could expect even better speeds, should the proposed method be implemented using a low-level programming language and a quality optimizing compiler.

Acknowledgements

The author is grateful to prof. Prutzkow Alexander Viktorovich of RSREU for his constant attention to this work, to prof. Mironov Valentin Vasilyevich from RSREU for his hospitality and beneficial discussions, and to Zavolokin Alexander Ivanovich from RSREU for his many valuable comments and helpful discussions.

References

1. A.V. Prutzkow, *Cloud of Science*, **1**, 88 (2014) [Rus]
2. A.V. Prutskov, Automat. Document. and Math. Ling., **45**, 232 (2011)
3. V.V. Mironov and A.K. Rozanov. Inform. of Education and Sci., **25** (2015)
4. A.V. Prutzkow, 2014 International conference on computer technologies in physical and engineering applications (ICCTPEA), p. 157 (2014)
5. https://tech.yandex.ru/mystem/

ITM Web of Conferences 6, 03014 (2016)
DOI: 10.1051/itmconf/20160603014

Real time prediction of track while scan data

Olga Selezneva[1, a]

[1]Saint Petersburg State University, Applied Mathematics Department, 198504 Saint-Petersburg, Russia

Abstract. The article covers several path prediction methods based on Kalman filter, compares them and estimates their advantages and disadvantages on example of searching a path of a maneuvering object on noisy pre-processed radar picture by evaluating their error values.

1 Task description

There is an ordered series of pictures (radar images), received at a fixed intervals of time. On one of them, we select a mark (tracking object). The task is to find this mark on the following images and to built its path of moving [1]. In is considered that the images are situated in the same coordinates (the radar is stationary), and the number of moving marks on the images is limited (sea vessels).

On the figure below there is a path built upon the center points of found marks. As in can be seen on the picture, it results rough because of mark positioning errors due to noisiness of images.

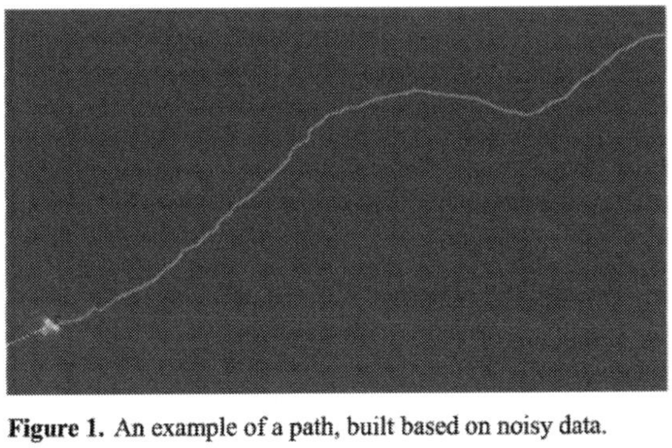

Figure 1. An example of a path, built based on noisy data.

The parameters of error in the geometric positions of objects are also unknown: they can appear just as because of the inaccuracy of the equipment (improper calibration of radar, imprecision of the equipment, noise on the data transmitting line), so due to the weather conditions, general situation and primary processing of images (for example, noise elimination and color correction) for finding geometric parameters of the mark. That is why for the further studying we will have to use simplified models of moving [2–4] and introduce a number of assumptions.

2 Kalman filter

Let us study a system:

$$x_k = Fx_{k-1} + Ga_k \quad (1)$$

$$z_k = Hx_k + \vartheta_k \quad (2)$$

Here x_k is a vector of projections of coordinates and velocities of the object to the axes Ox and Oy:

$$x_k = \begin{bmatrix} x \\ \dot{x} \\ y \\ \dot{y} \end{bmatrix}; \quad (3)$$

According to the Newtonian mechanics, we can write:

$$F = \begin{bmatrix} 1 & \Delta t & 0 & 0 \\ 0 & 1 & 0 & 0 \\ 0 & 0 & 1 & \Delta t \\ 0 & 0 & 0 & 1 \end{bmatrix}; \quad (4)$$

$$G = \begin{bmatrix} \Delta t^2/2 & 0 & 0 & 0 \\ 0 & \Delta t & 0 & 0 \\ 0 & 0 & \Delta t^2/2 & 0 \\ 0 & 0 & 0 & \Delta t \end{bmatrix}; \quad (5)$$

$$a_k = \begin{bmatrix} a_x \\ a_x \\ a_y \\ a_y \end{bmatrix}; \quad (6)$$

a_k – is an unknown vector of acceleration projections. We will consider that between revolutions (k−1) and k the object is moving with steady acceleration, which is limited by the capacities of sea vessels.

Covariance matrix of random interaction is:

$$Q = E[Ga_k(Ga_k)^T] = G[a_k a_k^T]G^T \quad (7)$$

[a] Corresponding author: olga.v.selezneva@mail.ru

z_k – is a vector of measurements of object's coordinates for every revolution.

$$H = [1 \quad 0 \quad 1 \quad 0]; \tag{8}$$

ϑ_k – inaccuracy of measurements. Due to the fact that the real value of inaccuracy is unknown, we will consider it to have normal distribution with zero mathematical expectation and mean square deviation σ_z. In this, the measurement noise covariance matrix will look like:

$$R = [\sigma_z^2]; \tag{9}$$

As the noise on the estimated images is monotonous, the adjustment of noise matrix R is to be performed only once.

Further, on the each step the stages of extrapolation and correction are used. The result of this work is shown below.

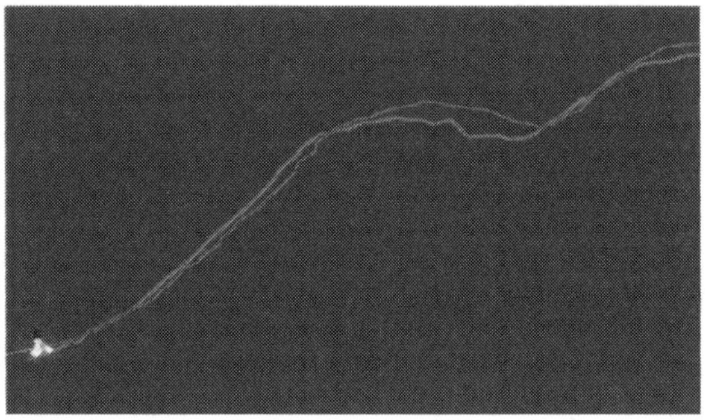

Figure 2. Comparison of a path constructed by Kalman's method and a path built on the centers of marks.

The Figure 2 shows two paths. The violet one is the path shown before, which is built upon the centers of found marks. The green one is a path, connecting the points received out of the presented model, which describe a predictable situation of the object. As it is seen from the figure, the received path goes closely enough to the one built upon the entering data. However, at the moment of maneuver, the paths are slightly separating.

Table 1. Values of errors for different objects

Object	N = 30	N = 40	N = 50	N = 60
1	6864.07	7257.87	8129.73	8438.21
2	6850.12	9109.79	12022.4	14179.8
3	21391.6	23961.2	27354.9	28560.4
4	7684.74	11508.8	14656.9	17017.6

The Table 1 represents the values of errors calculated according to the following formula:

$$Err(\mathrm{N}) = \sum_{\mathrm{i}=1}^{\mathrm{N}} \sum_{\mathrm{j}=1}^{\mathrm{n}} \left(x_{i,j}^{opt} - z_{i,j}\right)^2 \tag{10}$$

Here $x_{i,j}^{opt}$ are the values of coordinates of the object calculated using the filter for N tracking points, $z_{i,j}$ – values of measurements, n = 2 is space dimension of calculation.

The values in the table are calculated for four different tracks and for different number of measurements.

3 Conclusion

The negative side of this method for the task is the absence of data about errors of the model and the measurements, we have to use average empiric values, and this causes unpredictable errors. What is more, for different objects the optimal value will differ. Another disadvantage is a complexity of programming and resource costs for calculation. However, with enough computation capacities, this method is able to provide a higher accuracy of the path

References

1. S.Z. Kuzmin, *The basics of design of digital processing systems of radar data* (1986)
2. R.E. Kalman, Journal of Basic Engineering, **82**, 35 (1960)
3. P. Matisko, *16th IFAC Symposium on System Identification*, pp. 1523 (2012)
4. W.A. Fuller, *Measurement Error Models* (1987)

ITM Web of Conferences **6**, 03015 (2016)
DOI: 10.1051/itmconf/20160603015

Collection, transfer and processing of information in systems of monitoring of objects based on wireless sensor networks

Maxim Sergievskiy[1, 2, a] and Sergey Syroezhkin[1]

[1] *National Research Nuclear University MEPhI, 115409 Moscow, Russia*
[2] *Moscow Technological Institute, 119334 Moscow, Russia*

Abstract. Monitoring of the aircraft structures' during the pre-flight testing is a critical task of the aerospace industry. One of the most promising solutions, not yet widely applied, is continuous monitoring of aircraft structures using wireless sensor network technology. The brief summary of the proposed system is the following: special sensors send signals to the local motes (autonomous computing device equipped with a wireless transmitter). Information from motes is gathered by routers which then transfer the aggregated information to the datacenter. Applications of corporate network control and define flexible patterns for processing of the information received from sensors. This network structure allows to centralize data collection modes in the process of testing; implement continuous data collection at a defined frequency; process and display data in real-time.

1 Introduction

Internet of Things (IoT) – is an environment, which provides an interface for a variety of objects, equipped with computing and communication resources. In this case, Internet is understood broadly, not only as a method of transmitting data within a network using specific protocols and technologies, but also as a set of different services. Obviously, such a definition of IoT is very close to the definition of wireless sensor networks (WSN) [1]. However, the concept of IoT is broader than WSN concept, because the IoT brings together, firstly, animate and inanimate objects, and, secondly, the objects that do not have an active communication tools [2].

WSN consists of a number of small computational and communication devices - motes. Mote is a board, which size is usually less than one cubic inch, which consists of: a processor, memory (Flash and RAM), digital-to-analog and analog-to-digital converters, RF transceiver, power supply and sensors.

The sensors are connected to the board via the digital and analog connectors and can be very diverse: temperature, pressure, humidity, light, vibration, electromagnetic, chemical and others. The set of installed on mote sensors depends on the functions performed by the WSN. As the power source nodes use small batteries; typically, rechargeable batteries are not applied, since its charging is impossible in most cases. Motes serve for the collection, basic processing and transmission of the data.

Gateway is a special network's node, a sufficiently powerful computer, which performs the main functional processing of collected data. To retrieve data from the motes, node is equipped with a radio transmitter. Because of the limited range of the transmitter, gateway does not receive information directly from every network's mote, it can obtain data just from the motes that are located close to it. The problem of obtaining sensors data by gateway is solved as follows: motes can communicate with each other using transceivers operating in the radio bands. They send, information collected by motes sensors, as well as service information (status of devices and the results of data transmission).

Information is transferred from one mote to another by chain, and finally nearest to gateway motes send all the collected data to it. If some motes fail, the sensor network operation should continue after reconfiguration and changing its structure. But in this case, of course, the number of motes, sources of information, decreases.

To perform the functions a special operating system is installed on each node. Currently one of the most common operating system for WSN is TinyOS [3]. It is event-driven real-time operating system, designed to work in limited computing resources environment. This OS, as well as a number of others [4, 5], has special libraries and protocols that allow motes automatically establish communications with neighboring items to form a sensor network of a given topology. The controlling program of wireless sensor node describes all its operation logic, including such basic things as protocols of interaction with hardware, the primary processing of sensory data, and more complex processes, such as routing algorithms, encryption and data transmission.

The most important factor when working with wireless sensor networks is a limited capacity of the battery, mounted on mote [1]. It should be taken into account, that it is impossible to replace the battery in

[a] Corresponding author: sermax@yandex.ru

many cases. For this reason, firstly, motes should perform only simple primary processing, aimed at reducing the amount of transmitted information, and secondly, perhaps the most important, the number of data transmission and reception cycles should be minimized. To solve this issue special communication protocols were developed. The most common of which are the protocols of the ZigBee Alliance [6], which were created to coordinate activities of wireless sensor technologies. In general, to produce a standard, including protocol stack for wireless sensor networks, ZigBee used the previously developed the IEEE 802.15.4 standard, which specifies physical and medium access layers for wireless data transmission over short distances (up to 75 m) with low power consumption, but high degree of reliability.

The main purpose of the use of sensor networks is to control the state of objects during its operation. The critical components and systems can be equipped with a wireless data collection systems and diagnostic tools, for analysis and decision-making [7].

2 Problem statement

Now let's discuss a solution of important task - the control of modern aircraft structures' state in the process of testing and operation. This problem is relevant for the aircraft industry, because hidden defects caused by mechanical damage can lead to emergencies and accidents. Different manufacturers solve the task of improving the reliability and safety of the aircraft differently. They perform more preflight tests, analyze results and make estimates.

One of the most promising ways to solve this problem, not widespread yet, is the continuous monitoring of aircraft constructions in the process of testing and operation with the output on the dashboard of the necessary information. There are all preconditions to populate this approach:

- wide range of compact sensors (strain, temperature, pressure, vibration, location, etc.) with different mounting options;
- wireless sensor technology to collect information from sensors and send it to consumers; wide capabilities of control of information gathering modes;
- data processing techniques, implemented by custom applications.

The main aim of this work is to create a wireless system for monitoring of aircraft structures' deformation level during static and dynamic tests.

3 System architecture

The structure of the monitoring systems in most cases is the following: there are sensors connected to motes on the lower level. Several sensors can be connected to one mote; it is possible that the sensors are located on the mote's board - it depends on the tasks,which sensors perform. In our case, sensors are mounted directly on a controlled structure.

Motes are only used for collecting and converting the primary sensor data, which they send to each other and, eventually, to a special unit - gateway (base station) that has a wire connection to the server (the network). The network may contain multiple gateways; it increases its reliability and performance. Controlling of information collection modes and main processing of the obtained data is performed by applications on the corporate network. This approach allows to get rid of a large number of cable connections, since before wire connections were widely used in the airspace industry [8].

In case, when sensors are very tight, a star topology is considered to as the most effective. In this case, motes will transmit information to special routers that communicate with the base station. Routers are not equipped with sensors.

Thus, the network consists of a set of clusters, each formed by a router and motes with sensors, polled by router. Routers forward data to each other and, finally, the data comes to the gateway. The reliability of such systems is very high: even failure of a large number of motes or routers will not affect the operation of the system. Additionally, routers may be located outside of the deformable structure [9]. Fig. 1 shows a monitoring system consisting of a gateway router and sensor motes. Each mote has several sensors, connected to it by wires. To save energy motes are unable to receive and retransmit data from other motes, they only can send to router their own data.

Some routers have a direct link with the gateway, while others are transferring data by a longer chain, using other routers. This approach has both advantages and disadvantages. On one hand, it allows the use of only one gateway, but on the other, it increases utilization of some of the routers. Since in this domain network topology usually varies little during operation, these routers will fail earlier than others. Knowing the characteristics of a particular network topology makes it possible to increase the number of routers and efficiently balance the load between them, extending the network lifetime and avoiding potential loss of data.

The described network architecture can be attributed to the hybrid type, where some nodes (routers) form a mesh network, and the router and its motes actually use the cluster topology. An important task that WSN developer is faced is to increase the operating time of the network without having to replace the batteries. The most energy-consuming operations for wireless node is sending and receiving data. In the process of deformation level monitoring of aircraft constructions during static and dynamic tests measuring frequency reaches 200 Hz, that is, WSN should transmit a quite large data stream [10,11,12].

Let's determine the amount of payload data that should be transmitted to the gateway over the network, consisting of N motes with M sensors on each, if one deformation level measurement takes two bytes of memory.

$$Q = 2 \times N \times M \text{ (B)} \quad (1)$$

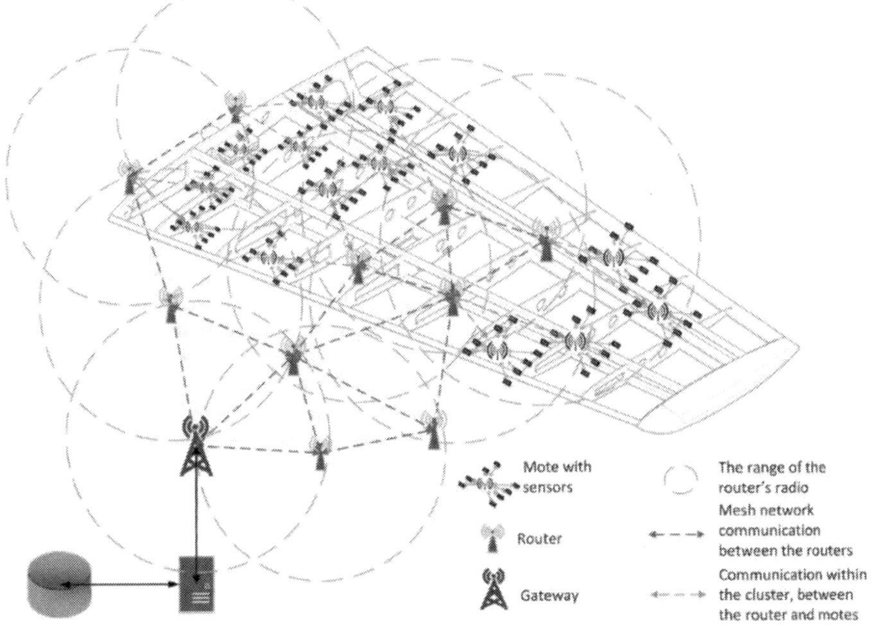

Figure 1. Structure of monitoring system

If the required measurement frequency of deformation is H Hz, the flow of information transmitted over the network as a whole, will be equal to:

$$S = Q \times H = 2N \times M \times H \text{ (Bps)}. \qquad (2)$$

For example, for a network consisting of 100 motes with 10 sensors on each, and a measurement frequency of 10 Hz, the flow of information will be 20 KB/s. This estimate does not take into account the fact that the overhead information, accompanying each message transmitted over the network, increases the total, transmitted over the network, traffic in about 7-10 times. Thus, the actual flow in this case is equal to 140-200 KB/s. Note, this is an estimate of the total data stream that arrives at the gateway, for routers and, especially, motes values of local flows will be significantly lower. Continuous processing and transmission of the data stream may trigger certain network components (routers or motes) failure in some cases. In order to maximize the network lifetime, you can apply several solutions related to the choice of its functioning modes. Let's discuss them in the next paragraph.

The process of developing of wireless deformation level monitoring system includes not only determining the network structure and configuration, but the solution of two interconnected problems - choice of hardware components and software creation.

4 Hardware components

To measure the deformation level of aircraft structures we use strain gauges model "FLA-5-17" by Tokyo Sokki Kenkyujo Company. Basic characteristics of the sensors are shown in the Table 1.

Table 1. Basic characteristics of the sensors.

Applicable specimen	Metal, Glass, Ceramics	**Backing**	Epoxy
Operational temp. (°C)	-20 ~+80° C	**Element**	Cu-Ni
Temp. compensation range(°C)	+10~+80 ° C	**Strain limit**	5% (50000×10^{-6}strain)
Bonding adhesive	CN, P-2, EB-2	**Fatigue life at room temp.**	1×10^{6} ($\pm1500\times10^{-6}$strain)

As a hardware platform for primary data processing and transmission, we use motes IRIS (Fig. 2) from MEMSIC.

Figure 2. Mote IRIS

They have a wide range of features including built-in processor, ADC, multi-channel radio transmitter, RAM, and interface for connecting sensors [3].

Special data captures and interface board are used in this WSN for strain monitoring. Both of these cards connect to themote through the 51-pin interface. To connect strain gauges FLA-5-17 to wireless motes IRIS a special data capturing board MDA300CA is used. This Board is attached to the IRIS Mote's extension connector and provides a set of digital and analog inputs for connecting a variety of sensors.

Every strain gauge connects to a data capturing board through any differential pair of channels and Ai + Ai-, which are used for connecting external sensors with a gain of 100. Thus, a single board can connect up to 10 sensors of the strain level. The dynamic range of channels is ±12.5 mV. The result obtained after analog-to-digital conversion of the sensor readings, can be translated into a voltage V (mV) according to the following formula:

$$V = 12{,}5 \times (ADC/2048 - 1) \quad (3)$$

For routers, we use the same IRIS motes, but they are not equipped with sensors. Sensor readings received by mote, should be transferred wirelessly to the server for further processing.

Special multi-purpose USB-interface board MIB520 (Fig. 3) of MEMSIC is the link between the wireless sensor network and the server. This board (gateway) with a transmitter module, integrated with IRIS mote, on one hand is able to exchange messages with the wireless network nodes, and on the other to transmit and receive data via USB-port of an ordinary computer.

Figure 3. MIB520 board

5 Software components

For development of software components of condition monitoring system, we use a special platform - MoteWorks of Crossbow Company [3]. This platform is based on the TinyOS operating system. Developers of the MoteWorks platform considered features of such systems and created the product, which allows create effective and reliable decisions.

The monitoring system software has two groups of components: network and server. Network components include a control application for motes and special software, to ensure the normal functioning of the network. Control application implements all algorithm required for monitoring and data transmission. For the data transfer, application uses stack of network protocols XMesh of MoteWorks platform. The stack of protocols XMesh supports multilink transmission of messages and conforms to the standard 802.15.4 [13].

Server software components of the monitoring system are running on the server special services, with main tasks to 1) collect, 2) store and 3) process the readings obtained by the network sensor. Server components uses XServe platform of MoteWorks as a basis, which collects incoming data on the interface card, converts them to a format specified by XML- template, and stores in a special database.

While monitoring of the aircraft structures state, experts rarely analyze obtained sensor data in the real-time, often they study them after experiments. Thus, often there is no need to deliver sensors data on gateway in real-time, and hence, a better approach from the standpoint of energy saving, would be an accumulation of a certain amount of data at the node, its compression, and only then transmission to the network. This operating mode allows you to switch the radio transmitter in the sleep mode, and thus save energy. In addition, it will allow solve another problem - avoiding conflicts arising from the simultaneous transmission of data from different routers.

Dependency of energy consumption on data transmission distance is elevated, which means that in

addition to the transmission time, the distance between transmitter and receiver and the transmitter's power also determines energy consumption. To reduce the cost of energy, required to data transmission, it is important to design the network in such a way to prevent the transmission over a long distances. Furthermore, the configuration of the domain allows us to pre-arrange the location of nodes, and hence it becomes possible to calculate the transmitter power that is required for reliable operation of the network.

In practice it is desirable to use minimum transmitter power, as this will not only reduce the energy consumption for data transmission, but also reduce the number of possible collisions [14].

6 Conclusions

In conclusion we highlight the key advantages of the use of wireless sensor networks for controlling and monitoring aircraft structures:

- lack of cables or a minimum number of cables;
- very small form factor of motes that basically allows to embed them in the body of various aircraft structures or connect to various devices;
- reliability of individual elements, and the whole system in the process of information collection and transmission;
- minimum energy consumption for receiving and transmitting radio signals, which allows you to use compact batteries;
- simplicity of a sensor network self-organization;
- scalability, allowing to ensure the deployment of networks with large number of nodes, which is important for a detailed analysis of aircraft structures.

The use of aircraft structures monitoring system, created on the base of wireless sensor network technology, will allow to organize the centralized management of the data collection modes during experiments; to carry out continuous data collection from sensors of various type with the set frequency of measurements; quickly to process and display data in real time.

References

1. C. Cordeiro and D. Agrawal, *Ad hoc and sensor networks: theory and applications* (World Scientific Pub. Co., 2006)
2. J. Hart and K. Martinez, Earth-Science Reviews, **78**, 177 (2006)
3. *Crossbow Technology*, (2014) www.xbow.com
4. *UC Berkeley. TinyOS Open WSN project* (2013). http://www.tinyos.net
5. A.S. Kosachev and V.N. Ponomarenko, *Real time operating systems* (Institute of System Programming, 2006)
6. C. Shen, S. Harte, E. Popovici, B. O'Flynn and R. Atk, Electronics Letters, **45**, 1098 (2009)
7. A. Mainwaring, J. Polastre, R. Szewcyk and D. Culler, *ACM International Workshop on Wireless Sensor Networks and Applications* (2002)
8. T. Haenselmann, *GFDL Wireless Sensor Network textbook*, (2006) http://pi4.informatik.uni-mannheim.de/~haensel/sn_book
9. A.J. Swati, R. Priyanka, International Journal on Computer Science and Engineering, **2**, 3089 (2010)
10. R. Kay and F. Mattern, IEEE Wireless Communications, **11**, 54 (2011)
11. E.F. Nakamura, A.A.F. Loureiro and A.C. Frery, ACM Computing Surveys, **39**, 9 (2007)
12. M.V. Sergievskiy and S. N. Syroezhkin, Modern Applied Science; **9**, (2015)
13. *Linear Technology* (2013). www.dustnetworks.com
14. A. Tiwari, P. Ballal and F.L. Lewis, ACM Transactions on Sensor Networks, **3**, 1 (2007)

ITM Web of Conferences **6**, 03016 (2016)
DOI: 10.1051/itmconf/20160603016

Results of agile project management implementation in software engineering companies

Sergei Suetin[1,a], Elena Vikhodtseva[2], Sergei Nikitin[2], Alexei Lyalin[2] and Irina Brikoshina[2]

[1]*Moscow Technological Institute, 119334 Moscow, Russia*
[2]*State University of Management, 109542 Moscow, Russia*

Abstract. Agile project management methodologies, tools and techniques have been becoming more and more popular among Russian and foreign software companies. Though the agile software project management methodologies appear to be more flexible and sound alternative to traditional project management approaches, the practice of agile project management implementation needs more research. The article presents the research on the practical results of agile project management implementation in Russian software engineering companies. The survey-based study covers 8 companies and 35 their projects managed with the help of agile methodologies. In contrast to some optimistic researchers of agile practices, the research findings show that in the investigated projects agile project management led to the deterioration of cost and schedule performance. However, the quality, both perceived by clients and assessed by internal technical analysts, improved after the implementation of agile software project management practices.

1 Introduction

In the last ten years, many theorists and practitioners of software project management has been engaged in the discussion about the applicability of the traditional project management methodologies, tools and techniques to the area of software engineering and development. Nowadays, it is clear that classical project management approaches, such as those described in PMBoK [1] or other standards, need serious revision and should be supplemented or even replaced by more flexible and dynamic approaches.

As it was expressed by Highsmith (2009), linear thinking, prescriptive procedures and standardized practices are no longer suited to modern conditions of software development [2]. One of the new directions in software project management is the agile project management methodology. Today agile tools and techniques are accepted and implemented by many companies. However, the current body of research still needs more empirical studies of the practical results of agile project management implementation in software companies.

2 Overview of agile project management methodologies

Basic principles of agile project management are described in the books of Highsmith (2009) [2], Chin (2004) [3], Larman (2003) [4], Abrahamsson et al. (2002) [5], Koch (2004) [6] and others.

The main ideas of agile software project management are:

- People and their face-to-face interactions are more important than processes and procedures,
- Reliable software is more important than technical documentations, plans and budgets,
- Cooperation with clients is more important than addiction to contracts,
- Openness to changes is more important than following plans.

On the basis of these general principles many various agile methodologies were developed with different tools and techniques. The most widely known agile methodologies are 'Scrum' [7], 'Crystal Clear' [8], dynamic systems development method (DSDM) [9], feature-driven software development [10], ICONIX [11] and others. Very close to agile is the methodology of extreme programming [12].

3 Practical results of agile project management implementation

Though agile project management methodologies has received a lot of attention from theorists and practicing project managers, the empirical research on the results of the implementation of agile tools and techniques remains quite scarce. Even fewer researchers have investigated the agile implementation results and consequences in software engineering companies.

Highsmith (2009) in his overview of agile practices presented the results of the survey according to which 89% of respondents reported about the increase in

[a] Corresponding author : s_suetin@mti.edu.ru

productivity, 84% - decrease in the number of errors and defects, 82% - decrease in projects' duration, 66% - cut of project costs [2]. Mah (2008) conducted two case studies and discovered that in one company agile management led to cost cuts on 61%, time savings on 24%, and decrease in the number of defects on 83%. In the second company he found cost cuts on 5%, decrease in project duration on 59%, and decrease in the number of defects on 11% [13]. Coforto and Amaral (2008) reported about excellent results of the implementation of agile project management in two software companies. According to their research the agile project management methodologies can increase creativity of employees, higher level of self-organization in project teams, and creation of additional value for companies and their clients [14].

Though the number of authors who reported about positive results of the agile project management implementation prevails, there are some sceptical reports that underline that agile project management can lead to additional risks, decrease in controllability and as a result to poor performance [15].

Thus, there is a need for further research on the possible results and consequences of the introduction of agile project management in software companies.

4 Research methodology

The research was organized as on-line and, partly, face-to-face survey of project managers and top managers from 8 Russian software engineering companies. The survey covered 35 software engineering projects finished within a year before the start of the research. In all projects under survey which agile project management practices were implements. The respondents were asked about the results of the projects realized with the help of agile project management methodologies in terms of cost, schedule and quality performance indices. Cost and schedule performance indices were calculated according to the traditional formulas of earned value management [16]. Quality performance indices in all cases consisted of two different metrics: index of the quality perceived by clients and index of the technical solution quality assessed by the internal technical analysts. Both quality performance indices were calculated as the ratio of the number of quality features of the project final results that fitted or exceeded the expectations (of clients or technical analysts) to the total number of quality requirements formulated up to the start of projects [17–18]. Hence, quality performance indices evaluated how much of the quality requirements were implemented in the final results of projects.

The values of the indices provided by the respondents were compared with the average valued of the same indices calculated on all projects of a company, including those that were realized with agile practices and those that were managed with traditional project management approaches. The variances between average values and the values of the indices from particular projects were analyzed with traditional statistical methods.

For instance, one of the respondents reported that in one of her project the cost performance index was equal to 1,1 whereas the average value of the cost performance index in all projects of the company was 0,95. Hence, the variance equal to 0,15 was taken into analysis. If the value of an index in a particular project was smaller than the average value the variance was calculated as negative. Therefore, the analysis of the variances between the values of particular projects and the average values can provides insights about the effectiveness of agile project management practices in terms of cost, schedule and quality.

5 Research findings

The distribution of the variance between the average cost performance index and the same index in the projects analyzed is shown in Figure 1.

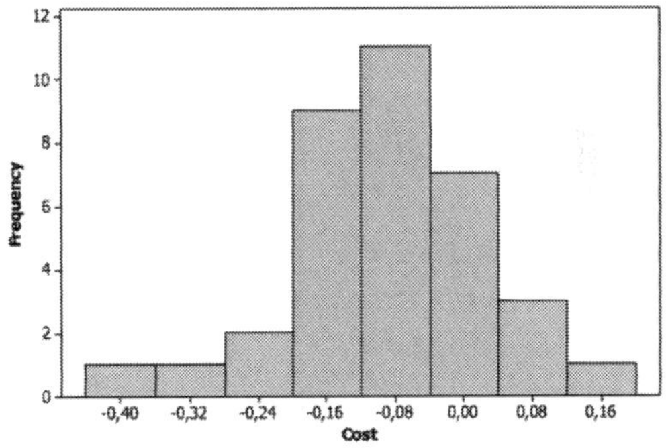

Figure 1. Cost performance index variance distribution.

The basic statistics on cost variance index variance are as follows:

- Mean value: -0,096;
- Standard deviation: 0,120;
- Minimum value: –0,430;
- Maximum value: 0,150.

The distribution of the variance between the average schedule performance index and the same index in the projects managed with agile project management practices is presented in Figure 2.

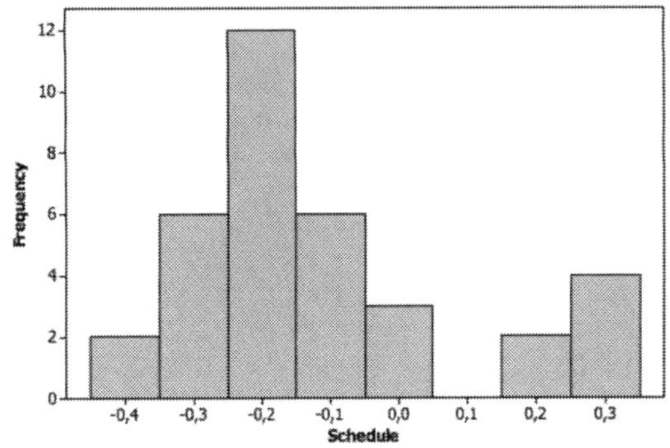

Figure 2. Schedule performance index variance distribution.

The basic statistics on cost variance index variance are:

• Mean value: –0,131;
• Standard deviation: 0,198;
• Minimum value: –0,420;
• Maximum value: 0,290.

In Figure 3 there is shown the distribution of the variance between the average quality performance (perceived by clients) index and the same index in the projects under investigation.

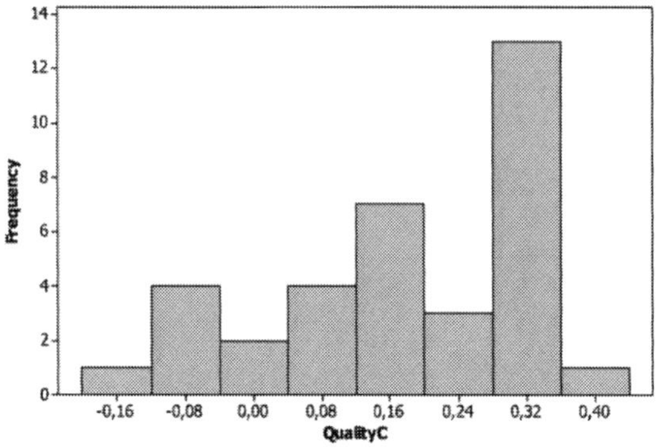

Figure 3. Client quality performance index variance distribution.

The basic statistics on client quality performance index variance are the following:

• Mean value: 0,178;
• Standard deviation: 0,152;
• Minimum value: –0,150;
• Maximum value: 0,430.

Finally, the distribution of the variance between the average value of internal technical quality index and the same index in the particular projects analyzed is presented in Figure 4.

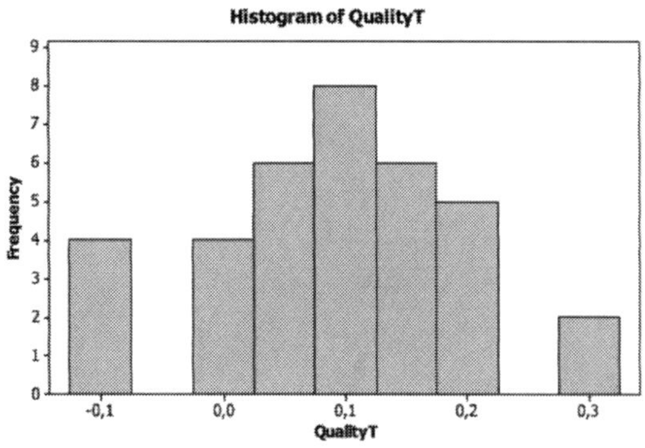

Figure 4. Technical quality performance index variance distribution.

The basic statistics on technical quality performance index variance are the following:

• Mean value: 0,090;
• Standard deviation: 0,104;
• Minimum value: –0,120;
• Maximum value: 0,290.

6 Discussion on findings

From the research findings we can conclude that in the companies under analysis the implementation of the agile project management methodologies brought the notable deterioration of the cost performance in software engineering projects. The cost performance index in agile projects worse than on average in all projects of companies (the mean variance is –0,096). There were 4 agile projects in which cost performance was better than in all projects. However, the improvements were not significant.

Agile project management practices were not able to improve the time performance in projects. Even more, the introduction of agile tools and techniques was accompanied by the decrease in project time performance. On average the agile projects were less effective in terms of time performance than all projects in companies (the mean variance is negative and equal to –0,131). Hence, the agile project management practices led to the deterioration of time performance which even worse than the deterioration of cost performance. However, it is worth noting that there was the group of 6 agile projects in which time performance was better than in all projects. Though the results of agile project management for cost and time performance are not impressive, the capability of agile management to create better quality is clear. From Figure 3 and 4 we can see that agile methodologies led to significant improvement of quality index from both perspectives – client and internal. The average increase in quality performance perceived by clients is even more than the similar increase in internal technical quality performance –0,178 and 0,090 respectively.

7 Conclusion

In contrast to the existing research [13, 14] the findings of the research presented showed the implementation of agile project management methodologies in software engineering companies led to the ambiguous results. In the project analyzed the agile project management brought about the deterioration of cost and time performance indices. However, the quality performance metrics increased after the introduction of agile tools and techniques.

We can recommend for practicing project managers to be more careful in their agile initiative and take into consideration the possible drawbacks of these initiative for the project time and cost performance. However, in the projects where clients emphasize the high priorities of quality and are able to pay for this by additional budgets and increase in project duration the agile project management can be implemented successfully, without any reservations.

References

1. *Project Management Institute* (2004)
2. J. Highsmith, *Agile Project Management: Creating Innovative Products* (2009)

3. G. Chin, *Agile Project Management: How to Succeed in the Face of Changing Project Requirements* (2004)
4. C. Larman, *Agile and Iterative Development: A Manager's Guide* (2003)
5. P. Abrahamsson, O. Salo, J. Ronkainen and J. Warsta, *Agile Software Development Methods: Review and Analysis* (2002)
6. A.S. Koch, *Agile Software Development: Evaluating the Methods for Your Organizations* (2004)
7. K. Schwaber, *The Enterprise and Scrum* (2007)
8. A. Cockburn, *Crystal Clear: A Human-Powered Methodology for Small Teams* (2004)
9. J. Stapleton, P. Constable, *DSDM: Dynamic Systems Development Method: The Method in Practice* (1997)
10. S.R. Palmer, J.M. Felsing, *A Practical Guide to Feature-Driven Development* (2002)
11. D. Rosenberg, M. Stephens & M. Collins-Cope, *Agile Development with ICONIX Process* (2005)
12. J. Highsmith, *Extreme Programming. Agile Project Management Advisory Service White Paper* (2002)
13. M. Mah, *Cutter Agile Product & Project Management Executive Report*, **9** (2008)
14. E.C. Coforto, D.C. Amaral, PMJ, **41**, 2, pp. 73-80 (2008)
15. M. Lindvall, , V. Basili, , B. Boehm, , P. Costa, , K. Dangle, , F. Shull, , R. Tesoriero, , L. Williams, , & M. Zelkowitz, *Empirical Findings in Agile Methods* in D.Wells and L.Williams (eds.) XP/Agile Universe, (Springer-Verlag, pp. 197-207, 2002)
16. Project Management Institute, *Practice Standard for Earned Value Management* (PMI Standards Committee, 2005)
17. N. Hill, J. Brierley, & R. MacDougall, *How to Measure Customer Satisfaction* (Gower, 2003)
18. I.V. Osipov, E. Nikulchev, A.A. Volinsky and A.Y. Prasikova, International Journal of advanced computer science and applications, **6**, 71 (2015)

ITM Web of Conferences 6, 03017 (2016)
DOI: 10.1051/itmconf/20160603017

Communication network structure parameters and new knowledge generation capabilities in companies engaged in industry control system engineering projects

Sergei Titov[1,a], Sergei Suetin[1], Natalya Titov[2], Sergei Nikitin[2] and Nikolai Malyshkin[2]

[1]*Moscow Technological Institute, 119334 Moscow, Russia*
[2]*State University of Management, 109542 Moscow, Russia*

Abstract. Engineering companies engaged in business of industry control systems need to manage the processes of generation of innovations within and across their projects. Generation and diffusion of innovations materialize through the communication networks of project teams. Therefore, it is possible to hypothesize that the characteristics of communication networks play role in generation of new knowledge. With the data from 14 industry control system projects of a Russian engineering company the communication network structure characteristics were calculated and the analysis of correlation between these characteristics and knowledge generation capabilities was performed. As a result correlation between centralization of communication and the number of new technical solutions developed in projects was discovered.

1 Introduction

With the advent of Internet technology in general and m2m technologies in particular [1] the industry control systems have been going through the constant change of the technological platforms. This implies the necessity to develop, disseminate and adopt new innovative solutions pertaining to the platforms, subsystems and elements of the industry control systems. The industry control system engineering is becoming extremely innovative sector of economy.

Engineering companies engaged in business of industry control systems need to manage the processes of generation of innovations within and across their projects. However, as Davies and Hobday (2005) noted [2] diffusion of innovations and knowledge generation in project-based companies are characterized by the problems of the extensive communication barriers between projects which hinder the effective dissemination of the innovative ideas and solutions across the projects of one company. Hence, the communications within and between projects can play significant role in innovation management and influence the speed and effectiveness of the diffusion of innovations.

2 Role of communications in industry control system engineering projects

Many researchers highlight the critical role of communications for the success of innovative engineering projects. For instance, Gupta and Wilemon (1988) analyzed the interaction between marketing and research departments in an engineering company and found out that the quality and the structure of the communications between these two types of departments notably effected the effectiveness of the innovation projects [3]. Pinto and Pinto (1990) ascertained that the high level of cooperation between the innovative project teams accompanied by the higher probability of the project success [4]. Allen, Lee and Tushman showed that the performance of innovation projects connected with the styles and quality of communications within the project teams [5]. Jagdev and Müller (2005) [6] and Henderson (2004) [7] determined the connection between communication competencies of project team members and success of projects. Ryynanen (2012) emphasized that effective communications are especially important for knowledge-intensive engineering projects [8]. Though many authors investigated the role of communications in engineering projects, these studies were largely of conceptual rather than of empirical nature. Yet another deficiency of the current body of research on communications in engineering projects is the insufficient number of quantitative findings. The article presented is trying to compensate for the lack of empirical quantitative research in the field of communication management in control system engineering projects.

3 Research methodology

The research methodology consists of the calculation of the formal quantitative characteristics of the

[a] Corresponding author: s_titov@mti.edu.ru

communication networks in industry control system engineering projects with the help of social network analysis [9] and the analysis of correlation between of these quantitative characteristics, on the one hand, and new knowledge generation capabilities of these projects.

The research hypothesis is that between quantitative structural characteristics of communication networks (such as density, average degree, centralization of a network) and knowledge generation capabilities there may be possible correlation that can be revealed with the help of statistical methods.

The research was conducted in a Russian engineering company realizing many industry control system projects. For the purposes of the research 14 different projects successfully finished in the year before the research were selected. These projects were comparable in terms of the number of team members, budgets, durations, scope and complexity of the project results.

In each of these projects the specific communication patterns evolved. These communication patterns can be described as networks consisted of vertices and arcs. Vertices represent the members of project team, and the arcs reflect the communications that can be considered as significant. The significance of the communications was defined as a frequency of the formal communications related to the problems, tasks, risks and other elements of a project within the project lifecycle. The significant communications were defined as those that occurred between project team members at least ten times every week during the project lifecycle. The data about communications (participants, frequencies) was derived from the project management information system used in the company. As a result the network models similar to one depicted in Figure 1 were constructed.

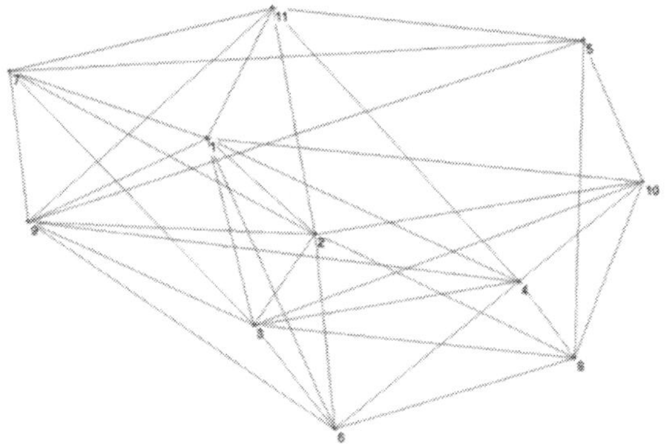

Figure 1. The sample communication network model.

For each communication network three different quantitative characteristics were calculated. These characteristics included:

- Density of the network,
- Average degree of the network,
- Degree centralization of the network.

The density and average degree measure how many significant communication links occurred in the project team communication network. The degree centralization is a measure of how the communication network are centralized.

The density of the network was calculated as:

$$Den = l/n(n-1), \quad (1)$$

where Den – density of the network, l – number of the arcs in the network, n – number of the vertices in the network (project team members).

The average degree of the network was found with the help of the following formula:

$$eg = \sum_{i}^{n}(Deg_i)/n, \quad (2)$$

where $AvDeg$ – average degree of the network, Deg_i – degree (number of the links) of the vertice i, n – number of the vertices (project team members).

The degree centralization was calculated with the formula:

$$CD = \sum_{i}^{n}(Deg_{max} - Deg_i)/(n-1)(n-2), \quad (3)$$

where CD – degree centralization of the network, Deg_{max} – the maximum degree in the network, Deg_i – degree of the vertice (participant) i, n – number of the vertices (project team members).

Knowledge generation capabilities were defined on the basis of the information registered in the company's knowledge management systems. Many projects in the company develop new technical solutions pertaining to industry control systems. Every technical solution is analyzed by the knowledge manager and then saved in the knowledge management data base. The knowledge manager assesses the potential of the new technical solutions in terms of the possibility to be used it in other projects. Each registered technical solution therefore has its rating which reflects the potential of the solution for the future projects. Hence, the knowledge generation capabilities of the project teams can be measured by the number of the new technical solutions and the average rating. Ratings are measure on the scale from 1 to 10 where 10 is the highest possible value.

To analyze the connection between structural characteristics of the communication networks and new knowledge generation capabilities the correlation analysis procedures were conducted with the help of MiniTab software. Pearson correlation coefficients and associated p-values were calculated.

4 Research findings

Using the data from the corporate project management information system the network models of communications in project teams were elaborated and the quantitative structural characteristics of the networks were calculated with the formulas (1–3). The results of the calculations are shown in Table 1.

From the knowledge management information system the number of the new technical solutions developed in the projects was derived and the average ratings of the new technical solutions were calculated. The number of the new technical solutions is provided and their average ratings of the future potential are presented in Table 2.

Table 1. Quantitative characteristics of the communication networks in industry control system projects.

Project ID	Number of project team members (Num)	Density of the network (Den)	Average degree of the network (AvDeg)	Degree centralization of the networks (CD)
A	14	0,1868	2,4286	0,2308
B	11	0,3273	3,2727	0,2111
C	11	0,6727	6,7273	0,1556
D	9	0,3889	3,1111	0,6250
E	15	0,2190	3,0667	0,4890
F	18	0,1634	2,7778	0,2132
G	13	0,3462	4,1538	0,1970
H	12	0,2272	2,5000	0,3818
J	17	0,2059	3,2941	0,3333
K	18	0,1568	2,6667	0,1544
L	10	0,3111	2,8000	0,7222
M	13	0,4359	5,2308	0,3864
N	12	0,3182	3,5000	0,6000
O	17	0,1838	2,9412	0,2167

Table 2. Number of the new technical solutions developed in the projects analyzed and their average ratings.

Project ID	Number of the new technical solutions developed in the project (NumNew)	Average rating of the new technical solutions (AvRat)
A	1	5
B	2	6
C	0	0
D	4	5
E	5	7
F	1	6
G	0	0
H	2	5
J	2	3
K	1	5
L	4	6
M	2	4
N	3	6
O	0	0

The correlation between each of the quantitative structural characteristics of the project communication networks, on the one hand, and two measures of the new knowledge generation capabilities was analyzed by calculating Pearson correlation coefficients and p-values. The results are shown in Table 3.

Table 3. Pearson correlation coefficients and p-values (in brackets).

Knowledge generation capability metrics	Number of project team members (Num)	Density of the network (Den)	Average degree of the network (AvDeg)	Degree centralization of the networks (CD)
Number of the new technical solutions developed in the project (NumNew)	-0,377 (0,184)	-0,083 (0,777)	-0,306 (0,288)	0,860 (0,000)
Average rating of the new technical solutions (AvRat)	-0,085 (0,772)	-0,394 (0,164)	-0,552 (0,041)	0,504 (0,066)

The correlation between the number of the new technical solutions developed in projects and the degree centralization of the project communication network can be considered as high with Pearson coefficient 0,860 and p-value 0,000. The weak correlation is found between the average new technical solution ratings and the average degree of the networks with Pearson coefficient 0,552 and p-value 0,041. The correlation between the average new technical solution ratings and the degree centralization of the networks can be also considered as weak (Pearson coefficient -0,504 and p-value 0,066). Other results cannot be considered as statistically significant.

5 Interpretation of research findings

The most notable and interesting result of the research is the high correlation between the new technical solutions developed in the company projects and the degree centralization of the project communications networks. The more centralized is the communication network the more new technical solutions related to industry control systems were developed. Of course, the correlation is now causation. But it is clear that centralization of communications plays significant role in new technical knowledge generation. In order to investigate further in the nature of the relationship between centralization of project communications and knowledge generation capabilities additional research is needed.

However, even from the research presented in this article and based on the data limited to the several projects from the only one engineering company we can recommend to stimulate the development of the more centralized communications in the industry control system project if there is a need for new technical solutions.

References

1. S. Krishnamurthy, O. Anson, L. Sapir, C. Glezer, M. Rois, I. Shub and K. Schloeder, *The Internet of Things, First International Conference, IOT*, pp, 68-86 (2008)
2. A. Davies and M. Hobday, *The Business of Projects: Managing Innovation in Complex Products and Systems* (Cambridge University Press, 2005)
3. A.K. Gupta and D. Wilemon, J Prod Innovat Manag, **5**, 20 (1988)
4. M.B. Pinto and J.K. Pinto, J Prod Innovat Manag, **7**, 200 (1990)
5. T.J. Allen, D.M. Lee and M.L. Tushman, EM IEEE-TEM, **27**, 2 (1980)
6. K. Jugdev and R. Müller, PMJ, **36**, 19 (2005)
7. L.S. Henderson, Int J Proj Manage, **22**, 469 (2004)
8. H. Ryynanen, Int J Bus Inform Syst, **11**, 324 (2012)
9. S. Wasserman, & K. Faust, *Social Network Analysis: Methods and Applications* (Cambridge University Press, 1997)

ITM Web of Conferences 6, 03018 (2016)
DOI: 10.1051/itmconf/20160603018

Usage of the game technologies engines for the purpose of modern geographic information systems creation

Kirill Zhigalov[1, 2, a]

[1]V.A. Trapeznikov Institute of Control Sciences of Russian Academy of Sciences, 117997 Moscow, Russia
[2]Moscow Technological Institute, 119334 Moscow, Russia

Abstract. Modern professional geographic information systems significantly lagged behind in quality of 3D graphics, which complicates their full application in the existing conditions. The main differences of the principles of game engines work from the principles of creation of professional geographic information systems structure are considered in the article. These aspects interfere with construction of modern from the graphic point of view, geographic information systems. The analysis of the contradictions considered in article will allow minimizing them at application of game engines (for example, Unity) for reduction in cost and acceleration of production of modern GIS of new generation.

1 Introduction

The three-dimensional graphics allows presenting better various processes and the phenomena to people without vocational education and spatial imagination. Unfortunately, modern geographic information systems were developed more than 10 years ago. At that time, the most part of loading on reproduction of graphics on monitors laid down on the system processor but not on the graphic processors. It causes their essential lag in a graphic component expressed not only in slow display of a scene, but also in impossibility to reproduce modern graphic effects (for example, transparency).

In a situation with games everything is absolutely opposite: they are constructed on all modern technologies and allow using all resources of the modern computer as much as possible. As, the majority of them are constructed on the unified graphic engines, such as: Unity, Unreal Development kit, Cry engine would, etc. logical to use them for fast creation of the modern geoinformation supplement. Nevertheless, there is some of obstacles to this decision connected with initial orientation of graphic engine to computer games:

• Only the relative system of coordinates, with the center in a graphic scene is used. While standard GIS use generally geographical systems of coordinates;

• The seamless repeating textures at most in HD permission (1920*1080 pixels) are used. GIS uses aero photo filming, space pictures, etc. They don't repeat and can have permission in some tens of thousands of pixels on each of the parties;

• Objects have to contain the minimum quantity of the triangles (grounds) in a scene, and the maximum quality of the picture is reached by textures. GIS aspires to the accuracy of mathematical models, respectively strives for the maximum number of triangles;

• Positioning of objects in a scene is carried out "approximately". It is necessary in GIS to have the exact geographic position of objects (with an accuracy of centimeters);

• There is no possibility to display the cuts of the objects, which are cut off by other objects.

2 Use only of relative system of coordinates

For game system and also 3D systems of modeling (3DsMAX, for example) there is no need to use difficult system of coordinates, such as the relative system of coordinates. Meanwhile all GIS programs use geographical systems of coordinates.

It looks naturally to use recalculation of coordinates for display them on the screen, input-output of data and their adjustment in such systems. At such implementation of a question the scene is building concerning the Center of the world - a reference point, from which all others will be shifted, at this parameters:

• Latitude;
• Longitude;
• Exceeding.

The software has to carry out transformation from relative system of coordinates to geographical angular or metric. Thus the internal system of coordinates remains in meters with the center in 0,0,0. The main transformations can be made in a code rather compactly and precisely through mathematics of quaternions. For recalculation between various systems of coordinates can be used Russian standard GOST P 51794-2008 [1]. In

[a] Corresponding author: kshakalov@mail.ru

more detail about it is possible to see formulas in it. It is possible to see an equivalent code in figure 1.

```
double n = (int)((6 + L.deg) / 6);
double l = (L.deg - (3 + 6 * (n - 1))) / 57.29577951;
double l2 = l * l;

double sinB = sin(B.rad);
double sinB2 = sin(B.rad * 2);
double sin2B = sinB * sinB;
double sin4B = sinB * sinB * sinB * sinB;
double sin6B = sinB * sinB * sinB * sinB * sinB * sinB;

double cosB = cos(B.rad);

double x = 6367558.4968 * B.rad - sinB2 * (16002.8900 + 66.9607 * sin2B + 0.3515 * sin4B -
    l2 * (1594561.25 + 5336.535 * sin2B + 26.790 * sin4B + 0.149 * sin6B +
    l2 * (672483.4 - 811219.9 * sin2B + 5420.0 * sin4B - 10.6 * sin6B +
    l2 * (278194.0 - 830174.0 * sin2B + 572434.0 * sin4B - 16010.0 * sin6B +
    l2 * (109500.0 - 574700.0 * sin2B + 863700.0 * sin4B - 398600.0 * sin6B)))));

const double pow10_5 = 10 * 10 * 10 * 10 * 10;

double y = (5.0 + 10 * n) * pow10_5 + l * cosB * (6378245.0 + 21346.1415 * sin2B + 107.1590 * si
    0.5977 * sin6B + l2 * (1070204.16 - 2136826.66 * sin2B + 17.98 * sin4B - 11.99 * sin6B +
    l2 * (270806 - 1523417 * sin2B + 1327645 * sin4B - 21701 * sin6B +
    l2 * (79690 - 866190 * sin2B + 1730360 * sin4B - 945460 * sin6B))));
```

Figure 1. A program code fragment on C ++, responsible for recalculation of systems of coordinates.

Recalculation accuracy on a test example was checked by converting data between angular system of coordinates, system of coordinates of SK-42 (which it is still rather widespread in Russia Federation) and local system of coordinates of the program. Accuracy of converting reached 100%

3 Use of the seamless repeating textures

In games there is no need to display the district precisely since it isn't real model. In geographic information systems the district has to be displayed rather precisely in this connection, the repeating seamless textures can't be applied.

The only way out is the greatest possible compression of entrance data (for example, photos) in graphic editors before you can see emergence of visual distortions. Usually, the standard image compresses to 70% which significantly increases software productivity.

4 Minimum quantity of triangles (planes) in models

In the most part of games, constructions and a parts of relief is replaced in a special way the made textures. GIS strives for the greatest possible geometrical compliance of each object. Nevertheless, amount of objects in a scene of GIS system can reach several hundred, and at the maximum compliance of each object to its real geometrical parameters, the number of at the triangles, displayed in the same time, will aspire to several million. Any modern graphic platform isn't able to make such quantity calculations. As a result, the task is reduced to a certain compromise.

For this purpose, during 3d modeling of objects for GIS it is necessary to choose parameters, important for the specific project, and apply only them. As shown in Figure 2 – fragments of ladders, lampposts and metalwork are simulated, and windows and walls are made in the form of textures on an equal surface.

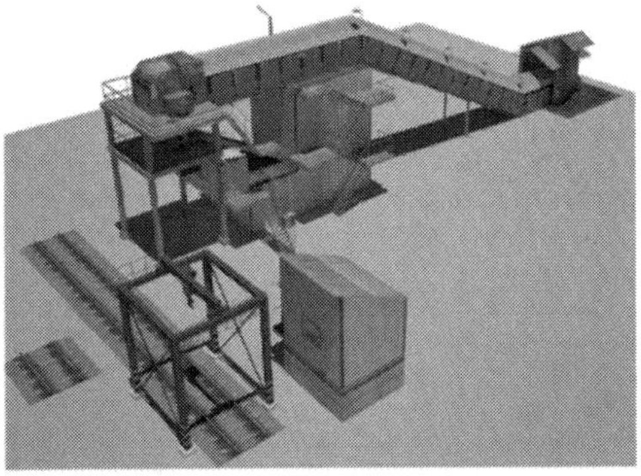

Figure 2. Example of production of model in the hybrid way.

5 Positioning of objects in a scene

In game systems 2 types of positioning are used:
- approximately;
- on two points.

Unfortunately, both types of positioning of objects aren't suitable for GIS of systems. It is connected with the insufficient accuracy of their placement at such approach. In geographic information systems the following approaches are applied:
- by the three points (characteristic points on available a relief or a scene get out and are compared with the corresponding or adjoining points on the positioned model);
- by coordinates (matching on model not less than 3 points in the system of coordinates which is used in GIS, then the model at its loading is automatically positioned in a geographic information system).

Respectively, it is necessary to make updates to a graphic engine for possibility of such actions. They will be enough, for receiving the qualitative, measured and detailed visual images.

5 Lack of possibility of display of cuts of the objects which are cut off by other objects

In games everything is presented in the form of models and cuts aren't required. In the geographic information systems focused on a markscheidery, for example, cuts are simply necessary for obtaining visual information on layers of rocks (see figure 3).

At creation of difficult systems of display, such as the pit surface with simultaneous display of layers, at us already turns out a cut of the object which is cut off by other objects (see figures 4, 5).

For such displays it is expedient to use the passes of a render involved for the minor purposes in games (for example: depths of color, or refraction). This method has also a reverse side – absence of these effects at the time of should be noted that at the time of writing of article there was a question of display of cut of layers in places of their crossing with the relief existing for other date. The question remains open.

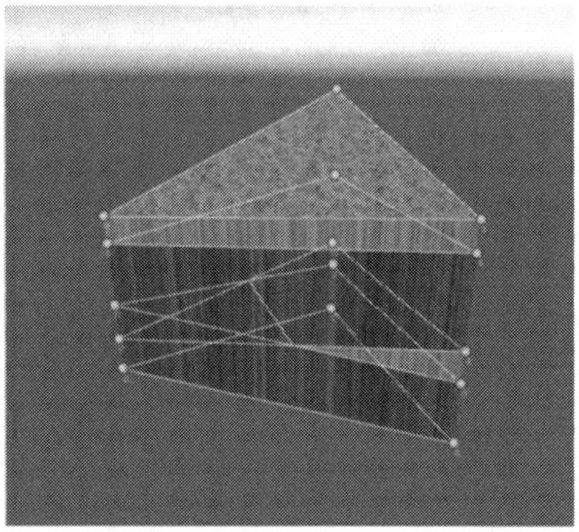

Figure 3. An example of visualization of rocks with use of cuts.

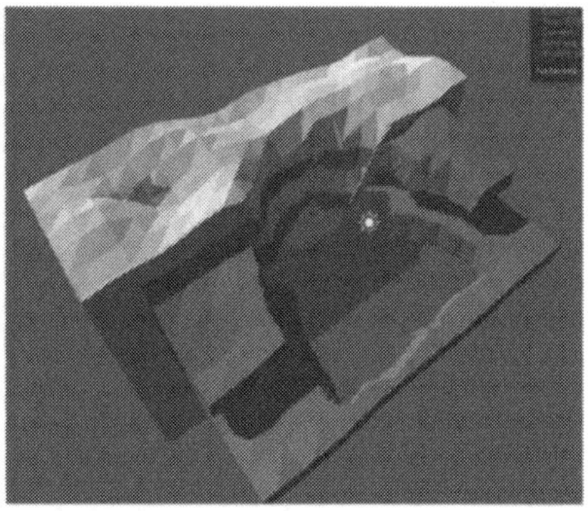

Figure 4. An example of display of a cut of the object which is cut off by other objects.

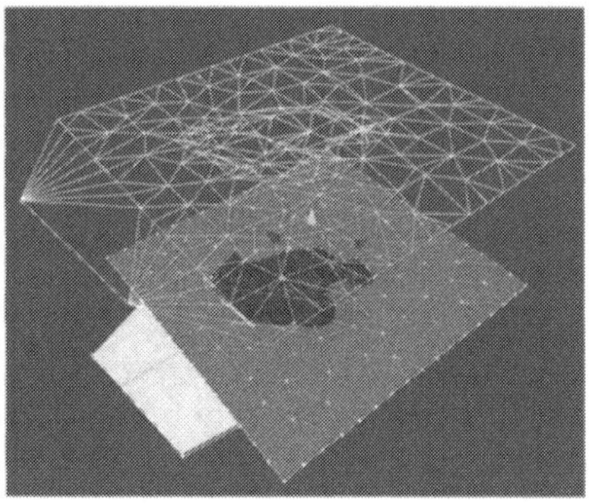

Figure 5. One example of the decision on crossing of the planes in a graphic look.

6 Conclusion

It should be noted that in practice this is not all the difficulties that occur when the integration of gaming graphics engines in the unusual structure. However, in spite of all the complexity of the gaming experience in major systems, this appears to be the most useful in the development of modern GIS systems in the coming years.

Reference

1. GOST P 51794-2008 (Russian Standard) *Global navigation satellite systems. Systems of coordinates. Methods of transformations of coordinates of the defined points* (2008)

AUTHOR INDEX